D1438694

RIFLE GREEN
IN THE
PENINSULA

*Badge of the Rifle Corps
on its formation in 1800*

Rifle Green
in the
Peninsula

Volume 1

An Account of the 95th Foot
in the Peninsular Campaign of 1808-14.
Volume 1 covers the Battles of Roliça, Vimeiro and Corunna,
together with the Military General Service Medal Official Entitlement
and Actual Entitlement as proven by the Paylists.
Fully illustrated throughout with
Maps, Photographs and Scene Reconstruction.

by

George Caldwell and Robert Cooper
Illustrated by James Dann

BUGLE HORN PUBLICATIONS

Correspondence: 49 Cromwell Road Great Glen Leicester LE8 9GU England
Tel/fax: +44 (0)116 2593124 Email: info@buglehorn.co.uk Web: www.buglehorn.co.uk

Rifle Green in the Peninsula
Volume 1

© Copyright G. J. Caldwell and R. B. E. Cooper 1998
Illustrations © Copyright J. Dann 1998

In preparation
Rifle Green in the Peninsula
Volume 2 in a series of 4

By the same authors
Rifle Green at Waterloo
Rifle Green in the Crimea
Rifles at Waterloo

Designed and Produced by
Citrus°
www.citrus.co.uk

Printed and Bound by
Bookcraft (Bath) Ltd

British Library Cataloguing in Publication Data:
A catalogue record for this book is available from the British Library.

ISBN 0 9516600 3 9

Contents

FOREWORD   6

INTRODUCTION   7

ACKNOWLEDGEMENTS   11

CALENDAR OF EVENTS 1808-09   12

PART ONE: Causes of the Peninsular War   14

Expedition for Portugal Prepares   16

Mondego Bay   18

Advance to Lavos   21

Obidos   26

Battle of Roliça   30

The Landing at Maceira Bay   41

Battle of Vimeiro   44

Advance and Occupation of Lisbon   67

Lisbon   72

The Advance on Salamanca   77

Moore's Advance against the French   87

Sahagún to Astorga   98

The Light Brigades' March to Vigo   113

Cacabelos   125

Battle of Corunna   148

The Army Returns to England   166

PART TWO: Military General Service Medal 1793-1814   174

Colour Plate Series   i, ii, iii, iv

MGS Medal Entitlement - Official and Actual   193

Battle Orders   212

BIBLIOGRAPHY   220

INDEX   221

Foreword

by Major Ron D. Cassidy MBE

When George Caldwell and Robert Cooper asked me to write an introduction to this book I was delighted to help. For some forty-seven years and for the last nine as curator to the Royal Green Jackets Museum, I have followed the fortunes of the 95th and subsequently The Rifle Brigade. The book will be of particular interest to those who follow the Peninsular War and the fortunes of the 95th. It gives an in depth view of the regiment in those early Peninsula days. It also manages to give the much wider story of other regiments, tactics and conditions throughout.

Here we see the authors, as they did with *Rifle Green at Waterloo* and *Rifle Green in the Crimea*, researching the facts, analysing their findings and producing a book that has for me put those times of the Peninsular War into perspective.

Early lessons about skirmishing are learnt, not without cost to life and limb. Fascinating tales about the women who accompanied their menfolk and the meagre rations they were supposed to exist on, it is no wonder they took in sewing and did washing to supplement their income.

This volume has already whetted my appetite for those volumes to follow. If they bring all the facts together as this one has done, then a more detailed history, lists of medal rolls and casualty lists will be hard to find.

Ron Cassidy

Introduction

by Philip J. Haythornthwaite

Coote Manningham, first colonel of the 95th Rifles, which regiment he had been instrumental in creating, delivered a series of lectures to his officers in the spring of 1803. He began with the statement that 'Light Troops are, as it were, a light or beacon for the General, which should constantly inform him of the situation, the movements, and nature of the enemy's designs; it is upon the exactness and intelligence of what they report that he is enabled to regulate the time and manner of executing his own enterprizes.' [1] Appropriately for one so involved with one of the most important military innovations of his time, one who knew him remarked that 'he seemed of a new order of men'; [2] yet Coote Manningham did not witness all the achievements of his regiment, for he died at Maidstone in August 1809, following his return from Spain, where he had commanded a brigade in Sir John Moore's army. Had he lived, the regiment which he had helped create must surely have fulfilled all his expectations, and more, by establishing a reputation during the Peninsular War which was second to none.

The evolution of light infantry in British service dated from the mid-18th century, but much of what had been learned had been forgotten by the start of the 'Great War' against France in 1793. The revival of light infantry tactics, and their development to a degree previously unmatched, is often attributed to that charismatic leader, Sir John Moore, who from a comparatively early period accepted the premise that the most effective light troops were not like those employed by some continental armies exclusively as skirmishers, but those who could equally well perform all the functions of ordinary infantry; as he noted when training composite battalions of light infantry in Ireland in 1798-99, 'Our Light Infantry...are in fact a mixture of the Yager, and the Grenadier.' [3] This was not a new concept, but had been expressed by Francis de Rottenburg, a light infantry expert of continental experience and Danzig birth, who commanded the 5th Battalion 60th Royal American Regiment, and was the author of a manual which influenced Sir John and many others, *Regulations for the Exercise of Riflemen and Light Infantry*, London 1798.

---

[1] Coote Manningham, *Military Lectures delivered to the Officers of the 95th (Rifle) Regiment, at Shorn-Cliff Barracks, Kent, during the Spring of 1803*, London 1803; r/p, intro. W. Verner, 1897, p. 1
[2] *Gentleman's Magazine*, October 1809, p. 902
3 'Sir John Moore's Light Infantry Instructions of 1798-99', ed. Maj. Gen. J. F. C. Fuller, *Journal of the Society for Army Historical Research*, Vol. XXX (1952), p. 70

The culmination of Moore's work on light infantry service occurred when he commanded at Shorncliffe camp, in Kent, where the training of three regiments - his own 52nd, the 43rd and 95th - laid the foundations for the Light Brigade, later Light Division, which became the most elite element of the Peninsular army. Traditionally, most of the credit has been given to Moore - for example William Napier, his most famous champion, remarked that Moore would have been known as the modern-day Iphicrates (the Athenian general of the 4th century BC, who improved the equipment of the light troops of his day), had he not won greater fame by dying like Brasidas (the Spartan general killed in battle in 422 BC). [4] Others, however, pointed to the contribution of Lt. Col. Kenneth Mackenzie (later known as Sir Kenneth Douglas of Glenbirvie, a dormant family title he adopted upon receiving a baronetcy in 1830) who was chosen by Moore to command the 52nd. Mackenzie 'commenced...a series of movements and exercise, in which Sir John Moore, at first, acquiesced with reluctance, the style of drill, march, and platoon exercise, being entirely new; but when he saw the effect of the whole, in a more advanced stage, he was not only highly gratified, but became its warmest supporter.' [5]

It was not just in the techniques of drill and exercise that Moore and his collaborators were so influential; the effect was much more profound, and concerned the 'discipline' of the light infantry in as much as it related to morale, professionalism and the relationship between officers and men. It was already recognised that light infantry service demanded a level of initiative and independence above that required by an ordinary 'line' soldier, and Moore added what he termed the discipline of the mind to that of the body. The new system was based upon the premise that the soldier, inspired by a feeling of personal and regimental pride, should be determined in all ways to do his best. Such sentiments were fostered by professional leadership, with officers using encouragement, emulation and explanation rather than punishment to obtain the necessary obedience. George Napier described how the system worked in relation to the 52nd, in which Mackenzie assembled the officers and told them 'that the only way of having a regiment in good order was by every individual thoroughly knowing and performing his duty; and that if officers did not fully understand their duty, it would be quite impossible to expect that the men either could or would perform theirs as they ought; therefore the best and surest method was to commence by drilling the whole of the officers, and when they became perfectly acquainted with the system, they could teach the men, and by their zeal, knowledge, and, above all, good temper and kind treatment of the soldier, make the regiment the best in the service.' [6]

4 William Napier, *The Life and Opinions of Sir Charles James Napier*, London 1857, Vol. I p.58
5 *United Service Journal* 1834, Vol. I p.235 6 George Napier, *Passages in the Early Military Life of General Sir George T. Napier, KCB*, ed. Gen. W.G.E. Napier, London 1884., p. 13

It was upon this grounding that the unique excellence of the Light Division was founded, and gradually spread from the regiments instructed under Moore's supervision to the rest of the army as the years passed, although the change from the previous practice was initiated more at battalion level than by official decree from above, and took a considerable time to gain general acceptance. The development of what might almost be termed a form of paternalism in the relations between the more forward-thinking officers and their subordinates was exemplified by George Napier's remarks on how a commanding officer should behave: '...the first and greatest duty an officer has to perform is that of preventing crime in the soldier, and the surest and most honourable means of doing so is to look upon the soldier as a fellow-citizen, who, by the admitted laws of society and for the general good of the State placed under you in rank and station, is nevertheless as good a man and as good a Christian as yourself, born in the same country, amenable to the same laws, and above all possessing the same feelings as the proudest peer in the land.'[7]

If many of these beneficial effects can be traced to some degree at least to the legacy of Moore and his immediate followers, it is not unlikely that from the very beginning something of the same existed in the 95th, so that the names of Coote Manningham and his lieutenant colonel, William Stewart, should be linked with those of Moore, Mackenzie and de Rottenburg in any consideration of the subject. For example, Coote Manningham's lectures recognised that the most effective light infantry was that skilled in more than 'the old and practised stratagems of a partisan only', and hinted at the revised role of the officer: 'British troops should never be permitted to get into slovenly habits, which produce both idleness and disease; this may be done without harassing the soldier, and the officers should set the example.'[8]

In addition to the attributes which came to be associated with the Light Division in general, the 95th added a number of unique features. Principal among these was the use of the Baker rifle, a weapon probably unsurpassed for accuracy by any comparable contemporary firearm; and the training and tactics which accompanied its use, which gave the 95th a sharp shooting facility immensely superior to even the best light infantry armed with smoothbore muskets. The dark green uniform, though not unique, was also distinctive, its black facings giving it a sombre aspect which not only distinguished its wearers but became a source of regimental pride. Matters of training, equipment and even superior leadership, however, could not alone produce the level of excellence in proficiency and morale enjoyed by the 95th;

[7] ibid. p. 270
[8] Manningham, op. cit., pp. 1, 42

equally important was the esprit de corps, and consequently indomitable spirit, produced by a combination of all these factors. It is perhaps a measure of this regimental pride that of all the many published memoirs of the Peninsular War era, more emanated from the 95th than from any other regiment: the works of, for example, John Kincaid, Edward Costello, Benjamin Harris, Jonathan Leach, Harry Smith, William Surtees and William Green include some of the great 'classics' of the genre, to which might be added the later publication of George Simmons' writings. It was during the Peninsular War that the regiment established and confirmed its reputation, a reputation for excellence fully deserved, to which the events recounted in this book will testify. In their mode of operation, as well as in the relationship between the ranks, the 95th proved itself to be not only Coote Manningham's 'light or beacon for the general', but equally a beacon for the future development of infantry service. The regimental toast, dating from the Peninsular War, was fully justified when it referred to 'the first in the field and the last out of it, the bloody fighting Ninety-fifth'.

Acknowledgements

Alan Barlow, Barbara Caldwell,
Samantha Caldwell, Major Ron Cassidy MBE,
Philip Clark, Carol Cooper,
James Cooper (Book Photographer), Robert Cooper Snr
James Dann (Illustrator), John Darwent,
Judith Farrington (Researcher), Derek Haighton,
Alan Harrison, Eileen Hathaway,
Philip Haythornthwaite, David Howarth,
Barry Gregson, John Gregson,
John Gretton, Barry Langridge,
Arthur Lloyd (Photographer), David Miles,
Terry Moore (Photographer), A. L. T. Mullen,
George Nichol, Peter Poulain,
Eric Price, David W. Rennie,
The late Ian Rowbotham, Bob Ruckman,
Alan Seldon, John Sly (Researcher),
P. J. Wardrop, Keith Webster.

Special thanks to the Rifle Brigade Trustees,
Rifle Brigade Club and the Royal Green Jackets Museum.

Crown-copyright material in the Public Record Office is reproduced
by permission of the Controller of Her Majesty's Stationery Office.

Calendar of Events

9th April 1808
Sir John Moore's force.
Three companies of the 1st Bn 95th under Major Dugald Gilmour, those of Norcott, Ross and O'Hare, embark for Sweden and upon arrival re-route to Portugal, arriving at Porto Novo near Maceira on the 25th August 1808, taking until the 29th to disembark.

8th June 1808
Sir Arthur Wellesley's force.
Four companies of the 2nd Bn 95th under Major Robert Travers, those of Crampton, Creagh, Leach and Pakenham, embark for Portugal and arrive at Mondego Bay on the 1st August 1808.

19th July 1808
General Worth Acland's force.
Two companies of the 1st Bn 95th under Lieutenant Colonel Thomas Sidney Beckwith, those of Cameron and Ramadge, embark for Portugal and arrive at Maceira on the 19th August 1808 and disembark on the 20th.

15th August 1808
OBIDOS, no MGS clasp.
One company of the 2nd Bn engaged.

17th August 1808
ROLIÇA, MGS clasp, 'ROLEIA'.
Four companies of the 2nd Bn engaged.

21st August 1808   VIMEIRO, MGS clasp 'VIMIERA'.
Two companies 1st Bn and four companies 2nd Bn engaged.

Sir David Baird's force.
Four companies of the 1st Bn 95th under Major Norman McLeod, those of Charles Beckwith, Elder, Miller and Pakenham and four companies of the 2nd Bn 95th under Colonel Hamlet Wade, those of Cadoux, Drake, Gray and Jenkins, land at Corunna on the 26th October 1808.

3rd January 1809   CACABELOS, no MGS clasp.
Nine companies of the 1st Bn engaged.

12th January 1809   The 2nd Bn 95th arrive at Vigo, embark and allow a few days for stragglers to arrive.

16th January 1809   CORUÑA, MGS clasp 'CORUNNA'.
Nine companies of the 1st Bn engaged.

17th January 1809   The 1st Bn 95th leave Corunna and return to Spithead, England on the 21st January 1809.
Some Riflemen returning as late as the 28th February 1809.

21st January 1809   The 2nd Bn 95th leave Vigo and return to Portsmouth, England at the beginning of February 1809.

Part One

Causes of the Peninsular War

In the years before the Peninsular War Britain was a great sea faring nation. Merchant ships sailed the oceans returning home with exotic and valuable cargoes, all in great demand. The Royal Navy equally sailed the seas with confidence having had the upper hand against the French navy and those of her allies. Napoleon considered and described Britain as a 'Nation of Shopkeepers' and set about to enforce the Continental System or blockade. This he did with the Berlin Decree of 21st November 1806 which was designed to stop the entry of British ships into European ports and the total ban on the trade of all British goods whether from Britain or her colonies. However, there was one country who decided to defy Napoleon, Britain's longstanding trading partner, Portugal, who for centuries had enjoyed a profitable trade with Britain. Napoleon, therefore, was determined to teach Portugal a lesson for her defiance towards him and to use Spain suited his purpose.

Spain was ruled by the weak and ineffectual King Charles VI and Queen Maria-Luisa, together with their treacherous son Ferdinand and the Prime Minister, the Queen's favourite, Don Manuel Godoy who was equally as corrupt. In the August of 1807, France and Spain put pressure on John, the Prince Regent of Portugal to declare war on Britain. This included confiscating the property of British interests and imprisoning British subjects in Portugal. Reluctantly, he was prepared to 'break off' diplomatic relations with Britain hoping it would be enough to pacify Napoleon. Unfortunately it was not. Napoleon, using Godoy to manipulate King Charles, entered into the secret Treaty of Fontainbleau 27th October 1807, which permitted the French army to enter Spain. Then together with the Spanish army invade and conquer Portugal to the benefit of France, Spain and Godoy, who was to acquire the principality of the Algarve, although in later life he denied it.

Straightaway, the 26,000 strong French army called the 'Corps of Observation of Gironde' under General Junot left Bayonne for Portugal. After a series of forced marches he arrived at Lisbon unopposed where he promptly disbanded the Portuguese army. A second larger French army, 55,000 strong, entered Spain and seized key frontier fortresses and then marched towards Madrid. On hearing this, Godoy recalled the Spanish army, assisting Junot and then tried to persuade the Royal Family to leave Spain for the Americas.

This precipitated unrest and he was accused of starting a riot amongst the populace of Madrid. For his own protection he was taken into custody. Ferdinand, feeling the time to be right, persuaded his father to abdicate in his favour. Then Napoleon, with his usual masterly touch, succeeded in luring the King, Queen and Godoy to Bayonne on the pretence of settling the domestic dispute. Once in Bayonne Ferdinand was pressurised into surrendering his claim to the Spanish throne. This left the way clear for Napoleon to install his brother Joseph as King of Spain.

The French army under Napoleon's brother-in-law Murat became 'cruel masters' in Spain. Unrest and bloodshed of the 'Dos de Mayo' resulted in the Asturias declaring war on France. Britain, in response to Spain's request for assistance, sent large quantities of guns, munitions, stores and, most important of all money which was followed in the July 1808 by a small expeditionary force under the command of Sir Arthur Wellesley.

Expedition for Portugal Prepares

On the 8th June 1808, four companies of the 2nd Battalion 95th Rifles, those of Captains Jasper Creagh, Jeremiah Crampton, Jonathan Leach and Hon. Hercules Robert Pakenham, under the command of Major Robert Travers embarked at Dover. They then set sail for Cork to join a force being assembled off the coast of Ireland for an expedition to South America. This destination, however, was later changed to Portugal after a request by that country for aid. The strength of the 95th companies allotted to the expedition was; 1 field officer, 4 captains, 13 subalterns, 1 staff, 20 sergeants, 8 buglers and 397 rank and file. They remained anchored for four or five weeks off the Cove of Cork awaiting the arrival of their commander. To keep the Riflemen in trim they were landed each day so as to practice their skills at skirmishing and the surrounding countryside echoed with the sound of their bugles and shouted commands. At the end of the day the Riflemen were transported back to the ships to spend the night out in the bay. To help break this monotonous routine whilst waiting for the expedition to receive its orders, the Rifles' officers amused themselves with boating trips to areas of outstanding beauty such as Glanmyre and with frequent visits to the city of Cork. At this point the men still did not know their true destination, but a long voyage was expected because of the amount of stores being shipped and the small number of horses on board the transports.

When General Sir John Moore returned from a futile expedition to Sweden he inevitably expected to take command of the force being assembled for Portugal. The Government, however, because of their political dislike for Moore appointed Sir Arthur Wellesley to its command, who then became the youngest lieutenant general in the British army. General Sir Brent Spencer [1] was also at this time with another force in and around Gibralter and was ordered to join Wellesley on his arrival off the coast of Portugal.

While Wellesley's troops [2] prepared to set sail, a further force was also being assembled at Harwich and Ramsgate under the commands of Brigadier Generals, Worth Acland [3] and Robert Anstruther. [4]

---

[1] Spencer's force of 5,000 men consisted of artillery, 1/6th, 1/29th, 1/32nd, 1/50th and 1/82nd Regiments. [2] Sir Arthur Wellesley's force of 9,000 men consisted of 20th Light Dragoons, artillery, 1/5th, 1/9th, 1/36th, 1/38th, 1/40th, 1/45th, 5/60th, 1/71st, 1/91st, and 4 companies 2/95th. [3] Acland's force of 1,332 men consisted of 2nd Regiment, 1/20th and 2 companies 1/95th. [4] Anstruther's force of 2,703 men consisted of 2/9th, 2/43rd, 2/52nd and 2/97th Queen's Germans.

The two companies of the 1st Battalion 95th in Acland's force were those of Captain Alexander Cameron and Captain Smith Ramadge under the command of Lieutenant Colonel Sir Thomas Sidney Beckwith.

Wellesley's convoy finally set sail on the 12th July with those of Anstruther and Acland leaving on the 19th. Wellesley on board the Crocodile, arrived at Corunna on the 20th July and having met with the Galicians who wanted British money and not troops, advised him to go to Oporto at the mouth of the Douro River. Here on the 24th July he met with the supreme Junta and the Bishop of Oporto, Don Antonio de Castro. They agreed that the best place for the British troops to land in Portugal would be the mouth of the River Mondego at Figueira da Foz, a hundred miles north of Lisbon. Here a small fort originally held by the French had been taken by the students of Coimbra University on the 24th June and then handed over to Admiral Cotton who garrisoned it with 300-400 British marines from the fleet. This encouraged Wellesley to attempt a landing, having first sent word for Spencer to join him. The transports set sail and arrived at Mondego Bay on the 30th July. The very same day that the French General Loison, massacred the whole population of Evora including the women and children. If ever the Portuguese had second thoughts about bringing the British into their war they were certainly now left in no doubt after Loison's barbarous action.

Fort at Figueira da Foz

Mondego Bay

The fleet remained anchored for two days at Mondego Bay while preparations were being made for the landing. The boats of local fishermen were hired to help with those of the transports to bring the troops ashore. Three days' rations had been cooked and issued to the men, while at the same time the arms and equipment were brought up from the ships' holds. It was now quite clear to the men that they were going to be in conflict with the French. Wellesley had also made provision for the women and children with the regiments, only six women per company were allowed. They were to receive half rations and the children a quarter, but no spirit or wine was to be issued to them. It was a problem for the army to protect the women and children from the effects of drink especially in hot climates or countries where wine and spirits were both plentiful and cheap. A fact which was later to become all to apparent in the retreat to Corunna.

Once Wellesley received the all clear from the naval signallers ashore, the landing began. On the 1st August the men of the 2nd Battalion 95th Rifles and the 5th Battalion 60th Rifles were the first into the boats and to land, followed by the 45th Regiment of Brigadier Henry Fane's brigade. Though the weather was fine and the sea calm, perfect for landing, it was still a difficult and dangerous operation. There was a heavy swell coming in from the Atlantic which caused the ships to roll, so much so that their yards practically touched the water. This rolling of the ships created chaos below decks, causing minor damage to the officers' mess, glass and crockery. It also made it very difficult for the men to leave the ships and board the local coastal craft or ships' boats. There was a sand bar across the mouth of the river leading to the beach head, which only allowed boats drawing no more than eleven feet to pass. Once over the bar there was a considerable surf running which made the passage to the beach quite treacherous. The 95th companies landed, however, with little more than a soaking for some of the men. Sad to say this was not the case for the rest of the army.

As the boats were rowed towards the shore crammed tight with the red coated soldiers, each with a pack and musket squashed between his legs, the fear of being drowned was all to real. The boats were being tossed high into the air which then came crashing down into the foam, but on nearing the shore, in most instances and before a second wave had a chance to dash them to pieces, groups of naked sailors armed with ropes waited to pull them ashore. When a boat did ground the sailors would dash into the foam and carry the soldiers to the beach and safety. A number of boats did end up swamped or capsized and unfortunately several men were drowned.

Because of the severe conditions in the bay it took five days to land Wellesley's entire force of; 9,000 men, guns, stores and a small number of horses. Getting the horses ashore was even more of a problem than the men. The troopers were instructed to stand upright with their mounts in the boats and keep hold of the horses' bridles ready in case of accident. This was to make it easier for them to jump into the saddle and allow the horse to carry them ashore, but some did manage to reach the shore without their riders. Once the terrified animals reached land after being confined for so long on board ship they galloped up and down the beach neighing and kicking out at their owners or anybody else who tried to restrain them.

General Spencer arrived at Mondego Bay on the 5th August and immediately started landing his own force. This took three days until finally on the 8th, the last of the men were landed. Meanwhile, Wellesley started to organise the commissariat and supply lines for the coming campaign using two companies of the Irish Waggon Train which he had brought with him as a nucleus.

He also engaged local drivers with ox-carts to serve the force for regular wages paid by the Commissary General's Department. (A civilian organisation under the responsibility of the Treasury!) This added a further 500 draft animals and 300 carts to his commissariat with enough horses to bring the mounted strength to 240 of his 390 light dragoons. Unfortunately, not enough horses could be obtained to furnish all of General Spencer's artillery.

In addition to the British supplies and ammunition, Wellesley landed 5,000 muskets to arm the Portuguese army which he had expected to join his force. However, the Portuguese General, Bernadino Freire proved to be an impossible ally and left Wellesley according to Napier 'with 250 cavalry and 1,000 infantry of the line and 400 light infantry,' [1] the latter under the command of an eccentric British officer in the Portuguese service, Colonel Nicholas Trant. Trant's troops were described as, 'a grotesque bunch of ragamuffins dressed in white jackets and immense feathered hats.'

Once the 95th Rifles reached the shore the captains formed their respective companies, collecting individual and company baggage, after having first secured the immediate area with some advanced picquets. It was while waiting in this position for further orders that they were surprised to be greeted by 'a host of padres, friars and monks, who having seen the troops land joined them on the beach with plenty of 'Vivas'. The scene was made even more ludicrous as practically every well wisher carried a large brightly coloured umbrella. More pleasing, however, to the Riflemen was the appearance of some members of the fairer sex who singled out for special attention certain members giving them presents of flowers and fruit.'

---

[1] Oman states that Da Luz Soriano, the Portuguese historian, provides the following figures; cavalry of the 6th, 11th and 12th Regiments 258 sabres, 6th Battalion of Cazadores 562 bayonets, 12th, 21st and 24th Line Battalions 1514 bayonets. The British commander repeatedly stated that he saw no more than 260 horse and 1,600 infantry.

Advance to Lavos

At last the order came for the Rifles to advance and the companies started to move off along the beach in a southerly direction keeping the sea to their right. Besides the heat and terrain the men struggled under a heavy load of personal arms and equipment which each man was required to carry. Rifleman Benjamin Harris gives us an insight as to what this contained.

'For my own part being a handy craft, I marched under a weight sufficient to impede the motions of a donkey; for besides my well-filled knapsack, there was the great coat rolled on its top, my blanket and camp kettle, haversack, stuffed full of leather for repairing the men's shoes, together with hammer and other tools (the lap stone I took the liberty of flinging to the devil), ship-biscuit and beef for three days. I also carried my canteen filled with water, hatchet and rifle, and eighty rounds of ball cartridge in my pouch.'

Sandy tracks through the pine trees to Lavos

Once the rest of Fane's brigade had landed and gained some order they also set off after the Riflemen along the beach. At first the initial advance was welcomed by the men, but that soon changed after marching a mile or so across an uninterrupted plain of hot, white sand, into which they sunk ankle deep at every step. The heat, weight of arms and equipment and their confinement of almost two months on board ship was starting to take its toll. After continuing for nearly another five miles the 95th halted and were soon joined by the rest of Fane's brigade. This was the limit of what the men could achieve on their first day's march. The brigade now united for the first time, bivouacked in a pinewood near the village of Lavos, where the shade from the trees was most welcome. Picquets were at once posted and patrols sent out to report on the surrounding countryside, while the rest of the troops set up camp for the night.

The following day, 2nd August, they were joined by Ferguson's brigade and then gradually by the other remaining brigades. Once the equipment, stores, ammunition and baggage were landed this was also brought to the camp. The arrival of the equipment brought further shelter from the fierce rays of the sun in the welcome shape of tents. There was no mistaking the arrival of the supplies for, the screeching of the solid wheels against ungreased axles of the Portuguese ox-carts could be heard long before they came into sight.

At Lavos the local peasants came into the camp with quantities of oranges, grapes, melons and figs for the men, this gave them an abundance of delicacies, which many had never tasted before. The Rifles were also given a live calf and 'they feasted like lords', for the first few days of their stay in Portugal, according to Rifleman Harris.

On the 3rd August, Wellesley published a General Order which was to have a far reaching impact on his campaign in the Peninsula,

'Lavos 3 August 1808,

G. O.

The Order of Battle of the Army is to be two deep and as follows, beginning from the right:
    Major-General Ferguson's Brigade.
    Brigadier-General Catlin Craufurd's Brigade.
    Brigadier-General Fane's Brigade, on the left.
    There will be a howitzer and three pieces of cannon attached to each of the Brigades of Infantry...
    When the Army moves from its left, the 95th and 5th Battalion 60th will lead the column in the ordinary course. When the Army shall move from its right, the 95th and 5th Battalion 60th must form the advanced Guard and lead the column from the right.' Supp. Desp., vi, 96.

The most significant fact in this General Order was the final adoption of the two-deep line from the more widely used three ranks. The importance of this change cannot be over-stated. It proved a decisive factor on many a bloody battle-field in Portugal and Spain culminating at Waterloo with Wellington's victory over the master tactician, Napoleon. Though two ranks had been employed occasionally before, the permanent use of the two rank system reduced the depth but increased the front by one half, which gave a valuable increase in fire power.

From a Rifleman's point of view the General Order states quite clearly that, 'what-ever' the order of march the Rifles were to lead the army as the advance guard. This latter fact was not always received in good spirit by other regiments who often made jealous remarks as to their own seniority and standing in the army in stark contrast to the newly raised Rifle Regiment. Much of this jealousy from the senior regiments of the army was attributed to the ignorance of the new system and role of the Rifles, which many had not yet seen in action and their true value appreciated.

With the arrival of General Sir Brent Spencer's five infantry battalions, Wellesley now re-arranged the army into six brigades. The 6th or Light Brigade consisted the 1/45th, four companies of the 2nd Battalion 95th Rifles and the 5th Battalion 60th Rifles, under the command of Brigadier General Fane with Brigade Major M'Neil and Assistant Commissary Lamont as staff officers, (Supp. Desp., vi, 101.); the composition being:

1st brigade	General Rowland Hill	1/5th, 1/9th, 1/38th
2nd brigade	General Ronald Ferguson	1/36th, 1/40th, 1/71st
3rd brigade	General Miles Nightingall	1/29th, 1/82nd
4th brigade	General Barnard Bowes	1/6th, 1/32nd
5th brigade	General Catlin Craufurd	1/50th, 1/91st

At 3 a.m. on the 9th August, Fane advanced with his brigade from Lavos southward, towards Leiria, with orders not to engage with the French if they came into contact with them. The tents and heavy baggage had been left behind, with the men carrying their personal kit and equipment as before. The heat and lack of drinking water was again a problem but they were at least free from the sand which made their previous march along the beach so tiring. The land they now crossed was a mixture of pinewoods and uncultivated heaths of white sandy soil with the occasional vineyard. A large proportion of the route was along lanes with high hedge-rows or prickly pears which shielded them from any welcoming breeze and instead trapped the heat causing the fast marching Riflemen to suffer severely. The night of the 9th they bivouacked on the side of a hill surrounded by gum cistus trees.

Daybreak, on the 10th August saw the general advance of the whole of Wellesley's force. The troops carried 60 rounds of ammunition per man, except the Rifles who we have seen carried 80 rounds; 90 mules carried a further 2,000 rounds each and were attached to the artillery with the main supply carts carrying another 500,000 rounds. The army also marched with seventeen days' ration of bread; four days' issue with each individual soldier;

three days' on mules for quicker access and distribution with another ten days' being transported on the carts; along with five days' allowance of salt meat and ten days' ration of spirits.

It was Wellesley's intention to march directly on Lisbon, keeping close to the coast so he could be kept supplied from the transports and at the same time be in a position to cover the disembarkation of Acland and Anstruther's brigades, which he expected at any day.

General Fane sent 200 Riflemen and a group of the 20th Light Dragoons in front forming the advance of his own brigade. Here they came upon deserters of the 4th Swiss Regiment, in the service of the French, clad in long red coats who were at once sent to the staff officers in the rear. From these Swiss troops they gained intelligence that the French had left Leiria, which encouraged General Fane to push on and enter the town.

At Leiria, the men were able to witness first hand, the lengths to which the French would go in exerting retribution on the local population. Terrible atrocities had been inflicted on the inhabitants which came as a shock to the troops, but soon this was to become all too common a sight. The destruction of the town was on a large scale and everything had been plundered or destroyed. Captain Leach along with fellow Rifles' officers entered the grounds of a convent to find its walls covered with the evidence which stood silent witness to the activities that had so recently taken place.

The French, meanwhile, under the command of General Jean Andoche Junot received news of the landing practically at the same time as the first British troops set foot on the beach at Mondego Bay.

Junot at once sent orders to Loison, who was near Badajoz with 7,000 men, to rejoin him and his force of some 19,000 men. On the 6th August Junot sent General Henri Delaborde with a force of about 2,500 men and five light guns from Lisbon with the task of trying to delay Wellesley as long as possible and gain him time to concentrate his own forces.

Delaborde advanced to Alcobaça on the 10th where he was joined by a further three battalions from Peniche which increased his force to 5,000 men. With this larger force he continued as far as Batalha. His plan had been to make this his first defensive position, but on arriving at Batalha found it was not suitable to oppose Wellesley. Delaborde now fell back to Obidos, a town some three miles north of Roliça. At Obidos he left a rearguard consisting of an infantry detachment and a few cavalry, taking his main force back to Roliça, where he detached six companies of his Swiss troops to garrison Peniche. This reduced his total fighting force to 4,350 men.

Obidos

Obidos caſtle looking north towards Caldas

On the 14th August, Wellesley left all the tents and baggage at Leiria and advanced through Batalha and Alcobaça, then on the 15th towards Caldas. By this time General Fane's brigade had already proceeded a short distance south from Caldas, while Major Robert Travers' 95th received orders to push on and attack the outposts at Obidos. He at once dispatched three of his eight companies as his own advance guard. These were Captain Pakenham's No 3 Company 2nd 95th with two companies from the 60th, [1] along with an officers' party of the 20th Light Dragoons, whilst he followed with the remaining three 95th companies and two of the 60th.

---

[1] Many authorities state that three companies of the 60th were with this advance, even Wellesley in his despatches quotes the same. However, the regimental history of the 60th states quite clearly that only two companies were with the single company of the 95th.

As the advanced Riflemen were approaching a windmill at Brillos, situated on rising ground adjoining Obidos, the French opened up with a fire of musketry from the windmill while a few shots came from the walls of the town. The Riflemen immediately attacked this position at the double, driving the French picquets before them, who then fell back on their comrades in the town. This made the jubilant Riflemen even more determined as they pressed home their attack, pursuing the defendants from the small houses and along the one long street past the old Moorish Castle and then down into the plains leading to Roliça. Having driven in Delaborde's outposts from the town with little harm to themselves, the men were euphoric and they continued driving the French light troops before them, at the same time distancing themselves from their own support companies with Major Travers. At Roliça, Delaborde had been watching the proceedings and the rashness of these Riflemen had not gone unnoticed. He ordered a body of cavalry and an infantry battalion from his force to cut them off, aided by his retreating advanced picquets.

The eagerness of the advancing Riflemen was now almost their undoing for they were confronted by a far superior force. Receiving a heavy fire from the advancing French infantry, Lieutenant Ralph Bunbury, at the head of Pakenham's company, received a musket ball in the head which killed him on the spot. He was the first casualty of the 95th. Travers seeing the trouble his advance guard were in proceeded at once to their aid with the remaining companies, but they were still outnumbered.

The French seeing the British skirmishers still unsupported made a charge and poured in a heavy and destructive fire on the Riflemen in a desperate attempt to cut them off. This would have succeeded if it was not for the timely arrival of Major General Spencer, who having reached Obidos could see from his elevated position that the Riflemen in the plain were outnumbered and that they were in considerable danger. He at once advanced with his brigade to their assistance and extricated Travers' force, but not without a little difficulty.

The cost to the Rifles in this overzealous attack was: Captain Pakenham slightly wounded; Lieutenant Bunbury killed; Riflemen William Dodd, James Martin and Mathew Maxwell killed; Patrick Doyle missing; with Thomas Wall wounded. The official return states: 1 officer killed, 1 wounded, 3 rank and file killed, 1 missing and 2 wounded. The paylist shows, William Duggin sick absent and Maurice Kelly sick General Hospital; one of these could be the missing casualty! All the 2nd Battalion 95th casualties came from Captain Pakenham's No 3 Company, which confirms the rashness of these men in engaging the enemy without support. The 60th Rifles did not get off lightly either, having casualties of; 1 Rifleman killed, 5 wounded and 17 missing, an indication as to how close the advanced party of Travers' force came to being cut off!

However, a valuable lesson was learned at a small price for their eagerness in wishing to engage with the enemy, which possibly saved them from heavier casualties in later actions throughout the Peninsular War.

Wellesley in his despatches to the Secretary of State for War, for the 16th August 1808 said, 'The affair of the advanced posts yesterday evening was unpleasant, because it was quite useless, and was occasioned, contrary to orders, solely by the imprudence of the officer, and dash and eagerness of the men: they behaved remarkably well and did some execution with their rifles.' Writing to the Duke of Richmond on the same date he says: 'We had yesterday evening a little affair of advanced posts, foolishly brought on by the over eagerness of the Riflemen in pursuit of an enemy's picquet, in which we lost Lieutenant Bunbury of the 95th killed and Captain Pakenham, slightly wounded and, some men of the 95th and 60th. The troops behaved remarkably well but not with great prudence.' Well. Desp., iv, 94 and Supp. Desp. iv, 115.

After Spencer's timely arrival the Riflemen moved back towards Obidos and halted on a knoll that formed part of the spur on which the town was built. It was about a mile from the town and close to the main road which led from Obidos to Roliça. Rifleman Harris says they formed around its summit standing three deep, the front rank kneeling, remaining in this position until daybreak to be prepared for any surprise attack.

Wellesley did not openly lay the blame for this affair and the death of Bunbury on any individual, but by stating that it was due to the imprudence of the 'officer' and eagerness of the men, left it open to interpretation. Reading between the lines this could only refer to Captain Pakenham or the unfortunate Lieutenant Bunbury, to single out the former as the culprit would not have gone down too well back home as he was his brother-in-law! This is further borne out in October of the same year when Wellesley in writing to Colonel Gordon at the Horse Guards on Pakenham's behalf for promotion to major, states that he is really one of the best officers of Riflemen that he has seen! GC/RC

Colonel Verner in his history of the Rifle Brigade puts the blame for this affair squarely on the shoulders of Major Robert Travers, which we feel to be rather unjust. The casualties highlight that it was Captain Pakenham's company and those of the two 60th with which the blame should lie. From a 95th point of view this would mean Captain Pakenham, for once Major Travers dispatched his advanced companies he would have had little immediate control over them. With the French picquets in retreat, the Riflemen's adrenalin would be flowing and possibly spurred on by trying to out do the 60th Riflemen, this would have been attributable to the rashness of their actions. Travers saw the situation his advanced troops had gotten themselves into and at once tried to retrieve the situation by bringing up the remaining troops to their aid.

At dawn on the 16th the Riflemen having made breakfast from the contents of their haversacks, left the knoll and joined the army who had now moved into the town of Obidos, which they occupied until the 17th to allow for the supplies to be brought up.

Delaborde, had taken up a defensive position at Roliça, with his advance posts on high ground two miles to his front, with a horseshoe of rugged hills to his rear and flanks, with the open end facing Obidos.

Meanwhile, Loison having received Junot's urgent request when at Elvas, was force marching his men to the aid of Delaborde and by the 9th August had reached Abrantes. Owing to the exhausted condition of his troops he made a halt for two days, then continued in the same manner until reaching Santarem on the 13th, when another extended halt was required. He finally reached Alcoentre on the 16th about 15 miles east of Obidos. Delaborde had hoped to hold off Wellesley until joined by Loison and decided to fight a delaying action at Roliça, even though his force was far smaller than the British, who had a numerical advantage of about four to one, greater than even Wellesley had thought. Delaborde made up for his lack of numbers by the expert positioning of his troops and then his excellent handling of them throughout the action.

Wellesley spent the night of the 16th in a small square palace in the main street of Obidos and was now making his own preparations for an attack, having first checked on the enemy positions from high ground, possibly the knoll on which the Rifles had spent the night being closer to the French position.

Battle of Roliça

Windmill south of Obidos castle looking towards Roliça

Having received information that Loison was only half-a-day's march away, Wellesley sent his force out of Obidos at 7 am in order to deploy for the attack. Using the three roads that lead south from Obidos, Wellesley took four brigades of infantry and two batteries (12 guns) straight down the centre road. Rowland Hill's 1st brigade, Miles Nightingall's 3rd brigade and Catlin Craufurd's 5th brigade, with a weak battalion of Portuguese caçadores, 400 cavalry made up of 250 Portuguese and 150 20th Light Dragoons. Trant, with his 1,600 Portuguese, he dispatched along the western road to threaten the French left. While Ferguson, with two brigades of infantry, a battery of 6 guns, three companies of the 60th Rifles and about 40 light dragoons were ordered along the east road to protect Wellesley's left flank, should Loison arrive from that direction. Ferguson's main objective was the right flank and if possible the rear of Delaborde's position, to cut his line of retreat.

Hill's brigade, Wellesley positioned about half a mile on his right, while Fane's brigade of Riflemen he had extended on his left. This was in order to keep open communication with Ferguson and the centre column when moving through the hills. At the same time the Rifles could cover the area between the two columns a distance of about one to one and a half miles.

Having sent three companies of the 60th Rifles to join Ferguson's force, Fane's brigade of Riflemen consisted of the four 2/95th companies and remaining seven of the 60th, just over 1,000 strong.

The French outposts began to fall back as soon as they came into contact with the advancing Riflemen. Wellesley's centre column, meanwhile, made a much slower but impressive advance towards Delaborde's position, halting every now and again to dress and regain the order of his regiments which had been lost when crossing the broken ground. All calculated to take up time and the attention of the watching French commander, while allowing his flanking troops of Trant and Ferguson to get behind the French defences. The Riflemen continued to push forward in a long skirmishing line, with the 60th on the right and the 95th on the left and they soon gained the hills on Delaborde's right flank.

Delaborde at this point was positioned on a knoll about hundred feet above the plain and it was on this that the British centre was advancing. Delaborde, however, was quite aware of Wellesley's ploy and sent his voltigeurs to engage with the British Riflemen. Whilst this action of the light troops was taking place, Delaborde was able to withdraw his main force retreating rapidly to his second and what turned out to be his main position. This was on the heights one mile south of Roliça, which rose in steep, broken spurs to about five hundred feet above a stream flowing down a ravine, securing his left flank. The right flank was also to some extent protected by another stream, the hill sides being quite steep had masses of bare rock protruding from the scrub, with a number of fir-trees scattered over the whole area.

With Delaborde escaping from the trap Wellesley had hoped to set, the main British line was at first halted. This resulted in the initial contact with his regiments' light companies and the French being broken off. Fane's Riflemen were, however, still heavily engaged with the French voltigeurs, who contested every foot of the broken ground. As soon as the Riflemen gained a position the French light troops would drop back to defend another. It was quite clear from their stubborn resistance that they were out to gain Delaborde time to regroup on the new defensive position beyond Roliça. The work was exhausting for the Riflemen who had to ascend first one hill, thickly covered in brushwood, which sapped the strength from their legs. Whilst the enemy, laying down at the top concealed in the heath poured a heavy and constant fire into their thinning ranks. By the time they had fought their way to the top of the hill the French had already retreated to the next, where they would again lay concealed firing into the advancing Riflemen, who then had to repeat the process.

After clearing the French from a succession of hills the Riflemen became separated from the voltigeurs by a valley which the enemy defended from a wood. From this position the Riflemen now engaged in a severe rifle fire exchange with the French.

Besides being exhausted from their labours, the heat was also causing a problem with a number of the men who were desperate for water. Captain Leach, having placed his company into the best possible positions to counter the stand made by the French, was also suffering like the men and almost dropping with exhaustion. Lieutenant Cochrane seeing the condition of his Captain came to his aid with the offer of some wine. Just as the lieutenant raised the canteen to Leach's lips a musket-ball smashed through his hand and the canteen, splashing the wine all over Leach's face, cutting his lip and sending him spinning. Captain Leach thought at first, from the force of the blow that he had also been wounded. With blood and wine running down his face he was relieved to find that he had escaped quite so lightly. Leaving a man to attend the wounded lieutenant and take him to the rear, Captain Leach continued the attack with his company.

Sergeant Alexander Fraser of Captain Crampton's company at this point fell to the ground screaming in agony and sitting in a doubled up position swayed backwards and forwards as if he had a terrible pain in his stomach. Rifleman Harris, a colleague of the wounded sergeant ran to his aid and gathered the sergeant in his arms. Fraser gripped hold of Harris' arm, his mouth foaming and the perspiration pouring down his face exclaiming, 'Oh! Harris! I shall die! I shall die!' and in a short time lay dead in Harris' arms. A musket ball had hit the sergeant sideways going through both groins. Harris then rejoined his company and continued to advance with the men, at the same time keeping up a constant fire on the retreating French voltigeurs. As a result the barrel of his rifle became so hot that it made loading difficult and he had to grip the weapon by the stock below the iron.

The Rifles kept pressing the French, forcing them from one stone gully to another until they came under a heavy fire from two houses held by the French light troops, which checked their advance. William Panton, a determined Rifleman of Crampton's company, however, was not to be deterred by this and advanced beyond the skirmish line to gain a better shot at the French. An officer of his company shouted to him to hold back, but he continued advancing and firing until he fell with a musket ball in his thigh. The ball must have hit an artery for in a short time Panton was dead.

Harris crept forward and reached Panton's body, using it as a rest and shelter. He then took revenge for the death of his comrades by picking off a number of the French. The Riflemen had to remain in this position for a while, not able to advance because of the severity of the fire against them, until a man jumped up in full view of his comrades and rushed forward shouting, 'Over boys! over! over!' Instantly the whole line of Riflemen responded and dashed after the leading Rifleman, fixing their sword-bayonets as they ran. The voltigeurs seeing this mass of Riflemen rise and rush at them, turned at once to make their escape and by the time the Riflemen reached the houses they were found to be empty. They then continued in pursuit of the retreating French light troops. At one stage the Rifles also came in range of the French artillery, Rifleman John Sammon was struck full in the face by a cannonball and he fell to the ground a headless corpse.

Wellesley, after the first halt now continued to advance with his column on the new position defended by Delaborde. On nearing this, the light troops of the French and the British forces once again made contact. The regiments of Wellesley's brigades now received orders which allotted each battalion to one of four dry water courses upon which to make an assault on the French position, with one battalion leading and a second in support. For some unknown reason, Lieutenant Colonel George Lake of the 29th Regiment, who commanded the leading battalion and was positioned third from the left of the assaulting line, made an unsupported attack.

This attack was premature and contrary to Wellesley's plans. Whether Lake had seen an opening that required a quick decision to gain an advantage over the reforming French defences, or like the Riflemen at Obidos had received a sudden rush of blood to the head, we shall never know.

Lake advanced with his light company and four battalion companies up the steep gully on the rugged hillside immediately to his front. This isolated him from the main force and as they neared the top, the gully angled to the right leading them into danger and the centre rear of Delaborde's position. They were instantly confronted by a force of Swiss troops who instead of attacking them actually tried to desert! The first priority, however, was to form line and regain some order and in attempting to do this they received a severe musket fire on both flanks. They were then charged in the flank and rear by a full French battalion in a most determined manner intent on driving them down the hill. Colonel Lake and a number of his men fell dead whilst a group of his officers and men were cut off and taken prisoner. Those men who managed to survive had no choice but to retreat down the gully they had just ascended.

Wellesley at once tried to retrieve the situation by making a general advance using the troops in his immediate vicinity. The 5th Regiment made a strong attack on the French left, whilst the 60th and 95th who had been in continual conflict with the enemy's light troops were now descending from the hills onto the French right flank. The 29th were rallied by the sight of the 9th Regiment advancing to their support ready to attack the position they had just left. Once reformed, they joined the 9th Regiment in the general advance. The British artillery also added their weight to the assault giving the infantry much needed cover and did such splendid execution with their guns, which spurred the men on in a most determined manner. Under a fiercely burning sun they laboured up the steep hills against a heavy musket fire, slipping on the loose stones which covered the ground. Men gulped for breath in the fierce heat, choking on the acrid smoke which filled the air, burning their parched mouths and throats.

Trant's force did not cause Delaborde any immediate problem to his left flank and in fact they did not play an active part in the battle, other than to be a potential threat. Ferguson, however, was the main cause for concern having at first descended from the hills too soon, now fell on Delaborde's right flank. His strong force added to that of Fane's, who had been in constant action from the beginning and was gaining ground rapidly. Besides engaging the whole of Delaborde's right flank they were also driving a wedge between himself and Loison, who he still expected at any time. He at once detached three companies from his main force to help guard that position, whilst he continued to organise and charge the British infantry attacking his centre. With his centre battalions, on three occasions he was successful in driving the British from the crest of the hill. In one of these repulses Colonel Stewart of the 9th Regiment fell mortally wounded. The 5th Regiment on the left of Trant's brigade gained the crest of the position and made a stand on Delaborde's left flank. Gradually the British line regiments gained the ridge establishing a strong presence.

The Riflemen of the 95th and 60th continued to attack the French right flank and put in such a destructive fire that they started to fall back.

The pass attacked by British troops at Roliça

2nd French position looking eastwards along the French lines

Delaborde now had no choice but to start to withdraw his force, which he did in a most admirable way. His four infantry battalions retired in pairs alternately, covered by his cavalry, who made a number of charges against the British infantry who constantly threatened to cut his line of escape. Delaborde reached the ridge near to the village of Zambugeira [1] about a mile from the main action with the British. It was protected on each flank by steep ravines and it was here that he decided to make a stand.

The advancing British troops pressed home the attack once again, with the Riflemen of the 95th and 60th putting in such a telling fire on the French right flank that their columns broke and fled in panic. Three of the five guns they had brought safely out of action were now abandoned and a number of men taken prisoner. The French continued their retreat still being pursued by the British light troops and fought their way to Quinta da Bugagliera. The fighting gradually died as Wellesley called a halt to the pursuit, having insufficient cavalry to finish off the routed French. By about four o'clock the action was over which was also about the same time that Loison's vanguard came into view. It was too late to have any effect on the outcome of the battle as the main part of Loison's force had already joined Junot at Cercal. They retired with Delaborde through the pass of Runa to the Cabeco de Montachique, which was nearly thirty miles south of Roliça, where they finally halted.

---

1 This village is actually called Azambugeira

The two opposing forces now counted the cost of the day's action. The French losses in the battle were: 600 killed and wounded, with Delaborde being amongst the wounded. The British losses were: 4 officers and 67 men killed, 20 officers and 315 men wounded, with 4 officers and 68 men missing. Though Wellesley's force was far superior to that of Delaborde only five and a half British battalions were actually engaged in the battle. They were 5th, 9th, 29th, 82nd, 5/60th and 4 companies 95th.

2nd French position looking towards Roliça and Obidos

The official losses for the 95th Rifles in the battle given as: 1 sergeant and 16 Riflemen killed, with 3 officers, 3 sergeants and 30 Riflemen wounded.

The casualties we have been able to confirm from the muster roll/paylists:

Killed:

Sergeant	Alex	Fraser	No 1 Company	
Riflemen	George	Dewer/Dwer	No 2 Company	
	Thomas	Halfpenny	No 1 Company	
	William	Panton	No 1 Company	
	Thomas	Robinson	No 2 Company	sick absent, DOW 7th Sept 1808.
	John	Sammon	No 2 Company	
	William	Wiggin	No 1 Company	
	John	Williams (2nd)	No 1 Company	

Wounded:

Captain	Jasper	Creagh		
Lieuts	Thomas	Cochrane		
	Dudley	St Leger Hill		
Sergeant	Patrick	Brown	No 1 Company	sick absent wounded
Riflemen	David	Beety	No 4 Company	sick absent wounded
	Edward	Burns	No 3 Company	sick absent
	Thomas	Calsin	No 1 Company	sick absent wounded
	Thomas	Connelly	No 1 Company	sick absent wounded
	William	Duggin	No 4 Company	sick absent
	James	Duncan	No 2 Company	wounded
	John	Eastam	No 2 Company	sick absent wounded
	John	Freer	No 1 Company	sick wounded
	Robert	Gray	No 1 Company	sick absent wounded
	William	Greyner	No 3 Company	sick absent wounded
	Chris	Holmes	No 4 Company	sick absent wounded
	William	Hurst	No 1 Company	sick absent wounded
	John	Jack	No 2 Company	sick absent wounded
	Alex	Johnstone	No 3 Company	sick absent wounded
	Patrick	McGovern	No 2 Company	missing POW returned
	Joseph	North	No 1 Company	sick absent wounded
	Edward	Ryan	No 1 Company	sick absent wounded
	Joseph	Sharples	No 1 Company	sick absent wounded
	John	Smith (2nd)	No 1 Company	sick absent wounded
	Danniel	Stott	No 2 Company	sick absent wounded

The 60th casualties were: 8 Riflemen killed, Lieutenants Steitz D'Arcy and de Gilse (the Adjutant), 5 sergeants and 34 Riflemen wounded, with 6 men missing.

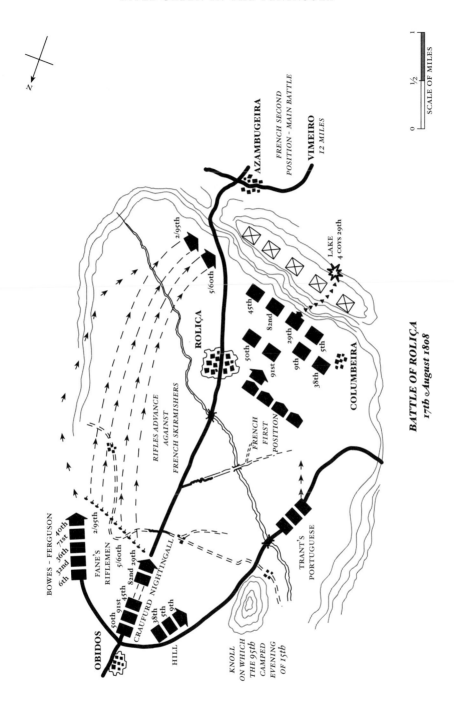

BATTLE OF ROLIÇA
17th August 1808

Wellesley in his despatch said 'although we had such superiority in numbers employed in the operations of this day, the troops actually engaged in the heat of the action were, from unavoidable circumstances, only the 5th, 9th, 29th, the Riflemen of the 95th and 60th, and the flank companies of Major General Hill's brigade; being a number by no means equal to that of the enemy. Their conduct therefore deserves the highest commendation.' Well. Desp., iv, 99 (Wellesley actually missed out the 82nd Regiment.) The same day as that despatch was written, Wellesley published a General Order as follows: 'Lourinha, 18 August 1808.

The Lieutenant-General was perfectly satisfied with the conduct of the troops in action yesterday, particularly with the gallantry displayed by the 5th, 9th, 29th, 60th, and 95th, to whose lot it principally fell to engage the enemy...'

The Duke of Wellington always regarded his victory at Roliça as an important event in his long roll of military achievements. Writing to the Duke of Richmond on the day after the battle he says: 'The action was a most desperate one between the troops engaged. I never saw such fighting as in the pass by the 29th and 9th, or in the three attacks made by the French in the mountains. These were in their best style...' Supp. Desp., vi, 118.

Though Delaborde received some criticism for standing and fighting and suffering such high casualties, he did, however, show remarkable skill in taking full advantage of the ground both to conceal his dispositions and the eventual withdrawal of his troops.

General Junot, meanwhile, had waited until the action at Obidos before making any move to go to the aid of his Generals, Loison and Delaborde. Leaving a garrison of 3,000 men to hold Lisbon, he finally advanced. After several delays and counter-marches caused by the conflicting reports he received as to the movements of the British, he eventually joined Loison on the 17th at Cercal. Here they could hear the guns at Roliça, but they were too far off to go to the support of Delaborde. On the 18th Junot and Loison fell back on Torres Vedras, where, on the 19th he was joined by Delaborde from Montachique.

Of the two roads leading south from Roliça to Lisbon, that to Montachique was the most direct, the other followed the coast to Vimeiro and Mafra. Junot, uncertain as to which one the British would take remained halted until the 20th, when he received reports that Wellesley was advancing along the coast road. Junot having gathered all the available forces he could muster, amounting to about 10,300 infantry; 2,000 cavalry with 700 artillerymen and train plus 26 guns, making a total force of approximately 13,000. He decided to attack straightaway, having already divided his force into four infantry brigades and a cavalry division. On the night of the 20th August the French army marched off to meet the British and by dawn of the 21st had covered ten miles bringing them to within four miles of Wellesley's force.

The Landing at Maceira Bay

Wellesley had previously left orders at Mondego Bay for Anstruther telling him to land south of Peniche, which was still in the hands of the French. Learning of the arrival of his reinforcements he personally reconnoitred and approved the beach at Maceira Bay for the landing, which was some twelve miles south of Roliça. Wellesley's army, meanwhile, had marched to Lourinha on the 18th and after a further march on the 19th reached Vimeiro, a small town on the Maceira, which was two and a half miles inland from the sea.

Expecting the French to attack from the south, Wellesley had positioned his force along the Valongo ridge that ran west to east from the sea towards the town of Vimeiro. The sea protected his right flank while his left was as equally protected by a deep cleft in the ridge, which divided the heights he defended from those that ran north to south covering the landing from the east, should the French try an out flanking movement. Through this cleft the Maceira River [1] flowed and close to its banks was the little town of Vimeiro. On these heights he placed the single battalion of the 40th Regiment with some picquets positioned further north. The lack of water in this area limited the number of men able to defend this part of the field. In reserve behind Vimeiro were the brigades of Ferguson and Trant with four guns. Immediately south of the town was a small hill where Wellesley placed Fane's brigade as an advance post. It was flanked by the heights of the main position. Though the ground here was fairly open in places, it was also broken and overgrown by scrub and cut up by vineyards and woods.

With the British covering troops posted and ready to defend any possible French attack the landing commenced on the 20th, with Anstruther's brigade being the first to get ashore in a heavy surf which caused many boats to capsize and several men to drown. The surf here was probably more dangerous than at Mondego Bay. However, a naval officer in charge of the landing wrote, 'the boats were almost constantly filled in going in by the surf but few if any lives were lost.' In the afternoon a part of Acland's brigade also landed, but the remainder did not get ashore until the following day, too late to take part in the battle.

---

[1] The river was actually called the Alcabrichel, but all British accounts refer to it as the Maceira taken from the village near its mouth (Michael Glover, *Britannia Sickens*).

General Anstruther's observations of the immediate position on landing are of interest, 'The spot where we landed is a sandy beach at the foot of an almost perpendicular cliff. On the summit are the ruins of an old quadrangular fort, to which we were conducted by a narrow winding path, very steep and difficult of ascent. Behind lies a heath where we took up our abode for the night.'

Once Anstruther's brigade was ashore it took its place in the line, part of Acland's brigade was also beginning to move up, bringing the strength of the army to: 16,312 infantry, 240 cavalry and 18 guns, with 2,000 Portuguese under Trant.

For the Light Division, the disembarkation was one of great significance for it brought the 1st Battalion 43rd Light Infantry, 721 strong, the 2nd Battalion 52nd Light Infantry, 654 strong and two companies of the 1st Battalion 95th Rifles, 200 strong, those of Captains Alexander Cameron and Smith Ramadge, under the command of Lieutenant Colonel Sir Thomas Sidney Beckwith. From this day a bond would be formed by these three regiments that would continue throughout the six years of the Peninsular War. During this time they would evolve into one of the finest fighting divisions in the whole of Wellesley's Peninsular army.

The 2nd Battalion 95th, meanwhile, had been taking up their usual out post and advance guard duties and it was whilst on out post duty covering the Vimeiro position on the 19th August, that Rifleman Henry Jessop collapsed and died from fatigue. His comrades buried him in a wood at daybreak, close to one of their out lying picquets.

Also at this time General Fane's brigade had some changes made to it. Wellesley saw the advantage of using his Riflemen in covering the advance of his infantry and containing the opposing French light troops. Possibly with the rashness of Colonel Lake at Roliça still fresh in his mind and not wishing a repeat of this, he ordered a company of the 60th Rifles to be attached to each of his five brigades. Two further companies were transferred to the brigades of Acland and Anstruther. This left Fane with only the three remaining Headquarter companies of the 60th and the four companies of the 2nd Battalion 95th. To make up for this loss the 50th Regiment was transferred from the 5th, to the Light Brigade.

The strength of the British army at Vimeiro now stood as:

1st brigade	Hill	1/5th, 1/9th, 1/38th	2,658
2nd brigade	Ferguson	1/36th, 1/40th, 1/71st	2,449
3rd brigade	Nightingall	1/29th, 1/82nd	1,520
4th brigade	Bowes	1/6th, 1/32nd	1,813
5th brigade	Craufurd	1/45th, 1/91st	1,832
6th brigade	Fane	1/50th, 5/60th, 2/95th	2,005
7th brigade	Anstruther	2/9th, 2/43rd, 2/52nd, 2/97th	2,703
8th brigade	Acland	2nd Queens, 1/20th, 1/95th	1,332
Cavalry	Taylor	20th Light Dragoons	240
Artillery	Robe	3 Batteries	226
Portuguese	Trant	(not engaged)	2,000

Whether these figures allow for the single company of the 60th attached to each of the first five brigades is unclear at this point. In the 60th Rifles' Regimental History it states that, 'In accordance with the G. O. of 21st August 1808, a Rifle Company was attached to each of the newly arrived 7th and 8th Brigades, leaving only three Battalion Headquarter Companies in the Light Brigade.' Whether Acland's brigade received a company of the 60th at this stage is debatable owing to them having two companies of the 1st Battalion 95th Rifles with them already? GC/RC

Battle of Vimeiro

The key to the British position was the small hill south of Vimeiro, on which Wellesley now added the brigade of General Anstruther to that of Fane having reinforced them with another six guns. The brigades of Hill, Craufurd, Nightingall, Bowes and Acland and eight guns held the western heights whilst those of Ferguson and Trant and four guns as already stated were in reserve behind Vimeiro, with the 40th Regiment posted north on the eastern heights.

Wellesley's original plan had been to advance against the French on the 22nd August, once all his reinforcements and stores had been landed. However, news of the arrival of Lieutenant General Sir Harry Burrard in Maceira Bay, who informed his subordinate that he would be spending the night on board ship, put these plans on hold. Wellesley at once rode down to the beach and was rowed out in one of the ship's boats to meet Burrard on the Brazen, which lay about a mile and a half from the shore. With the meeting concluded and Burrard remaining on board ship until the following morning, Wellesley returned to Vimeiro where he found himself in the unexpected position of commander of the land forces until the following day.

A cause for concern to Wellesley over the last couple of days had been the activity of the French cavalry, who because of their superiority in numbers had complete control of the surrounding countryside. They were able to take advantage of this by making constant patrols right up to the British position and on the 20th had effectively gained access to the rear and right of the British lines getting even as far as the landing place! The success of this latter patrol from a French point of view is questionable, for the patrol failed to report the landing of reinforcements unless at the time of their observations only stores were being landed. However, a more likely reason to have affected their judgement might be the fact that they had captured a number of women from the British camp? This patrol could not have been a total failure for Junot planned his attack on the evidence of a British weak left flank, based possibly on the single battalion of the 40th Regiment and some picquets protecting Wellesley's rear and flank.

Once Wellesley returned from his meeting with Burrard he issued a 'Night Pass Order', an order passed from brigade to brigade, rather than sending separate copies to each individual unit. This informed the brigades that on the 21st they were to remain halted, which countermanded the original order for an advance on the enemy. The men were also to remain accoutred throughout the night in readiness to turn out and be under arms at three o'clock in the morning.

Wellesley had already put out a line of outposts from General Fane's brigade to cover his front south of Vimeiro as soon as they reached the area after marching from Roliça. The picquets were drawn from the 95th and 60th Rifles, amounting to around a hundred and fifty men under the command of a field officer, Major Hill of the 50th Regiment. They were about a thousand yards in advance of General Fane's advanced post and occupied the wooded heights east of the Maceira River. Further in advance again, on the Torres Vedras road were the vedettes of the 20th Light Dragoons and it was to these in the early hours of the morning on the 21st August, a peasant gave information that a large column of French troops estimated to be around 20,000 men was advancing on the British position. This movement of a large body of troops was confirmed shortly afterwards, when in the still night air the clatter of horses' hooves and the rumble of guns and limbers could be heard as the French army crossed the wooden bridge over the Maceira River. This was at once reported to General Fane who called out his troops and sent the commander of the cavalry patrol, Sergeant Landsheit with the news to Wellesley. He received the report in relative calm, ordering his officers to their stations to get the troops under arms, but without any noise and neither drums nor bugles.

With Wellesley's army preparing to meet the advancing French forces, Junot had, meanwhile, completed his night march and halted his troops to rest and cook their breakfast. This was about four miles south east of Vimeiro, safe in the knowledge that his superior force of cavalry would shield him from any surprise attack by the British. At the same time he and his men were quite confident that they could beat the British, for they had already proved on many occasions that no continental army had been able to defeat them so far.

An illustration as to how sure the French were of actually achieving this is given by Lieutenant George Simmons of the 95th Rifles, 'When the French entered Lisbon before the landing of Wellesley's army an English family allotted to remain in the city because of the property they owned rather than return to their native country and lose everything to the French. While at the same time expecting to be dragged away to prison they were surprised to have billeted on them a French colonel and captain along with their servants. The English family fed and looked after their guests well and the French officers prevented any harm coming to them in time they became quite friendly. The captain one day took the wife to the window of the house and said "Look at my fine company of soldiers; have you anything like them in England?"

Her pride being hurt, she answered, "Yes indeed we have plenty." "Well, Madam, I hope one day to meet them on the battle field. I have fought in many battles, but never against the English, and really I have no good opinion of them as a military nation." She replied, "You may learn, Sir, to think differently ere long." When news reached Lisbon of the British landing the French troops were assembled and ordered to march to attack the invader. The captain informed the lady of the house, "I am going to fight against the English, and I will give you, my dear Madam, a good account of them when I return." She very good humouredly said, "Take care you do not burn your fingers." The captain's regiment marched and joined the French army previous to the Battle of Vimeiro, where his company was annihilated and himself badly wounded.

It was some days later that the English woman was seated at her window when she noticed a large crowd coming towards her. Eventually it approached near enough for her to observe that it was wounded men lying in great numbers on bullock carts. They passed along towards the hospital, with the exception of one cart, which stopped at her door. On it she perceived the French captain who not long ago was all bravado and confidence. She had him put directly into the chamber he had occupied before leaving and treated him with all the care possible. "My dear lady," he said as soon as he saw her, "Your countrymen have made me pay handsomely for my boasting. The fine fellows that daily paraded before your windows for so many weeks are now lifeless and inanimate clay, and will trouble you no more. Would to God it had been my fate also! I met the English, Oh, that morning was one of the most happy of my life! My men to a man had the same feeling. I was sent out to skirmish against some of those in green, grasshoppers I called them you call them Riflemen. They were behind every bush and stone and soon made sad havoc amongst my men killing all the officers of my company, and wounding myself without being able to do them any injury. This drove me nearly to distraction. In a little time the British line advanced, I was knocked down, bayoneted, and should have been put to death upon the spot if an English officer had not saved me. Our army has been defeated by your countrymen in a succession of battles, and you will have them with you soon in Lisbon.'" (Lt G. Simmons, *A British Rifleman*.) The French officer died some days later from his wounds.

After breakfast, Junot made a reconnaissance of the British position which confirmed that attacking the Valongo ridge held by Wellesley's army was not practical. He, therefore, changed his original plan still unaware of the reinforcements already added to the British force, issuing fresh orders for a major assault on the village of Vimeiro, Wellesley's centre. While at the same time attempting an out flanking movement to roll up the British left, no doubt confident that the latter would work, after the ease with which his cavalry had been able to enter the British lines only the day before. Because of the cavalry error in failing to report the landing of reinforcements for Wellesley, Junot had based the strength of the British army on the numbers employed in the field against Delaborde at Roliça.

At dawn Wellesley rode along the position with General Anstruther. Everywhere it was quiet, with the men waiting in anticipation for the enemy attack. He was still convinced at this point that the French would come from the south, in an attempt to break through his brigades on the Valongo ridge. If this was successful and they were able to reach the landing beach, Wellesley's force would be isolated from their supply ships and transports. With this in mind Wellesley told Anstruther that he thought the right flank was rather short of troops and ordered Acland's brigade, part of which had landed during the night, into this position as a second line.

Between eight and nine o'clock in the morning the French columns finally came into view, which at first puzzled the British troops, for instead of being in the famous dark blue of France, they were instead clad in 'dust coloured' clothes which we would now style as 'khaki'. Junot, in an attempt to add a degree of comfort for his men, while marching through Portugal under a tropical August sun, had provided them with linen frocks. Their long blue uniform coats, they carried rolled up and strapped upon their knapsacks.

Junot divided his army into five infantry brigades, which varied in strength from 1,000 to 3,000 men. (Oman states 2,000 to 4,500 men) Four of these he had formed into two divisions commanded by Generals Delaborde and Loison. The fifth, was his elite brigade consisting of the grenadier companies of every battalion serving in Portugal. These he formed into four battalions, commanded by General Kellermann. His new plan of attack was aimed at breaking through the British centre which if successful would have split Wellesley's force. Half would be trapped with their backs to the sea with little chance of making an escape across a beach that would be under a heavy and constant musket fire from the high ground which commanded it. Whilst the other half would only be able to retreat north east, along the road running over the Mariano ridge, which Junot intended to block. Further north was the French held fortress at Peniche whose garrison could be used to complete the rout.

The two brigades of Loison's division along with Delaborde's first brigade now began to move towards Vimeiro hill, while Delaborde's second brigade under the command of General Brennier, some 3,000 strong (Oman 4,531) with a regiment of dragoons and six guns, Junot had ordered to make a sweeping movement north east. This was to block the British escape route along the Lourinha road and at the same time threaten Wellesley's left flank where, as we have seen only one battalion of infantry the 40th was posted.

Fane's position on Vimeiro hill looking towards French attack

The huge dust clouds formed by the French troop movement were ample warning to Wellesley of Junot's intentions and he at once altered the positions of his own brigades to combat the change in direction of the attack. Ferguson's brigade, in reserve behind Vimeiro, he at once sent to the heights which formed on the other side of the cleft through which the Maceira River ran. At the same time sending orders for Craufurd, Nightingall and Bowes to join Ferguson by marching along the Lourinha road towards Ventosa, where they formed up, with two brigades in line each side of the road with one in reserve. Acland had been ordered to take up a position on the left of Vimeiro hill which was on the other side of the cleft and slightly behind Fane's force. While Hill remained on the right along the Valongo ridge, Craufurd's brigade of two battalions, Wellesley used as a link between his main force in the east and Acland. Trant's Portuguese had been posted to the north east to block any attempt made by the French of sweeping down and turning the British left, but in fact they took no active part in the action.

Junot, not to be outmanœuvred by Wellesley's change of position, detached Solignac's brigade from Loison's division to reinforce Brennier's force; possibly with the intention of making Wellesley release more troops from his centre ground around the village of Vimeiro which was Junot's main objective but by doing this he weakened his own frontal assault, while at the same time creating a gap of over a mile and a half between his main attack and the flanking movements of Brennier and Solignac. Advancing upon Vimeiro hill under the cover of a cloud of tirailleurs were the first two infantry brigades of Thomières and Charlot consisting of four and a quarter battalions with seven guns. In the second line were the four elite battalions of the grenadiers, with some cavalry and the reserve artillery.

The brigades of Anstruther and Fane on Vimeiro hill were now prepared for the defence of their position. Still on outlying picquet, however, some thousand yards in advance of the hill was the small force of Riflemen under Major Hill. On the summit of Vimeiro hill itself in line and partly hidden by these vineyards and scrub of the flat ground Anstruther had the 97th; 43rd and 52nd Light Infantry; with the 9th Regiment formed in column of companies immediately behind them in reserve. Fane's brigade, consisting of the 1st Battalion 50th Regiment, three companies of the 60th Rifles and four companies 2nd Battalion 95th Rifles, less the picquets, were formed up on Anstruther's left, with a belt of scrub about one hundred and fifty yards to their front. Also in reserve were the 20th Light Dragoons. The twelve guns of the artillery were posted in three groups of four, one on each flank, with the remaining group positioned between the two brigades.

It was about seven o'clock in the morning when the night picquets under the command of Major Hill first had sight of the French. It was a beautiful sunny day and the sun was reflecting from the tips of the enemy's bayonets as they advanced en masse on Wellesley's centre. Fane had ordered Major Hill to try to check the French advance as best he could by pouring in a running fire, retreating and firing. This small body of men remained in the woods until a number of them had been killed. Major Hill then gave the order to retreat on the main position. The French tirailleurs were putting in such a telling and heavy fire from in front of their advancing columns that they could not hope to slow their advance. The British artillery up to this point had been unable to add their fire without injuring their own men but with the picquets retreating first through the vineyards and then up the hill towards them they were now free from this obstacle. The retreating Riflemen eventually reached the position held by the 97th Regiment and once they cleared its front they passed around the right flank to the rear. Having gained the safety of the British line the picquets moved off to find and join their respective companies. Besides the Riflemen killed and wounded the outlying picquets also lost their Commander, Major Hill who fell having been wounded twice. Captain Leach of the 95th who was part of this force though not wounded was hit in the thigh by a large piece of stone which had been deflected by a round shot. This made him quite lame for some days but he continued to command his company throughout the battle.

General Fane and Major Travers were standing together at the beginning of the action with the former observing the movements of the French through his telescope, while at the same time keeping a watchful eye on the progress of his retreating picquets. After a short time he ordered Major Travers to form up his Riflemen and send them down to the foot of the hill in skirmishing order so they could attack the head of the leading column of the French, leaving only a small reserve with the 50th.

With the buglers sounding the call to arms one man, Private John Murphy of No 4 Company 95th, normally a lively and brave Rifleman, was showing some reluctance to take up his position; for that night he had had a premonition of his own death in the coming battle. Captain Pakenham, his company commander, had a sharp word with him and the dejected Murphy joined the ranks of his comrades. Murphy had just cause, however, to feel as he did for he was one of the first men to be killed that day in the 95th!

General Fane, now ordered his reserve Riflemen from the 95th and 60th to attack the head of Thomières' brigade. They immediately pushed on down to the bottom of the hill in skirmish order. The 50th remained in reserve on the original position to the left of Anstruther's brigade, except for three companies which had been detached from the flank, to their left. The French, however, continued to attack in such a determined manner and in overwhelming numbers which caused the Riflemen to give ground forcing them to retreat. This they did by firing and retiring at short distances where they would then halt and continue to fire into the French columns until they came up with the Riflemen again. They then repeated their actions until reaching the original position when they formed as reserve behind the 50th.

The French tirailleurs suffered casualties to their ranks as they continued to advance against the fire of the more accurate Baker rifles of the 95th and 60th positioned in a thin skirmish line at the bottom of Vimeiro hill. Even at a distance of nine hundred yards, the front ranks of the leading French columns were also feeling the same effect and many officers were singled out for their deadly fire. The two French brigades deployed to their left and advanced to the attack in line of half battalion columns, each company standing three ranks deep, supported by the fire of the seven guns which advanced with the two brigades.

General Fane whilst riding along in rear of the skirmishing line observed a Rifleman of the 60th, who were all German, make a couple of excellent shots which resulted in two French officers being shot down while trying to rally their men to attack. Fane shouted out to him, 'Well done, my fine fellow! I will give you half a doubloon for every one you bring down.' The Rifleman loaded his rifle in great haste and brought down another Frenchman, then looking back at the General said, 'By Got I vill make my fortune.'

An officer also noted a similar incident about this time. Seeing himself covered by a French marksman he shouted to a Rifleman of the 60th to shoot him. The Rifleman, however, took no notice of the officer and brought down a French officer instead. Luckily for the English officer the French marksman missed! Angrily the officer asked the Rifleman why he had shot the French officer, his cool reply was, 'It vas more plunder.'

The brigade of Thomières, advancing on the British centre, was the first to come into action and was heading for the ground held by Fane. He had only the 50th Regiment in position to oppose them, less three companies which he had previously detached from the flank to their left. While at the same time Charlot's brigade was approaching Anstruther, whose troops were still largely unseen by the French. This mass of enemy soldiers was, however, too strong for the thin line of Riflemen out in advance and they were now in danger of being over-run. The buglers were ordered to sound the retreat just before this could happen and the men began to fire and retire. This they achieved by retiring short distances and halting to continue firing into the column until the French came up to them again. They then repeated the action by doubling back in relays up to the main position. Anstruther sent four companies from his force to help cover their retreat because the French were so hot on the Riflemen's heels putting them in danger. This just gave them time to reform behind the awaiting 50th. Wellesley seeing Anstruther's troops forward movement immediately despatched one of his staff officers to order the two Brigadier Generals to hold their ground and not to advance without orders from him. These supporting companies also retired with the retreating Riflemen.

Rifleman Harris relates that while retreating with his comrades at this time accompanied by Corporal John Gillaspie of his own company and while firing and retiring the corporal gave a sudden jump and started to limp quite badly. However, he continued firing and retiring with his company back to the main position though in some considerable pain and discomfort, until at last he became so weak he fell to the ground from loss of blood. His comrades at once showed concern for his well being asking where he had been hit. Gillaspie was reluctant to divulge the nature of his wound, but in the end full of embarrassment told Rifleman Harris that he had been hit in the rear. Harris soon made it common knowledge to the company and the plight of the wounded corporal was made even worse from the chiding he received at the hands of his comrades. Eventually Gillaspie, a very sensitive man could take it no longer, one day he just sat down and cried like a child! Strange that a man who could face any amount of danger in the field was broken by the sensitive nature of a wound received in battle.

With the Riflemen and their supports rejoined on the main position, the 95th regrouped and formed the reserve close to the guns. The artillery now fired into the advancing French columns, without the fear of causing casualties amongst their own troops. For a very short time the French had enjoyed a trouble free advance and must have thought that they had scared the British troops off the field. However, Colonel Robe and his gun teams soon changed that and poured in a most destructive fire with their round shot, smashing lanes through the packed ranks of soldiers, while the howitzers fired for the first time in the field Major Shrapnel's spherical shot. This burst in the air above the determined Frenchmen, as if sending a volley of musketry from the sky. The 95th were close to the guns when they first fired. Seeing the effect of the first round shot as it carved out a path through the advancing column they gave a loud cheer. Though many men were falling, the brave French infantry gallantly pushed on.

Thomières' brigade, was the largest of the two French brigades advancing on Vimeiro hill and they continued up the slope after the retreating Riflemen faced by the single battalion of the 50th, some 945 strong. The artillery also caused this brigade severe casualties and disruption in its ranks. The French marched up as far as a hedge which was a little in front of Fane's force, where they halted. This was only long enough to regain their formation which once completed they then continued to advance under the cover of their own seven guns. Colonel Robe ordered his gunners to continue firing into the French for as long as it was possible giving Fane's Riflemen maximum cover which at the same time helped to reduce the ranks of the enemy even further. This they continued to do right up to the point when the French were almost upon them.

They then made good their escape, running for the safety of the British line, abandoning the guns.

As Thomières' brigade approached the 50th Regiment, the three companies which had been detached on the left now opened up a strong fire into the right flank of the French column which caused it to incline to its left. Colonel Walker, the commanding officer of the 50th, wheeled up two companies from his right wing and ordered them to fire into the angle made by Thomières' front and left flank, then charged. Hit by a fire on both flanks the French column was severely shaken and disorganised. The drivers of the three leading French guns panicked at seeing this attack in their rear and at once cut their traces leaving the guns, only to plunge back through the ranks of their own infantry. Three more companies of the 50th added their volley fire into the shaken French column, before its outer companies had a chance to deploy and counter the charge made by Colonel Walker, who was also joined by the remaining companies of his battalion. Faced by this determined rush the whole French brigade finally broke, retreating headlong down the slope in wild confusion. Some companies of the 60th from the reserve joined in the 50th's rout of this brigade while the remaining Riflemen added their collective fire to the defeat. Rifleman Brotherwood lying alongside Harris had been one of the outlying picquet and now in the skirmishing line, having been firing away at the French, ran out of ammunition. Seeing the French in full retreat and not being able to wreak further destruction on them, in sheer frustration took his razor from his pack, rammed it down the barrel of his rifle and fired it after the French. Also in the ranks of the 95th skirmishers were three brothers: John, Michael and Peter Hart, who were noted for their reckless and fun loving nature. They had no regard for danger and treated life as one big joke, while at the same time they were perfect Riflemen, fine fit specimens of British youth and excellent runners. Their recklessness brought them into conflict with Lieutenant John Molloy of their company in this action, who for their own good had to keep them in check, 'Damn you!' he shouted at them, 'Keep back, and get under cover. Do you think you are fighting here with fists and that you are running into the teeth of the French.' Meanwhile, Colonel Walker continued after the fleeing Frenchmen with his battalion until he saw a body of French cavalry drawn up in a position to threaten his flank. He called an immediate halt to the pursuit.

Delaborde had led the attack on the right with Thomières' brigade, though still suffering from the wounds he had received at Roliça. Just as his attack was being defeated, Charlot's brigade was about to engage Anstruther. This able brigadier with one of the strongest brigades in Wellesley's army was well positioned to cope with the threat of this French left hand column.

He had the 97th Regiment deployed in his first line with the 43rd Light Infantry in echelon behind its right flank, the 52nd Light Infantry were also in echelon and in rear of its left flank, while the 2nd Battalion 9th Regiment were formed in column of companies in reserve. As the French emerged from the small wood immediately in front of Anstruther which was only one hundred and fifty yards distant, he ordered the 97th Regiment, who up to this point had been concealed by a dip in the ground, to advance and pour volley fire into them. This shook the French and after about three bursts of musketry fire the 97th advanced down the hill against the bewildered French troops. Though this movement was contrary to Wellesley's orders, once the 97th were in motion Anstruther had little chance of holding them. Instead he seized the opportunity that had been presented to him and ordered the 52nd to double round by the rear to give support to the 97th's right flank. This in turn, turned the French left flank, combined with the 97th's frontal attack and the French were pushed back to the edge of the wood. Here Anstruther halted to reform the 97th and after leaving strong picquets amongst the trees marched them back to the original position to rejoin the rest of the brigade. This attack was just as effective as that made by the 50th, therefore, the attack on Vimeiro hill had been defeated at both points, with the French suffering heavy losses. To make matters worse they had also left all their guns behind and both Generals Delaborde and Charlot were wounded.

Junot, as we have previously described, had sent a brigade and six guns to reinforce Brennier's outflanking movement. Because of this he now found himself with only the four infantry battalions of the grenadiers in reserve and four guns, with which to renew the attack. Junot even at this point was still very naive as to the true fighting spirit of the British troops. However, he was soon to learn that they could not be classed in the same breath as other continental armies, or as Fortescue put it, 'having never tasted defeat before had no reason to believe they could be defeated.' Junot made his second attack along much the same route that Delaborde had led Thomières' brigade. Two of the battalions under General St. Clair advanced in column of platoons supported by the fire of his four guns which now and again unlimbered and fired on the British position. The grenadiers pushed on, despite the heavy artillery fire of Colonel Robe's guns, only to encounter the accurate fire of the Riflemen of the 95th and 60th, who once again had been pushed forward in skirmish order. They then came under more infantry fire, that of the 52nd and 97th and after enduring heavy losses and having nearly the whole of the two leading platoons struck down by rifle fire, they broke and rushed headlong down to the shelter of the deep hollow below the eastern heights.

Acland's position looking towards Vimeiro

Whilst this fight was in progress, Junot had sent General Kellermann with the two remaining battalions of grenadiers to attempt to turn Fane's left flank and secure the village of Vimeiro from the northeast. This put the 50th and Riflemen in a dangerous position. The brigade commanders seeing this danger immediately sent reinforcements. Anstruther not being under attack was able to release the 43rd Regiment to the rear of Fane's brigade to cover the village and hold the cemetery, also putting two companies into the front houses which took Kellermann in the flank. Acland, posted on the spur of the opposite Eastern heights, opened up on Kellermann with his guns while at the same time sending the two companies of the 1st Battalion 95th under Captain Cameron, supported by two light companies from the line battalions, to take him in the right flank. The grenadiers, though exposed to artillery and rifle fire on their right, musketry fire on their left and the resolute 50th in their front still bravely advanced. The 50th were able to hold off the frontal assault, but the flank attack reached the walls of Vimeiro. It was here they encountered the 43rd at the cemetery and some of the most desperate fighting of the whole battle was to take place amongst the tightly packed buildings and enclosures of the village. This was the last throw of the dice for Junot and everything hinged on the success of this final assault. It was equally just as important to Wellesley, for had the grenadiers succeeded in gaining the village, the French would not only have pierced the British centre but would also have been in a position to capture their transport park. The grenadiers, opposed to the 95th, Harris describes as, 'Fine looking young men wearing red shoulder knots and tremendous looking moustaches.' The Riflemen though were not in awe of their enemy for, whenever they knocked one over they would shout out, 'There goes another of Boney's invincibles.' Lying near to Harris at this time, firing, was Rifleman Joseph Cockayne of his company, who was in high spirits and delighted in the losses he and his comrades were inflicting on the advancing French troops. The heat and the constant biting of the cartridges was, however, making the men quite thirsty. Rifleman Cockayne lifted his canteen to his lips shouting at the same time to Harris, 'Here's to you old boy' when a French bullet smashed through the canteen striking Cockayne in the head killing him instantly. At the same time another Rifleman close by fell from the same hail of bullets with a musket ball lodged in his thigh.

Though Wellesley had time to deploy his forces to combat Junot's change of tactics before the battle began, the huge mass of carts, bullocks, mules and supplies under the care of local Portuguese drivers, was a problem and had to remain where they were, in and around Vimeiro. To have attempted to move them through the narrow defile between the two heights and along the tracks would have brought utter chaos to the troop movements taking place.

It was at this point in the imminent defeat of the grenadiers that General Fane ordered the advance of the whole line against the retreating enemy. Rifleman Brotherwood of the 95th came rushing up to the General and presented him with a green feather, which he had torn from the cap of a French light infantryman he had killed. 'God Bless you General' he said, 'Wear this for the sake of the 95th.' Fane took the feather and stuck it in his cocked hat and advanced with the men.

It was now time for Fane's cavalry to take part in the action; three squadrons of the 20th Light Dragoons and two of Portuguese under Colonel Taylor had all this time been waiting in position behind Vimeiro hill. At last the General called them forward and Fane gave the order, 'Now 20th, now we want you. At them, lads, and let them see what you are made of.' The 20th then came trotting up and wheeling to the left, advanced with the Portuguese on either flank, but on nearing the fleeing French the latter gradually slowed up and left the dragoons to confront the French. The 20th continued on alone, riding into the fugitives who were falling back from the unsuccessful attack, sabring and cutting them to pieces. In no time the British cavalry resembled the butchers of the commissary, their white leather breeches, hands, arms and swords were covered in blood as they took their period of inactivity out on the French infantry. Unfortunately, they advanced

too far and were engaged by some French squadrons who outnumbered them five to one and exacted a swift revenge for the treatment metered out to their infantry. This resulted in more than half of the 20th Light Dragoons being either killed or wounded, their Colonel, Charles Taylor being amongst the former.

Throughout the whole of the battle Major Travers had been most conspicuous riding about the field shouting instructions and encouragement to the Riflemen. At the close of the battle he came riding down in great haste to where his Riflemen had made their final halt. He was in very high spirits and was well liked by his men. On joining them he shouted, 'A guinea, a guinea to the man who will find my wig!' To which the men burst into fits of laughter having discovered their leader's secret that he was as bald as a coot, which up to this moment he had been able to conceal from them.

Meanwhile, the proposed attack by Solignac and Brennier was in progress, for it was too late for Junot to halt or alter his previous plans even though the failure of his central assault now made this movement futile. The situation, however, was far worse than Junot expected, for his two brigades were about to mount an attack without any co-ordination. Due to Brennier having marched further north than was necessary, he came upon the road from Vimeiro to Lourinha which he then continued along in a south westerly direction towards Vimeiro, taking longer than expected. What little chance of success the French might have gained was now lost. With Solignac advancing from the direction of the Toledo valley, at one point close to the actual hamlet of the same name, [1] moving north and uphill towards the Mariano ridge in parallel columns of battalions preceded by a thick screen of skirmishers. The only troops he could see were the skirmishers of Ferguson's brigade.

---

[1] Michael Glover's observations are worth noting here…'The direction from which Solignac and later Brennier attacked are hard to determine. The brigades of Ferguson, Nightingall and Bowes were originally formed astride the Mariano ridge facing the village of Ventosa, i.e. facing uphill towards the north-east. All the authorities agree that Solignac attacked uphill and could see only the skirmishers in front of the main British line until it was too late to draw back. It follows, therefore, that he must have attacked from the Toledo valley, probably along the Toledo-Ventosa track, rather than attacking from Ventosa (as shown in the maps of Fortescue, Oman and Weller) which would have been downhill, with the British cavalry visible for some distance. Brennier, on the other hand, attacked downhill. He probably came down the Lourinha-Vimeiro road to Ventosa and struck off right into the ravine west of the Toledo-Ventosa track where Solignac had abandoned his guns.' (*Britannia Sickens*)

The French advanced with confidence, their guns positioned in the intervals between the columns. Solignac's brigade was, therefore, the first into action but unknown to them, behind the crest were seven British battalions. These quickly re-forming to their right with their backs to the Lourinha-Vimeiro road having previously been positioned across the Mariano ridge facing the village of Ventosa. In front were Ferguson's three battalions: 36th, 71st and 40th with, on their left the 82nd of Nightingall's brigade. In the second line were Bowes' two battalions, 6th and 32nd, with Nightingall's remaining battalion of the 29th.

Once formed the British front line advanced to the crest and now at a range of less than a hundred yards, poured a rolling volley fire of half companies into the French columns. The battalions at each end of the British line then brought up their wings so as to add their fire into the flanks of the French column. The British re-loaded and in complete silence, started to advance down the slope. This caused the enemy to retire but whenever they showed any presence of reforming, General Ferguson had the 36th Regiment charge them, which they did on three occasions. Meanwhile, the 71st charged six guns of the French artillery which were attempting to withdraw. The French eventually broke with the 36th and 40th in hot pursuit driving them eastwards and away from Junot's main body. It was at this time that Brennier entered the field and charged downhill with his dragoons who had been protecting the flanks of his brigade. They fell upon the 71st and 82nd Regiments who were guarding the captured guns of Solignac's brigade. Taken by surprise they were forced to leave their prizes and retreat up the westward slope of the re-entrant. On reaching the top they reformed with the 29th and charged back down the hill again. It was now that some desperate fighting took place before the French finally broke retiring under the cover of their dragoons, leaving General Brennier wounded and a prisoner.

With both Brennier and Solignac's brigades beaten and retreating eastwards away from the main body of the French who were retreating in a south-easterly direction, there was no chance of them uniting to stand against the British. Junot on seeing his army in retreat made no attempt to rally them and got into his carriage, giving no orders to his officers drove through his columns and returned to Lisbon leaving them to fend for themselves.

From Wellesley's point of view the battle had only been half won, the British having suffered a total of 720 casualties, while capturing all but nine of the French guns and taking 300 prisoners. The three brigades of Hill, Bowes and Craufurd had not fired a shot and of the rest, only the 43rd, 50th, 71st and 82nd had suffered serious casualties.

Vimeiro hill looking towards Ventosa

The French were beaten but not destroyed though this could still have been achieved by the quick deployment of Hill's brigade followed by those of Anstruther, Fane and Acland towards Torres Vedras, reaching it before the French. Once this position was held the French would have had no option but to reach Lisbon by crossing the rugged and roadless country of the 'masif' of Monte Junta.

With this in mind Wellesley gave preliminary orders to this effect then reported to the Commander-in-Chief, saying, 'Sir Harry now is your time to advance, the enemy is completely beaten and we shall be in Lisbon in three days. We have a large body of troops which have not been tried in action. Let us move from the right on the road of Torres Vedras and I will follow the French with the left.' However, Sir Harry Burrard declined to move from the ground they held until Sir John Moore joined with his force. Wellesley tried to change his mind by convincing him that the men were well provided with food and ammunition with plenty of mules, reserve ammunition, stores and provisions, but he again refused. Having already beaten the French as a complete attacking unit with only part of his army, it would have been even simpler to complete a victory on a scattered and spent force. Another opportunity presented itself only a few minutes later which could still have had a great impact on the day. General Ferguson's aide-de-camp, Captain Mellish, arrived with a message that he had the whole of Solignac's brigade penned in a ravine but could not make them prisoners without permission to make a short advance. Burrard again refused to sanction any move forward, ordering Ferguson back to the original position. The chance was lost and Solignac, who could not have believed his luck, escaped. Sir Arthur turned his horse's head and with a cold contemptuous bitterness, said aloud to his aide-de-camp, 'You may think about dinner for there is nothing more for soldiers to do this day.' The French after twenty four hours of continuous marching reached Torres Vedras in a most sorry state with their nine remaining guns. Having lost 2,000 men in the battle those who had completed the march were badly shaken and demoralised by the unexpected defeat. Junot's view was that they were in no condition to fight another battle.

At the end of the day the men slumped to the ground exhausted and many went to sleep in that same spot, while others went looking over the battle field in search of plunder. Rifleman Harris, an old hand at this game was out on this errand when he came upon a wounded Frenchman and taking pity on him was in the process of giving him water when Rifleman Stewart Mullen of his regiment came up. 'You should be better off bashing his brains out, Harris, after all the damage he has done us today,' was his observation of the scene as he passed on his way over the battle field. If Mullen had held back a little longer he would have got his wish for it was not long after Harris' kindness that the Frenchman died.

Harris continued to search the battle field and passing over the area in which the 43rd confronted the French grenadiers, saw at first hand an example of the desperate fighting which had taken place there. For locked in death as in battle were a man of the 43rd and a grenadier, their weapons still in their hands having killed each other at the same moment with their bayonets.

Though plundering the dead had its rewards it was also at times dangerous. Harris came upon the body of an officer of the 50th Regiment who had already been plundered. His shoes, however, were far more serviceable than Harris' own and it was while in the process of exchanging his own for those of the dead officer that a shot whistled past his head. Taking up his rifle he looked about the battle field but the culprit had taken cover. Harris continued the exchange while at the same time being aware to the possibility of having another shot taken at him. In due course a second shot rang out which also missed and being quicker to the danger caught sight of a French light infantryman about to take cover. Harris fired a loose shot which brought his man down. Rushing over to him he drew his sword bayonet, but their was no need for the Frenchman was already dead. Harris having at first drank the contents of the Frenchman's calibash was in the process of searching him for any plunder when an officer of the 60th approached and told him the best place to look was in the lining of the coat or in the Frenchman's stock, exclaiming, 'I know where these rascals keep their coin better than you do!' Harris was rewarded with several doubloons, three or four Napoleons and a few dollars which had been in a yellow silk purse, wrapped in a black silk handkerchief in the lining of the coat. Happy with this find Harris returned to where he had left his company, just in time, for the buglers were sounding the call to fall in for the roll to be called. Once the extent of the day's casualties had been recorded the men were told to lie down and get some rest which they did enranked upon the battle field.

Once the roll had been called the females belonging to the 95th who had missed their husbands came along the front of the line to enquire from the survivors whether they knew anything about their men. Mrs. Cockayne had made such a request without gaining any news as to her husband's fate and the poor woman stood before the Riflemen sobbing. Harris, who had been with her husband when he was killed could not bring himself to tell the woman of his death. At length, Captain Leach tried to resolve the woman's distress and asked the men if they had news of Rifleman Cockayne's whereabouts. Harris had no choice now but to give the woman the sad news, she, however, wished to find his body and Harris took her to where he remembered Cockayne being killed. When they reached the spot she embraced the stiffened body gazing upon his disfigured face for some minutes, then taking a prayer book from her pocket, with tears streaming down her face knelt down and repeated the service for the dead. When she had finished she seemed much comforted. Harris called to a passing pioneer who helped them to dig a hole in which they placed the unfortunate Rifleman. Mrs Cockayne returned with Harris to the company in which her husband had served and laid down near to them with some other females who had suffered a similar loss. The company to which Rifleman Cockayne belonged was still her home and she marched with it to Lisbon where she eventually procured a passage home to England.

Normally when a woman lost her husband in battle it was not unusual for her to marry one of his comrades and continue serving with the regiment. Some of these women became favourites with the men and were an important part of the regimental system. Washing clothes for the officers and sergeants, sewing for the men, or cooking for their husbands, for the former she would receive payment. In this way the unit was kept organised and happy.

When the men were not needed for duties or the troops were in winter quarters they were also a welcome distraction from boredom. With this in mind Harris offered to marry Mrs. Cockayne, who he also described as a handsome woman, but she turned him down, saying that she had had enough of soldiers and was still in shock from the death of her husband but thanked him for his kindness.

On returning to his company Harris, still feeling little need for sleep, decided to search the battle field once more with a couple of comrades. While in the process of doing this he witnessed the cruel fate of a French officer, who was running towards his position pursued by half a dozen horsemen. Harris held up his hand and called to them not to hurt him. One of the horsemen, however, cut him down with a desperate blow when close beside Harris, while a second, wheeling round as he leaned from his saddle, passed his sword through the officer's body. Harris was alarmed at this treatment of the French officer and was unhappy to notice amongst the Portuguese horsemen, a trooper of the light dragoons. He now decided to return to the battalion and after a short sleep was awoken by the company buglers sounding to arms. Once formed the men were marched off to take up the picquet duties for the night.

The following day the men were formed into burial parties whilst others had the task of transporting the wounded to the surgeons. The Rifles' Assistant Surgeon, Thomas Ridgway, had set up in the churchyard at Vimeiro two long tables taken from the houses nearby and placed end to end amongst the graves. Those men who required limbs to be amputated, both English and French, were constantly lifted on and off the tables as soon as the operation was performed. The surgeons with their sleeves rolled up resembled butchers with their hands and arms covered in blood, whilst severed arms and legs piled up in the yard. Rifleman Harris had been part of the group transporting the wounded and saw first hand the horrors inflicted by man upon his fellow man in battle. Having deposited his latest casualty he was about to leave when Ridgway called him over to help hold Rifleman Hugh Doughter, an Irishman of the 95th. The doctor needed to cut deep into the man's shoulder to remove the musket ball, but his twisting and writhing was making it difficult to perform the operation. When the ball was eventually extracted, Harris being no longer needed returned to the hill upon which the Rifles were bivouacked. Here he was ordered by Captain Leach to get his shoe making implements from his pack so that he could repair the men's waist belts, many having been torn during the action. This was possibly due to the men constantly throwing themselves down onto the rough ground from which position they fired for most of the day.

The casualties for the 60th Rifles are given as:

14 rank and file killed
Lieutenants Koch and Ritter, 1 sergeant and 22 rank and file wounded.
1 Rifleman listed as missing.

So far, we have only been able to extract a total of 27 casualties from the muster/paylists including the missing for the 2nd Battalion 95th. We are not able to give any figures for the 1st Battalion 95th as there are no returns though one would have expected a few casualties. In the works by Napier and Oman they list two men as missing in the general list of casualties for the Battle of Vimeiro. The two men of the 95th given in the roll opposite would seem to confirm their findings, these men having been taken prisoner, possibly when part of the original outlying picquets at the beginning of the battle?

The official casualty figures for the four companies of the 2/95th are:

3 sergeants, 34 rank and file killed.
4 officers, 3 sergeants, 40 rank and file listed as wounded.
2 rank and file missing.

Sergeant	John	Mills	No 1 Company	killed
Riflemen	Alex	Cameron	No 1 Company	killed
	Joseph	Cockayne	No 3 Company	killed
	James	Mathews	No 2 Company	killed
	John	Murphy (2nd)	No 4 Company	killed
	Peter	Rock/Rook	No 4 Company	killed
	John	Smith (3rd)	No 4 Company	killed
Lieutenants	William	Cox		wounded
	Dudley	St. Leger Hill		wounded
	William	Johnston		wounded
	Henry	Manners		wounded
Corporal	John	Gillaspie	No 3 Company	sick wounded
Riflemen	Patrick	Burns	No 3 Company	sick absent wounded
	Patrick	Comaford	No 2 Company	sick wounded (Also as Comeford)
	Thomas	Clayton	No 3 Company	sick wounded
	Joseph	Davis	No 4 Company	sick wounded
	Hugh	Doughter	No 2 Company	sick wounded
	William	Duggin	No 4 Company	sick absent (in Aug)
	George	Hakrow	No 1 Company	sick absent wounded
	William	Harrold	No 4 Company	sick absent wounded
	Daniel	Larkin	No 4 Company	sick absent wounded
	Alex	McCummin	No 3 Company	sick absent wounded
	John	Royle	No 2 Company	sick absent wounded
	John	Washbourne	No 1 Company	sick absent wounded
	Thomas	Williams	No 1 Company	sick wounded
Riflemen	Joseph	Hindle	No 3 Company	missing from 21st Aug rejoined from French prison 6th Sept 1808
	William	Miles/Mills	No 4 Company	missing 21st Aug POW

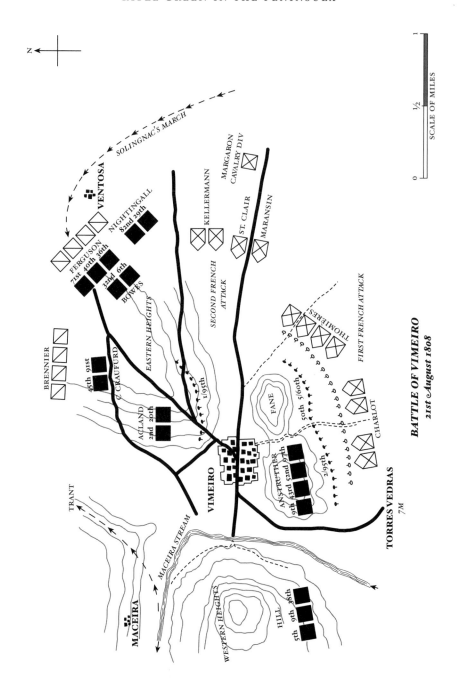

BATTLE OF VIMEIRO
21st August 1808

Advance and Occupation of Lisbon

Though Wellesley's request to follow up Junot's retreating French army had been rejected, the arrival of Sir Hew Dalrymple as the new Commander-in-Chief gave him fresh hope of being allowed to finish the job he had already started. However, this was soon dashed once more as Sir Hew refused on the grounds that having just landed he did not have sufficient knowledge of the situation to order an advance. On leaving Wellesley, Sir Hew made his way up the difficult track leading from the beach to join Sir Harry Burrard. At the same time, scores of baggage carts which first had to be unloaded were trying to negotiate the same track taking large numbers of wounded men to the beach for transportation to the ships. To reach Sir Harry's position Sir Hew had to cross the battle field of Vimeiro which was still strewn with hundreds of bodies of both the British and French which were becoming most offensive in the heat. The heaps of unloaded stores and all the usual clutter of battle all adding to the scene. Every building in the surrounding area was full of wounded British and French soldiers waiting for medical attention or transport to take them to the beach. To Sir Hew, this sight represented one of utter chaos which confirmed that he had made the right decision when confronted by Wellesley.

Rumours were also rife of British reinforcements having landed on the coast, while columns of Portuguese troops had been reported moving on Santarem. It was from this strong position Wellesley, Burrard and Dalrymple entered into talks with the French to negotiate terms for a treaty, which would force them to withdraw from Portugal. Junot, therefore, held a council of war which agreed to a capitulation under the best possible terms. General Kellermann was sent with an escort of two squadrons of cavalry which at first was thought to be an attack by the French army which caused some panic until Kellermann arrived under a flag of truce. The outcome of which led to the Convention of Cintra and the cessation of hostilities. The French evacuated Portugal, handing over the fortresses intact, but instead of being prisoners of war, were allowed to leave with all their military baggage and equipment to be returned to a French port, conveyed in British ships.

There is no place in this history for the politics which surrounded this Convention or, who was to blame for its final outcome, but suffice to say that because of it, all three generals were recalled to England to answer to the Government for their actions. The command of the British army was now placed on the shoulders of that most capable officer, General Sir John Moore.

However, before we pass over this sorry piece of British military history we will outline the details agreed in the treaty which will help to explain the movements of the force from this point.

Cease Fire resolved between Sir Arthur Wellesley, Lieutenant General and Knight of the Order of the Bath and Lieutenant General Kellermann Grand Officer of the Legion of Honour, Commander of the Order of the Iron Crown, Grand Cross of the Order of the Lion of Bavaria, both officers having been empowered to negotiate by the Generals of the respective armies.

Headquarters of the English Army. 22nd August 1808

Article 1. From today there will be a cease-fire between the armies of His Britannic Majesty and His Imperial and Royal Majesty, Napoleon I so that a Convention for the evacuation of Portugal by the French army may be negotiated.

Article 2. The Generals commanding the two armies and the Admiral commanding the British fleet at the mouth of the Tagus will meet at a time and place to be agreed in order to negotiate and conclude the said Convention.

Article 3. The River Zizandre will be established as the line of demarcation between the two armies; neither army will occupy Torres Vedras.

Article 4. The commanding General of the English army will inform the Portuguese who are under arms of this cease-fire; and for them the line of demarcation will be established from Leiria to Tomar.

Article 5. It is provisionally agreed that in no case will the French army be considered as prisoners of war, that all members of it will be transported to France with their arms and baggage, with their personal property of every kind, nothing having been abstracted from it.

Article 6. No proceedings shall be instituted against any person, be they Portuguese, French or of a nation allied to France on the grounds of their political conduct; such people will be protected, as will their property, and they will be at liberty to leave Portugal during a period to be agreed upon, together with their belongings.

Article 7. The port of Lisbon will be recognised as neutral as regards the Russian fleet; that is to say that while the town and port are in possession of the English, the said Russian fleet will not be molested during its stay, nor will it be stopped when it wishes to leave, nor will it be pursued after it has left until after the delay recognised by Maritime Law.

Article 8. All French artillery, as well as the horses of the cavalry will be transported to France.

Article 9. This Cease-Fire can only be broken by giving forty-eight hours notice.

Done and agreed by the undersigned generals at the place and time stated above.

Arthur Wellesley   Kellermann Lieutenant-General.

Additional Article. The garrisons of the fortresses occupied by the French forces will be included in the present Convention, should they not have surrendered before 25th instant.

It is quite clear from the articles listed opposite that the French, a defeated and demoralised army gained more than it could ever have hoped for, while the British could only stand by and watch as the French made the most of their good fortune. Instead of returning to France a defeated and disgraced army they were greeted more like gallant victors, but more importantly they returned as part of the army in Spain. The personal property the treaty mentioned turned out to be as much plunder as the French could get away with. Such items included church plate which had been melted down and two state carriages belonging to the Duke of Sussex. They even went to the extent of taking the Portuguese Royal family's cambric sheets from Mafra which Loison then had made up into shirts! Junot not to be out done by all of this had taken the liberty of removing a Bible from the Royal Library to France, which his wife later sold for 85,000 francs, having earlier claimed that all the horses and mules from the Royal stables were his personal property. However, some items did escape the French, such as the Royal Library and the National History Museum which had been crated up ready for embarkation. The French Paymaster-General was arrested on board ship after having removed £25,000 from the Portuguese Bank as part of his military chest.

While the convention of Cintra was taking place Sir John Moore arrived off the coast of Portugal at Mondego Bay where he started to land his force. He had already succeeded in landing several regiments when he received orders to re-embark and make for Maceira Bay instead. This caused further delay in joining with the British land force and to add to this the conditions at Maceira Bay were quite treacherous. One boat containing members of the King's German Legion overturned and most of the men were drowned.

The landings at Maceira Bay finally commenced on the 25th August and took four days to complete. With this force came another three companies of the 95th Rifles from the 1st Battalion, under the command of Major Dugald Gilmour. The company commanders were Captains Amos Norcott, John Ross and Peter O'Hare, who upon arrival were placed in General Fane's brigade. Here they were reunited with the two 1st Battalion companies of Cameron and Ramadge, these two companies having been transferred from Acland's brigade straight after the Battle of Vimeiro. Fane's brigade now contained nine companies of 95th Riflemen, four from the 2nd Battalion and five from the 1st Battalion.

Also with Moore's force were 600 cavalry of the light dragoons, an arm in which the British were sadly lacking. The 1st Battalion 52nd Light Infantry, the Rifles' comrades from Shorncliffe, were also part of this force. Once the troops were ashore they marched off to join the main army, which meant crossing the Vimeiro battlefield and all its horrors from the previous conflict.

This gave the newcomers an immediate insight into the struggle which had secured Wellesley a fine victory.

With the Treaty of Cintra signed, the advance on Lisbon took on a more leisurely and relaxed air. The outposts of the British army consisted of three companies of the 1st Battalion 95th Rifles, 1st Battalion 52nd Light Infantry and 1st and 2nd Battalions King's German Legion under the command of Major-General Hon. Edward Paget who had already pushed on and encamped near to Torres Vedras on the 29th August. The whole of the British army marched into Lisbon on the 9th September and Paget's 'advance corps' moved to the heights of Belem on the 11th, where they encamped. It was here that they were joined by the two remaining companies of the 1st Battalion bringing their strength back to five companies.

The four companies of the 2nd Battalion, meanwhile, had previously marched with Fane's brigade close to Torres Vedras on the 23rd August, where they halted until the 31st when they then marched to Sobral. Advancing once again on the 2nd September to Burcelles, they halted until the 10th, when they finally marched into Lisbon, bivouacking in the suburbs on a large public pleasure ground known as, 'the Campo Grande'. With the arrival of the baggage, the 2nd Battalion were placed under canvas, their camping ground making easy access to the city. The five companies of the 1st Battalion moved across the Tagus on the 25th September and were cantoned in the Alamtejo.

The 60th Rifles, meanwhile, had been reduced to three companies having provided a further two companies, one each to the newly arrived 7th and 8th brigades. This lack of manpower in the 60th Regiment had prompted the commanding officer, Major Davy to apply to the Commander-in-Chief, who at that time was still Sir Hew Dalrymple, for permission to enlist into his corps 'deserters' from the French army. These consisted of Hanoverian and Swiss troops who had previously served in the ranks of Napoleon's army and were only too pleased to quit and fight against him. Sir Hew, however, did not approve of deserters from the enemy being enlisted into a corps that would be doing duty with the advanced posts and refused, to the 60th and General Moore's regret. When Sir Hew returned to England from the 1,000 deserters enlisted into the ranks of the British army, over one hundred Swiss were allowed to join the 60th and the Hanoverians joined their compatriots in the King's German Legion.

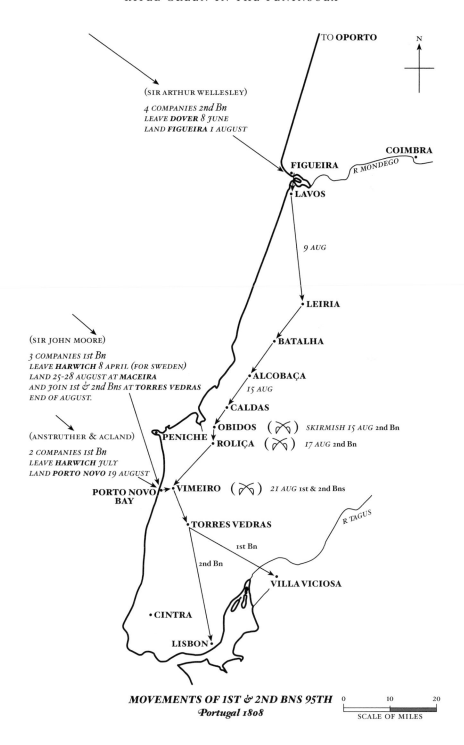

TO **OPORTO**

N

(SIR ARTHUR WELLESLEY)

4 COMPANIES 2nd Bn
*LEAVE **DOVER** 8 JUNE*
*LAND **FIGUEIRA** 1 AUGUST*

COIMBRA

FIGUEIRA   *R MONDEGO*

LAVOS

9 AUG

LEIRIA

(SIR JOHN MOORE)

3 COMPANIES 1st Bn
*LEAVE **HARWICH** 8 APRIL (FOR SWEDEN)*
*LAND 25-28 AUGUST AT **MACEIRA***
*AND JOIN 1st & 2nd Bns AT **TORRES VEDRAS***
END OF AUGUST.

BATALHA

ALCOBAÇA
15 AUG

(ANSTRUTHER & ACLAND)

2 COMPANIES 1st Bn
*LEAVE **HARWICH** JULY*
*LAND **PORTO NOVO** 19 AUGUST*

CALDAS

OBIDOS   (⚔)   *SKIRMISH 15 AUG 2nd Bn*
PENICHE
ROLIÇA   (⚔)   *17 AUG 2nd Bn*

PORTO NOVO
BAY

VIMEIRO   (⚔)   *21 AUG 1st & 2nd Bns*

TORRES VEDRAS

R TAGUS

1st Bn

2nd Bn

VILLA VICIOSA

CINTRA

LISBON

MOVEMENTS OF 1ST & 2ND BNS 95TH
Portugal 1808

0   10   20

SCALE OF MILES

Lisbon

With the 2nd Battalion companies settled in the public park encampment in the suburbs of Lisbon, it was now a good time to take stock of the condition of their arms and equipment after two major battles and the constant skirmishing. One of the main causes for concern was the desperate plight of the men's boots and shoes. Their belts also required some attention for many had been terribly cut up during the fighting from continually throwing themselves to the ground for cover. Captain Leach and Lieutenant Cox, therefore, took Rifleman Harris, the senior shoemaker of his company into the city to buy the necessary implements and leather to begin these repairs. The French at this time were very much in evidence about the city as the Riflemen walked through the streets. It is possible that this trio of Riflemen were amongst the first British troops to enter the city since the French surrender. The two Rifles' officers cut quite dashing figures in their dark uniforms with the pellise hanging from one shoulder and they were singled out for special attention by the local dark haired beauties, much to the disgust and annoyance of the French.

Having walked about for some time without any success the officers decided to go into a hotel for some refreshment. They sent Harris to the taproom below, which as it happened was full of French soldiers, many sporting the evidence of their recent meetings with the British. After a short time one of the men offered Harris a drink which he declined, he still held a hatred of the French for the death of so many of his friends and comrades at the Battles of Roliça and Vimeiro. This angered the Frenchman and his comrades, who by now were a little the worse for drink. One particular wounded soldier with a large moustache was trying to coax his comrades into some form of action against the single Rifleman. At this moment Captain Leach and Lieutenant Cox made a timely entrance in search of Harris and defused the situation. Captain Leach who could speak French informed Harris he was lucky that they came when they did, as the situation was about to turn very nasty. All three Riflemen then retreated to the security of the street to continue their search until eventually purchasing the materials and equipment they required.

The following day Captain Leach entered Benjamin Harris' tent and ordered him to pick out three of the best craftsmen from the shoemakers in the battalion. He was to take them into the city to find a shop which they could use to repair the men's boots and shoes, adding that they had a long march in front of them and they would be in need of strong footwear. Harris picked his party of craftsmen and took them into the city, each man carrying a sack of damaged footwear, where he found a shop almost at once. It was another matter, however, to make the resident shoemakers understand what they wanted, Harris finally solved this by emptying the contents of his sack onto the floor of the shop and sat down to repair the boots. This put the owners of the shop at their ease. Now established in the shop Harris took his little band of shoemakers there every day and they became very friendly with the owner and his wife who also had pretty daughters. This routine continued until all the officers' and men's footwear was repaired, which lasted to just before the British advanced into Spain. This was probably well calculated by Harris to last this length of time not only to have excused them from battalion duties, but to have kept them in the company of the shop owner's daughters a little longer, one of whom became quite attached to Harris.

The initial hostility shown to Harris by the French on first entering the city with Captain Leach and Lieutenant Cox changed as soon as the British began to arrive in even greater numbers. Though the French still remained in the city in strength the two armies gradually began to fraternise with each other and were soon to be seen arm in arm as they visited the various drinking establishments. The French infantry remained camped in the squares of the city while the transports were being prepared to take them home. Conditions, however, were far from what the British expected in and about the city for Lisbon was a very dirty and squalid place. The French had, even prior to the British occupation, tried to redress this with little success. The dirty conditions combined with the stifling heat during the day and the bitter cold at night began to take effect and the health of the British army began to deteriorate. It did not help matters that wine was cheap and in abundance, while the troops and their women had plenty of free time in which to indulge in their excesses. With so many troops in and around the city at the large camp at Queluz, typhus and dysentery broke out and soon spread throughout the camp even to the extent of affecting the people of the local villages close to it. Much of this was avoidable; the refuse from the army's slaughter house was one of the causes for concern, while the area used as a hospital, was only separated from the depot stores by a long ditch and was being used by the dysentery patients. Captain Leach of the Rifles succumbed to the conditions and was confined to his sick bed for many weeks. A number of the 2nd Battalion rank and file also fell to the same fate, many did not recover in time to advance into Spain. These men would later gain the honour of representing the regiment at Talavera and we shall meet them later in the next volume of this history.

In spite of all this the officers of the army, including the Rifles, visited the opera and attended a number of balls which were almost daily being arranged, much to the discomfort of the French. At length the French began to leave the city and as their numbers decreased the Portuguese took advantage of this fact. Any unsuspecting individuals were soon murdered and the incidences increased which alarmed the French high command. On the 5th September, General Kellermann begged the British to appoint an officer with the power to protect them and keep order in the city. British troops were eventually drafted in to form picquets to this effect. An officer and picquet of the 45th Regiment had a first hand experience of this when a Frenchman came running to his guard room to claim protection. He was closely followed by another two men with the same request, when a large mob suddenly appeared expecting the French to be handed over to them.

The officer ordered the picquet and guard to take up a position between the French and the enraged Portuguese mob, who continued to press forward too close to the bayonets of his men. As the situation was about to get out of hand he ordered three of the men to load with ball cartridge and told the mob he would shoot anyone who tried to force his way to the Frenchmen. This caused the mob to finally break up and move off cursing the intervention of the British. They were not exactly popular with the Portuguese, because of the outcome of the Convention of Cintra in which they had not been consulted, so incidences of this nature only added to these feelings.

The French, to the relief of the British were finally all away by the 18th September. They marched down to the harbour with bands playing, colours flying and bayonets fixed, with all the honours of war. The Portuguese national flag was once again hoisted above the city, accompanied by the ringing of the church bells the city erupted into scenes of jubilation. The streets rang out to the sound of the inhabitants singing and laughing while the sky was filled with bursting rockets.

It was around this time that the 2nd Battalion was transferred to another brigade which lasted, to their relief, for only a short time; for the brigade was commanded by a newly promoted Scot from the 79th Highlanders who did not take too kindly to Riflemen and thought that the kilts were by far better at soldiering than any other troops in the British service. The coming campaign would have changed his thoughts on this but the Riflemen did not get a chance to show their mettle in his company.

Prior to Sir Hew Dalrymple's return to England plans were in preparation for an advance on Madrid via Almeida, but at this time French troop strengths in Spain had been vastly underestimated. The orders Dalrymple received on the 6th October from the secretary of state, Lord Castlereagh, gave definite instructions for a line of operations based on Wellesley's view which he previously received by letter. These plans were eventually inherited by Sir John Moore along with the logistics of such a campaign with very little time to gather and collate his own intelligence reports.

Besides the troops already in Portugal under his command, Sir John was about to receive substantial reinforcements from England under the command of Sir David Baird. The transports for this force were concentrated at Falmouth and the fleet eventually left on the 6th October, reaching Corunna on the 13th. The troops who made up this force were: 1st and 3rd Battalions 1st Foot Guards, 3rd Battalion 1st Regiment, 2nd Battalion 14th Regiment, 2nd Battalion 23rd Regiment, 1st Battalion 26th Regiment, 1st Battalion 43rd Regiment, 53rd Regiment, 2nd Battalion 59th Regiment, 76th Regiment, 2nd Battalion 81st Regiment and four companies 1st Battalion 95th Rifles and four companies of the 2nd Battalion 95th Rifles, with three batteries of artillery and the 7th, 10th and 15th Hussars. The extra cavalry would give Moore the mobility he required to undertake his advance into Spain. However, for some inexplicable reason the cavalry was shipped out last when logic would have required them to be in the vanguard of such a force to cover the advance of the infantry. [1]

From a 95th point of view the arrival of Baird's force would mean a further eight companies of the regiment on service in Spain giving a combined strength of seventeen companies. [2] Both detachments of the Rifles had marched from Hythe to Falmouth, the 1st Battalion companies being those of Captains Latham Bennett, George Elder, George Miller and Charles Beckwith under the command of Major Norman M'Leod, Captain Beckwith's company was under the command of the senior lieutenant as Beckwith was already staff. The 1st Battalion were placed on board the transport Margaret; two men had been left behind sick at Falmouth while another was left sick at Harwich.

---

[1] The 15th Hussars did not leave England until the 2nd November and when they finally reached Corunna the rest of the transports with the remaining cavalry regiments on board had only just arrived even though they had left a few days before.
[2] Verner in his history of the Rifle Brigade is in error here for he states that five companies of the 1st Battalion and four of the 2nd Battalion were embarked for Spain.

The 2nd Battalion with a total strength of 25 sergeants, 8 buglers and 405 rank and file were embarked upon the transport Nautilas of Shields under the command of Lieutenant Colonel Hamlet Wade and Major James Stewart. The captains of companies being: Loftus Gray, Daniel Cadoux, John Jenkins and Francis Drake; two men are listed as being left sick in the General Hospital at Falmouth.

As Sir John made plans for his advance into Spain it was becoming quite clear that feeding the army was going to be a problem. This was increasing with each day, as large numbers of women and children who had come out with the original forces finally arrived in the city. The official number of wives permitted to travel with a regiment of six per company on active service had been greatly exceeded, officers often turning a blind eye to the extra women slipping on board the transports while others had smuggled themselves out since. In an effort to get rid of the women Moore offered them a return passage to England and on the 10th October issued a General Order to this effect;

'In the course of the long march the army is about to undertake and where no carts will be allowed, the women would unavoidably be exposed to the greatest hardship and distress, commanding officers are, therefore, desired to use their endeavours to prevent as many as possible, particularly those having young children, or such as are not stout, or equal to fatigue, from following the army. Those who remain will be left with the heavy luggage of the regiments. An officer will be charged to draw their rations, and they will be sent to England by the first good opportunity: and when landed, they will receive the same allowance which they would have been entitled to, if they had not embarked, to enable them to reach their home.'

Very few women, however, took up Sir John's offer, most refusing to leave their men and prepared for the long march across the mountains. The day after this order the advance guard of the army left for Almeida under the command of Brigadier General Robert Anstruther. As the column prepared to cross into Spain he ordered the men to wear in their caps the red cockade stamped in gold with the words 'Viva Ferdinando Septimo' as a compliment to the Spanish.[3] The troops marched along the banks and fields that bordered the River Tagus which were full of wild flowers and aromatic shrubs, while the autumn sunshine warmed them as they marched. The men were full of life and vitality, happy in the knowledge that at last they were to be in conflict with the French. It was also a chance to get away from the sickness in the city. They were very confident that they could now finish the job they had started at Roliça and Vimeiro. Nobody could contemplate how quickly the situation would change in just over a month.

---

[3] It is doubtful that this was a spontaneous gesture on behalf of the general but more of a propaganda move on the order of Moore. GC/RC.

The Advance on Salamanca

The plan of campaign had been for the whole of the British army in Portugal to act in co-operation with the Spanish armies in the north of Spain. It was the desire of the Government back home that Moore and earlier his predecessors should co-operate with the auxiliary Spanish forces in the field which had been estimated at not less than 100,000. While the armies of France opposed to them in Spain would be less than half that number.[1] (p.78) Moore had been given the choice of taking his force by sea and landing them at Corunna where they would join Baird's force or march them by land from Lisbon to Valladolid, where he hoped to concentrate the whole of his forces. He decided to move by land and gave his reason for doing so, 'the passage by sea is precarious, an embarkation unhinges and when I get to Corunna I should still have to equip the army before I could stir, and in Galicia it might have been impossible to have found sufficient means of carriage.'

Having made the decision to move by road Moore had to work out the best possible route for his columns, while at the same time he was aware that winter was not far off. Once it started the roads would become very difficult to traverse especially for his baggage, supplies and artillery. It was impossible to gain any information on the condition of the road systems in Spain from the locals, but it was generally agreed that the roads north of the Tagus were impassable to artillery. Moore finally decided on advancing his forces on four separate fronts and divided his troops accordingly:

Beresford's brigade	1/9th, 2/43rd, and 2/52nd.
Fane's brigade	1/38th, 1/79th and four companies 2/95th
	To proceed via Coimbra and Celorico.
Bentinck's brigade	1/4th, 1/28th, 1/42nd and five companies 5/60th.
Hill's brigade	1/5th, 1/32nd, 1/91st with one battery of artillery
	via Abrantes and Guarda.
Anstruther's brigade	1/20th, 1/52nd and five companies 1/95th.
Alten's brigade	1st and 2nd Light Infantry Regiments King's German Legion
	via Elvas and Alcantara.

Sir John Hope's division took the fourth route, which was chosen for no other reason than to accommodate the artillery, it was not ideal but this was the only one possible. The force consisted of; 2nd, 36th, 71st, 92nd Regiments and five companies 5/60th, the 3rd Light Dragoons of the King's German Legion,

18th Hussars and six batteries of artillery. It proceeded by way of a road that led south of the Tagus close to Elvas and Badajoz, which crossed the Tagus at Almaraz and then on to Talavera, the Escurial pass, Epinar and finally to Arevalo. Of all the columns this had the most difficult task, besides being close to the enemy Sir John was very short of money and supplies and his transport was very poor. This put a terrible strain on his baggage animals, so it was inevitable that they would sustain quite a loss amongst them and the horses. Sir John had to advance his column in six smaller parties each one a day's march behind the other, which caused some considerable delay.

Besides the columns entering Spain, Sir John Moore also left a division of nearly 9,000 men in Portugal for the protection of Lisbon. This force was to be under the command of Sir John Cradock, whom he expected to arrive any day. This division comprised of 3rd Buffs, who at this time were the garrison of Almeida, the 1/6th, 9th, 29th, 40th, 45th, 50th, 82nd and 97th Regiments along with the remainder of the 20th Light Dragoons and six batteries of artillery. Moore was also expecting the arrival of the 3/27th and 2/32nd Regiments who had left England at the same time as Baird's force. They were to replace the Buffs and 50th who were to join Moore's force. The 6th and 82nd Regiments also joined the main army later, Sir John finally left Lisbon on the 27th October and joined the army at Salamanca on the 13th November. The news on arrival was not good, reports were constantly being received of French successes against his Spanish allies who were to provide the bulk of his force. Moore was confident of his own position once all his force had arrived, but he felt it would be difficult at this time to join up with Baird, who was force marching south to meet him from Corunna.

The 2nd Battalion in Fane's brigade as part of Beresford's division, had reached Sacavem by the 15th October. The following day they crossed the Tagus by means of a floating bridge and continued their march north through Portugal via Villafranca, Leiria, Coimbra, Pombal and Celorico arriving at Pinhel on the 10th November. Much of this country was already well known to them from the previous campaign. It was here that the Riflemen were ordered

---

1 (From p. 77) The strength of the French army in Spain at the 10th October 1808 was:

1st	Army corps	Marshal Victor	34,000
2nd		Marshal Soult	33,000
3rd		Marshal Moncey	37,700
4th		Marshal Lefebvre	26,000
5th		Marshal Mortier	26,700
6th		Marshal Ney	38,000
7th		General St. Cyr	42,000
8th		General Junot	25,700
Reserve			42,400
A total of			305,500

to fix into their caps a 'red cockade' as they were about to enter Spain. By the 11th they had reached Almeida and entered Salamanca on the 17th. It was while on the march through Portugal on their way to the frontier that a few of the Rifles were involved in an incident which caused them to fall foul of the officer commanding the 79th Regiment. The brigades were halted at a convent for some days to rest and while there the 79th had been drawn up in square to witness the punishment of a member of their regiment. From the windows in the convent overlooking the parade some of the Rifles had gathered to watch the proceedings. During the parade a piece of masonry was thrown from one of these windows and it landed at the feet of the colonel of the 79th Highlanders who was most indignant at such an act. He at once called an inquiry into who was to blame for such a deed but because it was getting dark it had been impossible to pick out the culprit. As a result three men had been confined under suspicion of being the offender, one of these men called Baker was adamant that the perpetrator of the deed was Corporal Robert Liston, one of those confined. Liston was placed under arrest and marched to Salamanca, a prisoner where he was tried by court martial and sentenced to receive 800 lashes! The whole brigade was turned out to witness his punishment which he received without hardly a sound at the hands of the drummers of the 9th Regiment. Liston protested his innocence and even many years later in civilian life declared that he had not committed the act. He was a good soldier and many believed he was wronged and that it was more than likely to have been Baker who had thrown the brick.

It was also on this march that General Beresford [2] had to halt the column and lecture the men on the subject of their buttons, or the lack of them. He made it clear that any man who was found wearing a greatcoat that could not be fastened would be severely flogged. This came about because a number of men had developed the habit of tearing off their buttons and hammering them flat to make them look like English coins which they then passed off to the Spanish in payment for the local wines. [3]

---

[2] Major General William Carr Beresford was described as an ugly man. However this probably was due to the fact that he had injured his left eye in a shooting accident many years before which when added to his rugged and weatherbeaten features made him look a man not to be trifled with.

[3] Most authorities on the subject tell us that the buttons of the Rifles were plain with no markings or regimental distinctions i.e. 95, Bugle Horn or Rifle Regiment inscription and that they were made from a dull metal, lead! We have found no record so far of a button to a rifleman for the period to confirm this. However, it does seem strange that a simple peasant would accept a flat, plain piece of metal as a coin, even if it were from another country, when most would only part with their wares on receipt of silver dollars! An incident on the retreat to Corunna would seem to confirm our belief that the buttons did have regimental markings on them. The colonel of the 1/95th had the buttons cut off a soldier of bad character in the regiment who had to be left behind so that the French would not know which regiment he belonged to when made a prisoner.

The 1st Battalion Rifles under the command of General Paget left Lisbon on the 27th October marching for Elvas from where they turned north to Alcantara on the Tagus, with further marches via El Bodon, Ciudad Rodrigo, arriving at Salamanca on the 13th November. They, like the 2nd Battalion, also placed the 'red cockade' in their caps prior to entering Spain. Eventually arriving at Salamanca, the Rifles enjoyed their stay in the city with its large population and numerous shops, especially as the wine was very cheap.

Of the two wings of the 60th Rifles, Major Davy's companies in Beresford's brigade had reached Rio Mayor on the 16th where they halted until the 17th October. By the 19th they had reached Leiria, an area they knew well from first landing in Portugal. Then from the 23rd to the 26th they halted at Coimbra and by the 4th November had reached Trancoza. On the 9th November the commanding officer issued the following Battalion Order;

'The Major as yet has had much reason to be satisfied with the behaviour of the men on the march, and only regrets that the misconduct of a few individuals should have reflected on the character of the whole. He strongly recommends the continuance of the meritorious conduct which has procured the good wishes of the inhabitants of the towns of Portugal through which they have passed.'

The five companies under the command of Major Woodgate which had originally been doing duty with General Hope's division at Elvas was eventually transferred to Lord Bentinck's brigade.

On the 13th November the Headquarter companies were at Villa de Pedro Alonzo, when the following Regimental Order was issued;

'It is with deep concern that the Major discharges a most painful duty-that of announcing to the Battalion that in consequence of the misbehaviour of the five companies detached, they have been sent back to Lisbon. Under these distressing circumstances the Major calls upon every individual of the Regiment to use his utmost efforts to vindicate and maintain the well-merited reputation that the Battalion has acquired in the field: and doubts not that with the cordial co-operation of the whole they will be able to do away that disgrace which must otherwise for ever reflect upon the character of the Battalion. This order to be read in German.'

The Headquarter companies had reached Salamanca by the 16th November and it was here that to Major Davy's distress he was ordered to concentrate the whole of the battalion in Portugal. The battalion, however, did not move off until the end of the month by which time the French were in close proximity to the British forces. It was now that Major Davy's earlier folly of recruiting from Junot's vanquished army came back to haunt him for on the return journey as escort for the heavy baggage, a number of these men deserted back to the French. It was from three of these deserters that Napoleon was able to learn important intelligence as to the true position of Moore's forces.

With both detachments of the Rifles settled in Salamanca we will now follow the progress of Baird's force anchored off the coast of Corunna which they reached on the 13th October. A setback for an early meeting between Moore and Baird was caused by the Spanish Junta objecting to him landing his troops! This was not resolved until the 26th October and as a result the infantry was not fully landed until the 4th November. Baird was further distressed on landing because of the lack of transport and not being able to obtain the supplies he required. The Spanish like the Portuguese would only accept hard cash in silver dollars and not the British Government bills with which he had been issued. Baird did his best to raise the money but could only manage to secure 6,000 dollars, the Galician Junta eventually came to his aid with a loan of 92,000 dollars. The British Minister in Madrid, John Frere arrived in the harbour a couple of days later with a war chest of £410,000 and gave Baird a further £40,000. He was also given 50,000 dollars brought from the British Warship Tigre and Sir John Moore had also sent him £8,000.

In a short time Baird had gone from one extreme to the other with his funding. He was now able to purchase the transport and supplies he required. The inhabitants of Corunna, however, did not show much enthusiasm for their British allies, their attitude did change but not towards the British. This came about upon the arrival of some 9,000 Spanish troops in Corunna under the command of General Marqués de la Romana. These same troops only a short time before had been performing garrison duties in northern Germany for Napoleon, albeit unwillingly.

Baird now sent his forces off to join Moore, but could only, like Hope, send them in separate parties of about 2,000 men in each column, so as to keep them properly supplied. The draw back of such a plan, though again he had no alternative, was that his whole force was stretched out along the one hundred and forty miles from Corunna to Astorga. The last detachment of infantry left Corunna on the 10th November and it would be another five days before the first cavalry detachment was to follow. Baird left a single infantry regiment and a battalion of detachments to guard the ammunition and military stores at Corunna and also to garrison the citadel.

It was from Corunna and its surrounding area that the Spanish had raised and equipped some 5,000 volunteers for General Blake's army. These men received a very small amount of training and drill which made them only competent at soldiering up to platoon level. Once this was achieved they were equipped and sent off as soon as possible to join the Spanish force under Blake! It is little wonder that these men were no match for the seasoned troops of Napoleon. Should this practise be widespread in the remaining armies of the Spanish, the campaign would be doomed from the start.

On landing, the 1st and 2nd Battalions of the 95th Rifles were organised as the advance guard and set off on the road to Astorga. On reaching Betanzos, about three leagues [4] from Corunna, they experienced the defectiveness of the supply system at first hand. Once halted for the night the quartermasters went to draw the rations for each battalion from the officer in charge of the commissariat department, who had been sent forward with the express purpose of supplying the troops on arrival. The officer here refused to issue the Rifles with any bread, the problem being that the bread had been baked by the Spanish authorities and he did not understand their system of weights and measures. As he had left his own instruments behind he was afraid to issue the rations in case he gave the wrong amounts. The men were billeted in the convents of the towns they passed through, while in general the officers were quartered on the local population. The men slept in the corridors of the convents on straw which had been placed there for a degree of comfort.

The Rifles continued their march via Lugo, Villafranca, Cacabelos and Astorga which they reached on the 19th November. The actual road from Corunna to Astorga was of good quality and quite broad which made marching easier for troops who had spent some weeks cramped up on board the transports with little time to exercise prior to the march. The records, however, show that eleven men are listed as being sick in quarters with the regiment with a further fourteen left sick at Corunna. [5]

Both Lugo and Astorga were large towns surrounded by strong Moorish walls; the former had once been the Metropolis of Spain and was of great antiquity. The walls were of extraordinary thickness and in good condition, further strength was gained from its commanding position. The town's water supply came via an aquaduct which ran from the River Miño. It also contained four hospitals which the British converted into barracks and magazines which were later filled with their sick and injured.

Astorga, on the other hand, was situated in a vast sandy plain extending as far as the eye could see, with ancient walls at least twelve feet thick and supporting massive lofty towers. In the foundations of the walls, caverns had been formed which the local down and outs were using as shelter. The city itself was a very gloomy place for its streets were very narrow and dirty,

---

4 A Spanish league was equal to about four English miles and one furlong.
5 It is also interesting to note from a medal collecting point of view that fourteen men are listed as being left behind in Corunna. Thus in theory if any of these men lived long enough to have claimed the MGS medal they would be entitled to the clasp for Corunna, providing that they were still in the city on the 16th January 1809, having taken no part in the retreat and all of its hardships. While the men of the 2nd Battalion who had marched every inch of the retreat finally embarking at Vigo were not entitled to a medal or clasp for their troubles!

but its houses were quite large and well furnished. The shops were well supplied which enabled them to keep up with the demands of the British force stationed in and around the city. With this in mind Baird made it one of his supply depots.

The Rifles were able to rest here for some days, until the 2nd Battalion companies were pushed forward to the village of Zalada about a league in front of Astorga. A day or so later they were pushed on even further to La Bañeza about four leagues from Astorga, while the detachments of Baird's infantry force arrived in Astorga and assembled in and around the town.

Meanwhile, back in Corunna the first cavalry detachment left on the 15th November, five days after the last of the infantry. It was very slow going for them for some time, due to the condition of the horses as they had been in close confinement on board the transports for so long. It was, therefore, necessary for the cavalry to advance only by short and easy marches until they could regain their strength. In spite of this the animals still suffered from exhaustion and the change of food. At Betanzos the first halting place for the Rifles, the evidence of their poor condition was all too plain to see for around seventeen horses lay dead on the side of the road. The main cavalry force, therefore, as a result of these slow marches had only gone a little way past Lugo when they were joined by Sir David Baird with a brigade of infantry and three batteries of artillery. They had come over the mountains and down into the plain of León to Astorga.

The march to Astorga by the cavalry had finally taken its toll on their suffering mounts and a large number were declared unfit for further service. Colonel George Quentin of the 10th Hussars was ordered to return to Corunna with these poor animals, which meant that the cavalry were vastly understrength, each regiment only able to muster around 400 men in field.

It was while at Astorga that the troops of Baird's force had first sight of their Spanish allies; the army of the Marqués de la Romana entered the city, strangely equipped and very undisciplined. It amused the men to see them marching in file in double quick time headed by a single drummer for each regiment. The force was no more than 2,000 strong and part of it was dressed in British uniforms! Their arrival caused terror and confusion amongst the inhabitants of the city for they were informed by their fellow countrymen that the French had entered León which was only ten leagues from Astorga. With this news the shops were immediately shut and boarded up, valuables packed and those with transport began to leave with their effects.

On the 13th November Moore entered Salamanca and was met by the President of the Junta, the Marqués de Carralto, who informed him that his house and servants were at his disposal. Whether this was to soften the blow for Moore was then told that three Spanish armies had received severe set backs at the hands of the French. General Joachim Blake's force, the army of Galicia, was attacked by Marshal Ney at Durango and they retreated in confusion towards Bilbao. Napoleon, meanwhile, had reached Vittoria by the 7th November and with the Spanish armies opposed to him in isolation of each other, he was able to crush Blake's force at Espinosa, the remains of which quickly scattered into the Cantabrian Mountains. Napoleon's next target was the army of Estramadura, commanded by the twenty year old Conde de Belveder, which he almost destroyed at Gamonal just north of Burgos. He then moved on Burgos which he occupied making this his advance base, it having previously been the base of the army of Estramadura. Moore's troops, meawhile, continued to advance toward Valladolid, which had been suggested to Moore only a few days earlier as a suitable place for the British forces to concentrate! In a short space of time Napoleon had destroyed the centre of the Spanish forces gathered for the defence of their country placing the British in an awkward situation.

Baird having learned of the setbacks to the Spanish forces remained at Astorga and was now considering a retreat to Corunna. He, therefore, sent Moore details of his intentions. Soult had been reported as being only 100 miles away at Reinosa, while Marshal Lefebvre-Desnouettes was even nearer on the banks of the River Carrion. Sir David received a report that a further French force was also marching towards his position, he immediately ordered the withdrawal of the 2nd Battalion 95th Rifles from their outpost at La Bañeza and they retired to Zalada.

Meanwhile, Moore was still waiting at Salamanca for the arrival of Sir John Hope's division, his own force at this time being only around 17,000 strong with a light battery of artillery. For every day he waited, his position became more precarious for constant reports were coming in of French troop movements. At the same time he was not sure of how reliable these reports were and he still had no idea of what the true situation was with the Spanish forces.

He had not received a single despatch from his allies informing him of their intentions or movements. Whether Moore would have been encouraged by the arrival of the Spanish troops is another matter judging by the report sent by Lord William Bentinck from Madrid. Bentinck described the army of Castile, which had a reported strength of 11,000 men as; 'To form any idea of its composition, it is absolutely necessary to have seen it. It is a complete mass of miserable peasantry, without clothing, without organization, and with few officers that deserve the name.

The General and principle officers have not the least confidence in themselves. This is not an exaggerated picture, it is a true portrait.'

Moore's orders for entering into Spain had been made quite plain, he was, 'to co-operate with the Spanish Armies in the expulsion of the French and not to act alone.' In a letter Moore wrote to his brother at the time it is quite clear how he was feeling, 'I am in a scrape from which God knows how I am to extricate myself, I sleep little; it is now only five in the morning and I have concluded since I got up this long letter.' He eventually decided to leave Salamanca once Hope arrived with his division but events overtook him and forced a change of plan. A despatch received on the 23rd November reported the overwhelming defeat of the Spanish armies of Castaños and Palafox on the bank of the Ebro at Tudela. This report virtually ended any chance of combined operations against the French for there were now no Spanish forces with which to carry out the original plan. He wrote to Baird and Hope explaining the situation telling them of his plan to retreat to Portugal, advising Hope to do the same, with Baird to proceed for Corunna. Both commanders were in complete agreement with his orders but the news was not welcomed by the men or some of the more senior officers of the brigades.

In the eyes of the men they were running from an enemy whom they had every confidence in beating especially after the successes at Roliça and Vimeiro. However, they did not have an overall picture of the situation or see how precarious their position was, while their general had the added responsibility of their well-being to consider, having been entrusted with the finest army ever to leave the shores of Britain. In fact the only army the country could muster, defeat or loss of this army would have had far reaching implications for the defence of the British Isles, which would be dependant on an over stretched navy and militia! Britain would be ripe for an invasion.

Sir David Baird received Moore's orders to retire to Corunna towards the end of November and ordered the retreat to begin at once. The Rifles fell back as far as Cacabelos while the rest of the divisional troops occupied Villafranca and its surrounding area. Cacabelos was well known for its fine wines and this fact was not lost on the men, who devised all kinds of ways to obtain it. One idea thought up by the Riflemen was to borrow the jacket of a comrade in the 43rd Regiment in which he would go to steal some wine. When the irate owner tried to pick out the culprit he was unable to find him for the Rifleman would have changed back into his original uniform. This worked equally well in reverse!

With Napoleon marching on Madrid, the Spanish in an attempt to delay him attacked his advance guard at the narrow pass of Somosierra with around 12,000 troops. They managed to check the French initially but this was short lived for their cavalry were soon able to break through the Spanish defences. Napoleon's Polish Light Horse caused havoc in the Spanish ranks; the French having brushed aside this token resistance, the way was now clear to continue their advance on Madrid.

The French at this point were also within striking distance of the British force under the command of Sir John Hope who had been trying to reach Moore. At one time the French cavalry were only about twenty miles away, Sir John was quite aware of this and on his nightly halts ordered his troops to form square, sleeping fully armed. With the bad weather setting in Hope had already suffered much hardship on the march and a number of artillery horses died of fatigue. This forced him to abandon six of his guns which he had buried concealing them from the enemy. Hope had already received a message from Sir John Moore to make for Salamanca instead of Ciudad Rodrigo.

Moore was still at Salamanca on the 3rd December when he at last received news from his Spanish allies which caused him to alter his original plans for a full scale retreat to Lisbon and Corunna. Fresh orders were now despatched to Hope and Baird telling them to join him once more. As luck would have it the only troops to have returned to Portugal by this time were the 5th Battalion 60th Rifles as escort to the sick and heavy baggage.

Moore's Advance against the French

The reason for Sir John Moore's change of mind was brought about by a letter received from the Supreme Junta asking him to act with the army of Andalusia under the command of Castaños, which had escaped the French and was still intact. It was reported that this force was 25,000 strong and situated just north of Madrid. It would be joined by the combined forces of Generals Heredia and San Juan which numbered another 22,000 troops. Besides these forces the report claimed that Madrid had troops pouring in to defend the city everyday, even the women and children helping in the building of the defences. A ditch had been dug around the whole of the city and a number of outworks were in the process of being built. Including the force to defend the city the Spanish estimated that they could muster around 60,000 men which, when added to Moore's 20,000, they believed were more than a match for the 20,000 French troops advancing on the city. The report also confirmed that the French only had 80,000 troops in the whole of Spain!

Sir John, however, had learned a lot about the Spanish in his short time in command and was very wary of these allies. He suspected that the 60,000 was not more than 30,000, made up of those troops of the routed Spanish armies of the north who had escaped the French. Moore later discovered that the numbers quoted to him in the report also included the force already defeated at the pass of Somosierra! All Moore's natural instincts told him to continue his retreat. His orders, however, to support his allies and to listen to the constant requests from the Spanish, who at last seemed to show some nationalistic aim to combine and drive the French from their country, with their cries of help to divert the French from attacking Madrid, gave him no choice and he agreed to go to their aid. [1]

The news that the retreat had been halted and that the British were instead to go on the offensive changed the whole mood of the army. The leaden footed, sullen troops of the retreat had now changed into smiling happy soldier-like men once more with a spring in their step as they marched to do battle with the French. To confirm the Spanish reports for himself, Moore sent Colonel Graham to Madrid to assess the situation, giving him a letter to present on arrival to Tomas de Morla and the Prince of Castelfranco.

---

[1] For the intrigue surrounding this decision to help the Spanish, see pages 75 and 76 of Christopher Hibbert's *Corunna*.

On the 1st December Moore had already sent out some regiments to secure the surrounding areas of Salamanca. The Rifles, who were always in the forefront of such work, had in the course of their duty occupied the village of Villaris which they secured by barricading it against a possible cavalry attack.

In the short time it had taken Moore to issue his orders for a general advance he had already been betrayed by his Spanish allies! For on the 3rd December, de Morla and the Prince of Castelfranco struck a deal with the French. As a result the Spanish General San Juan was refused entry into Madrid to help in its defence and Napoleon entered the city unopposed. The Spanish troops, believing that San Juan was part of this treachery, promptly murdered him. Graham returned to Salamanca on the 10th December with the news of Napoleon's occupation of Madrid. Moore, however, was not the least surprised for the Spanish had ceased to amaze him in the way in which they pursued the defence of their country.

Sir John Hope arrived at Salamanca on the 4th December after a series of hard forced marches under very trying conditions, expecting to be attacked by the enemy at any moment. It was still clear to Moore even with the arrival of Hope that he was no match for a head on confrontation with Napoleon and his numerically stronger army. However, he still believed that he could be of service to the Spanish. By taking a leaf out of Napoleon's own book of tactics, Moore decided to cut the Emperor's communications with France! The French at this time still had no idea where Moore's forces were and believed them to be actually heading back to Portugal. Had they spread their search patrols a little further they would undoubtedly have encountered Hope's force and the outcome would have been completely different. Moore, however, having received a report from one of his patrols that the French had left Valladolid, decided to reach this place himself. From there he could cross the Castilian plain and the River Carrion, forcing Napoleon from Madrid and up into the mountains. If his plan succeeded he would have no option left but to retreat to Corunna. With his heavy baggage, reserve ammunition and sick safely on their way back to Portugal Moore's forces would at least be more manoeuvrable to attempt this outrageous plan.

When Baird received his revised orders for an advance he was still at Villafranca while his cavalry and the Light Brigade were at Astorga. On the 6th December, Baird ordered his cavalry, consisting of the 7th, 10th and 15th Hussars under the command of Lord Paget to Zamora where they were to join with Sir John Moore's force. Setting off at once in the direction of Benavente followed by the infantry marching via Astorga and La Bañeza and then on to Benavente, which they reached on the 15th December. Baird had already made Astorga, Villafranca and Tordesillas depots for his provisions which would now be vital to the supply and success of the coming campaign.

Moore finally marched his force out of Salamanca in two separate columns on the 11th December, having made it clear to his generals that should the Spanish situation change he would have no choice but to order a full scale retreat on Corunna. It was a bright clear day when the columns left Salamanca but the ground was very hard after a severe frost which extended to the whole of the plain and beyond towards Valladolid. The left hand column with the Rifles leading the way were to make for Toro where they were eventually to join up with Lord Paget's cavalry. The first march took them thirty miles to Zamora, a large town that could only be entered by a bridge of planks placed across a ditch, for the stone bridge had been demolished to prevent the enemy cavalry entering. There were, however, no fortifications except for an ancient stone wall and dry ditch, which meant the town could be easily taken by determined forces.

On the 13th December they continued their march a further twenty miles up the Douro to Toro, which was a similar sized town to Zamora but surrounded by a mud wall, its main defence being an ancient castle. The town of Toro was a very gloomy place for its streets in general were very narrow and terribly dirty. The mud was over a foot deep in places - even without rain, all kinds of abominations were littered amongst its filth. Pigs roamed the streets wallowing in the mud and the stench was most offensive, which had little effect on the inhabitants. The chief manufacture of the town was leathern bottles and skins for keeping wine which first came to the notice of the troops when they were moving up country at the beginning of the campaign. At that time a number of muleteers were on the roads transporting wine stored in pigs' skins on their noisy carts. The muleteers themselves also attracted some attention for they wore a sort of cuirass made of strong buff leather with broad-brimmed hats and they always travelled well armed.

The right hand column which was covered by the cavalry of General Stewart made for Alaejos and Tordesillas. Captain Dashwood, General Stewart's aide-de-camp carried out a valuable service for this column on the 12th December. He entered the village of Rueda dressed as a Spanish peasant, wearing a brown cloak and a large broad brimmed hat. There he found that it was occupied by a French cavalry patrol and a detachment of infantry. The French were completely unaware of how precarious their situation was, so sure were they that the British were in full retreat to Portugal. Once it was dark the 18th Light Dragoons advanced to the village and quietly surrounded it gradually closing in until just after midnight when they charged in and attacked the surprised Frenchmen, killing eighteen of the enemy in the attack and capturing another thirty five. The French cavalry were the 22nd Chasseurs from General Franceschi's cavalry division. Stewart's cavalry then continued their advance passing through Tordesillas until they joined up with Paget's cavalry on the northern bank of the Douro.

Sir John did not leave Salamanca himself until the 13th December, when he made for Alaejos and by the 15th had altered the objective of the army. A chance encounter by one of his officers in a Spanish village gave him vital information on the disposition of the French army. A French cavalry officer had been killed by the inhabitants of the village of Valdestillos, near Segoves, who then sold the contents of his sabretache to Captain John Waters. It contained important dispatches from Marshal Berthier in Madrid to Marshal Soult at Saldana, from which Moore was able to confirm the size of Soult's force of two infantry divisions and four cavalry regiments. Berthier also informed Soult that he could march from Saldana and take León, Zamora and Benavente as there were no troops to oppose him. The British were still believed to be at Salamanca and in full retreat on Lisbon. Confirming that Lefebvre-Desnouette's corps was at Talavera making for Badajoz and Bèssieres corps was in pursuit of what remained of General Castaños' army pushing them towards the coast at Valencia; Mortier's corps was in Aragon making for Saragossa to help in the siege; Junot was advancing on Burgos with his leading division already in Viullonia.

Armed with this vital piece of intelligence, Moore grasped the opportunity to attack and inflict a serious defeat on the unsuspecting Soult. On the 15th December the British force was ordered to march north, Valladolid no longer being their objective. To attack Soult, Moore needed to concentrate his forces and issued orders to that effect. Baird was to make for Mayorga and the other divisional commanders were ordered to join him. By the 19th December, the 15th Hussars in Baird's force had reached Mayorga, however, the weather had taken a drastic change for the worse. It had become bitterly cold and snow had started to fall. Moore finally joined from the south with his force on the 20th December, his army at last united. Its strength was 25,000 men, of which 2,450 were cavalry, 1,287 artillery with 66 guns (Oman).

For the Riflemen in Moore's force this had meant marches on the 19th of twenty miles to Villa Mayor, fifteen miles to Villalon on the 20th and a further eighteen miles to Villada on the 21st December, all in terribly cold conditions. Meanwhile, back in Madrid on the 19th December Napoleon held a grand review of his troops.

With the army united for the first time Moore was able to change his troop formations and arranged his infantry into four divisions, with two separate Light Brigades and a single cavalry division. The 1st infantry division was to be under the command of Baird, the 2nd Hope, the 3rd Fraser and the 4th, the Reserve division, under Edward Paget. Baron Charles Alten and Brigadier Robert Craufurd each commanded a Light Brigade. Lord Paget was in overall command of the cavalry with Generals Slade and Stewart as his brigade commanders.

The formation of the divisions being:

Sir D. Baird's 1st Division

Warde's brigade	1st Bn 1st Foot Guards
	3rd Bn 1st Foot Guards
Bentinck's brigade	1st Bn 4th Regiment
	1st Bn 42nd Regiment
	1st Bn 50th Regiment
Manningham's brigade	3rd Bn 1st Regiment
	1st Bn 26th Regiment
	1st Bn 81st Regiment

Sir J. Hope's 2nd Division

Leith's brigade	51st Regiment
	2nd Bn 59th Regiment
	76th Regiment
Hill's brigade	2nd Regiment
	1st Bn 5th Regiment
	2nd Bn 14th Regiment
	1st Bn 32nd Regiment
Catlin Craufurd's brigade	1st Bn 36th Regiment
	1st Bn 71st Regiment
	1st Bn 92nd Regiment

Lt. Gen. Fraser's 3rd Division

Beresford's brigade	1st Bn 6th Regiment
	1st Bn 9th Regiment
	2nd Bn 23rd Regiment
	2nd Bn 43rd Regiment
Fane's brigade	1st Bn 38th Regiment
	1st Bn 79th Regiment
	1st Bn 82nd Regiment

Maj. Gen. Edward Paget's Reserve Division

Anstruther's brigade	20th Regiment
	1st Bn 52nd Regiment
	1st Bn 95th Rifles
Disney's brigade	1st Bn 28th Regiment
	1st Bn 91st Regiment

The Light Brigades

Col. Robert Craufurd's	1st Bn 43rd Regiment
1st Flank brigade	2nd Bn 52nd Regiment
	2nd Bn 95th Rifles
Brig. Gen. Charles Alten	1st Light Bn King's German Legion
2nd Flank brigade	2nd Light Bn King's German Legion
Lord Paget's cavalry division	7th, 10th, 15th Hussars, 18th Light Dragoons
	3rd Light Dragoons King's German Legion

Artillery and Staff Corps

Moore made Sahagún his next objective on the 21st December. With the snow continuing to fall the troops marched north east, with Paget's cavalry in advance of the infantry. On reaching the outskirts of Sahagún the 10th and 15th Hussars came in contact with a party of French troops and captured five of them. Those who escaped were able to raise the alarm and the town was soon alive with the sound of the French getting to arms. Paget ordered General Slade to take the 10th Hussars and attack the French at the front of the town while he went with the 15th to the rear to cut off any attempt they might make to escape. By the time Paget had reached this point Slade had still not made his attack. As a result of this delay, formed up and ready to meet him were the 8th Dragoons and 1st Provisional Chasseurs of the French cavalry, around 600 strong against his 400 hussars. The French made an impressive sight mounted on their large horses, black horse hair flowing from their brass helmets. Paget gave the order to charge and with the added momentum of racing downhill the 15th soon covered the short distance to the waiting French dragoons. They only managed in this time to fire off a few of their carbines before the 15th reached them with their full force of flashing steel and determined men and beasts. Within a short while the French dragoons broke and fled followed closely by the British cavalry. The final outcome of this encounter was that twenty Frenchmen lay dead in the snow and a further one hundred and seventy had been captured; of these, two were colonels while eleven others were officers.

With the French cleared from Sahagún, Moore was able to establish his headquarters in the town in the Benedictine convent aware that Soult would soon receive news of the action. His true position, therefore, would soon be common knowledge to the French. They, however, would not be able to mount an immediate counter attack for it was still snowing and a thick fog had also set in which concealed the British position. The troops were able to rest for the whole of the 22nd December while stores were brought up from Mayorga.

The Rifles during this time had marched to Sahagún where they hoped to halt for the night but were ordered to continue a couple of miles further to the old convent of Trianon. When they arrived the troops already stationed here being in an advanced position were on the alert expecting the French to attack at any moment. When the Riflemen finally halted outside the convent walls soldiers from various regiments came swarming out to meet them. They rushed up to the Riflemen eager to shake their hands, cheering as they did so. The difference in the appearance of both sets of troops was quite marked, for Sir David's force were all fresh faced, ruddy cheeked well fed men, their clothing and equipment was almost new and at this point still quite clean. Moore's Riflemen looked the complete opposite, gaunt, way worn and ragged, with faces burnt to a dark brown, their accoutrements and uniforms were well worn and torn and a number were without shoes. On the 23rd December the Rifles lost their first man of the campaign when Sergeant James Wiseman, of No 1 Company 2nd Battalion 95th, died.

The butchers belonging to the Rifles now set to work slaughtering a chance find of oxen and sheep which were found within the walls of the convent, while the men started making fires out in the open snow so that they could cook the freshly killed meat. Once they had eaten they were ordered into the convent to rest, laying on the floor of a long passage, but keeping their knapsacks on and their rifles to hand. The tired men were soon in a deep sleep. A little later Quartermaster Surtees, who had joined with Baird's Riflemen entered the convent passage looking for Rifleman Harris. By the light of a single candle and after calling out his name he finally came upon the tired Rifleman. The quartermaster then ordered Harris to collect all the company shoemakers together for it was urgent that they follow him. After a short time and amidst numerous curses several men were roused to follow the quartermaster, who then led them to the top of the convent by a staircase from where they had to cross an area that was in ruin This was achieved by using the exposed rafters for there were no floorboards. Once on the other side the men entered a room which was full of barrels of gun powder and a large pile of raw bullock hides. Surtees, now informed them that General Craufurd had ordered that they should sew up all the barrels into the hides with the hair on the outside. Harris eventually cajoled his tired fellow Riflemen into completing their general's wishes and they were then allowed to return to the convent passage to rest until the buglers sounded the reveille.

These four companies remained at the convent for most of the next day until towards evening, when they were told to leave the women and baggage behind and move to the head of the Light Brigade which was about to advance towards the enemy. On the way to the front they were joined by the remaining companies of the battalion who had halted to allow them to take up the post of honour at the head of the brigade, cheering them as they marched passed calling them the 'Heroes of Portugal'. The snow by now was really thick on the ground and as the brigade set off the men realised that it was Christmas Eve which brought back many happy memories of the times spent with their families and friends back in England. A Rifles' officer, who was not very well while on the march, rather than go through a small stream which crossed the road made a small detour across a bridge a little way from the road. This, however, was his undoing for General Craufurd came up at this very moment and on seeing the officer leave his section immediately flew into a rage. He now ordered him to march through the stream back and forth several times and thus used him to set an example to his men, for if their general could do this to a sick officer, what chance would they have if they stepped out of line? No doubt it had a similar effect on the other regimental officers.

Previous to this the Riflemen of the 1st Battalion 95th in the Reserve division had marched from Toro to Puebla on the 16th December with Baird's advance guard. They continued with further marches on the 17th to Villapando, 18th Castro Nuevo and finally reached Santabas on the 20th, where they were united with the four remaining companies of the 1st Battalion 95th under the command of Sir Sidney Beckwith. This brought the 1st Battalion strength up to nine companies and the 2nd Battalion mustered eight companies, therefore, the regiment had seventeen companies on active service with Sir John Moore's force. (Not eighteen as stated by Cope and Verner in their regimental histories.) The Reserve continued their advance to Grajal del Campo on the 21st, the whole of the force finally halting on the 22nd December to rest and try to repair their footwear and get the guns in proper order for the proposed advance. The supplies for the Reserve at this point had still not arrived. In the morning of the 23rd the Reserve received orders that they would march that evening on the road towards the River Carrion. General Paget, with the men's welfare at heart, tried to encourage them to lie down and rest for he assured them they would need all their strength for the coming campaign. That evening having been ordered to dress in light marching equipment the Riflemen and the Reserve set off at four o'clock for the Carrion, the whole country now being covered in snow.

Baird's column was to march for Valencia while Hope headed towards Benavente, for as we have seen it was Moore's intention to make a night march to the Carrion where he planned to force the bridge and attack the French at Saldana the next day. Craufurd's brigade as previously noted were the most advanced of the advance guard and were already well on their way to carry out the first part of this plan. The Riflemen continued the march almost asleep on their feet until they were suddenly jolted awake by the sounding of the alarm and the word that the enemy was upon them. The men rushed forward in extended order, with Captain Pakenham galloping to the front to take note of the enemy strength and position. On trying to gain a bank along the side of the road his horse knocked Rifleman Harris to the ground, then in its panic promptly got its legs tangled up in the Rifleman's equipment, nearly breaking his neck in the process. Luckily for Harris, Captain Pakenham finally managed to control his horse and cleared the bank and the prostrate Rifleman, only to find it had all been a false alarm. The brigade now continued its march, this time with General Craufurd at its head. They had not proceeded very far when a dragoon came galloping up to the General with orders that he was to return to Sahagún. Craufurd immediately halted the column and ordered them to about turn and retrace their steps. The Rifles finally reached Sahagún just as dawn was breaking. It had now become bitterly cold and the ground had begun to freeze making it hard for the men to keep on their feet. Their only crumb of comfort after a night march in which a number of regiments of the rear divisions had not even left the town, was the welcome sight of their wives and children who came rushing out to meet them, who hours before had seen them depart not knowing if they would ever see them again. The entire 2nd Battalion now entered the same convent which had previously held the four companies from Moore's columns before the advance. This time the men were ordered to remain in their ranks and they stood leaning on the muzzles of their rifles, dozing as they stood.

Moore received a message from the Marqués de la Romana that a large French force was marching to the aid of Soult, this was further confirmed by one of Moore's own officers who had just returned from the Castilian plains.

Napoleon actually learned of Moore's true position on the 19th December, having it confirmed by three deserters from the 60th Rifles. He was now advancing personally at the head of a 40,000 strong force, having first sent a message to Marshal Ney to abandon his advance on Saragossa and instead to support Soult in Old Castile. He, meanwhile, would try to cut off Moore from his retreat on Corunna. The French suffered from the lack of accurate intelligence just as much as the British and circumstances were changing the commander's plans almost daily. Moore's army was in fact fifty miles further north than Napoleon had expected.

Sir John now had no option but to order the retreat but at the same time he informed the Spanish General la Romana that it would be impossible for him to confront the French with such a small force. He requested his co-operation in so far as to leave the road to Astorga free for the British and pass through the Cantabrian Mountains, whilst la Romana took his force across the River Esla to hold the bridge at Mansilla to gain them more time. He now evacuated Sahagún, ordering Baird to take his division along the higher road to Valencia de Don Juan, while the divisions of Hope and Fraser would retreat along the lower road to Castro Gonzalo

After an hour's rest the Rifles were ordered out of the convent yet again and they moved off in the wake of the retreating army. General Craufurd sat upon his horse watching them as they marched passed. A thaw had begun to set in and it now started to rain, the general moved forward towards a group of Riflemen who were avoiding a small rivulet, 'Keep your ranks there men!' he said 'Keep your ranks and move on no straggling from the main body.' No man could escape the ever watchful eye of their General who would continue to stretch his iron fist of discipline over their well being, for which many a man would be most grateful in the coming weeks.

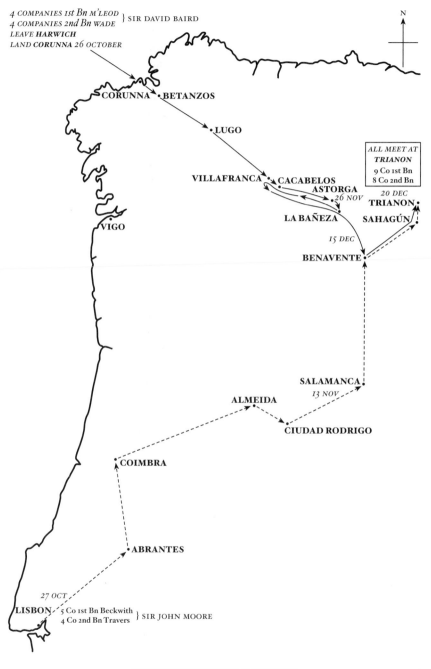

N

4 COMPANIES 1st Bn M'LEOD
4 COMPANIES 2nd Bn WADE } SIR DAVID BAIRD
LEAVE HARWICH
LAND CORUNNA 26 OCTOBER

CORUNNA • BETANZOS

• LUGO

VILLAFRANCA • CACABELOS
ASTORGA
26 NOV

ALL MEET AT
TRIANON
9 Co 1st Bn
8 Co 2nd Bn
20 DEC
TRIANON •

LA BAÑEZA   SAHAGÚN

VIGO

15 DEC

BENAVENTE •

SALAMANCA
13 NOV

ALMEIDA

CIUDAD RODRIGO

COIMBRA

ABRANTES

27 OCT

LISBON   5 Co 1st Bn Beckwith
         4 Co 2nd Bn Travers } SIR JOHN MOORE

MOVEMENT OF 1ST & 2ND BNS
27th October 1808 - 20th December 1808

0   30   60
SCALE OF MILES

Sahagún to Astorga

The troops still waiting in Sahagún to join the initial advance on the 24th, were not very pleased once it was made known that they were to retreat without confronting the enemy. They marched out of the town under a black cloud of depression, for they felt in their hearts that they were still a match for any French army and only needed the opportunity to show Moore their true fighting spirit. It did not help matters either when passing the area in which the cavalry had tasted glory, for the French cavalry still lay where they had fallen as a stark reminder. The bodies, stripped naked by the villagers, lay unburied on the frozen battlefield. The sight was all the more pitiful with the village dogs sniffing around them while the birds were pecking out their eyes. It was also discovered that one of the bodies was in fact that of a woman.

The weather conditions having changed, the rain made marching difficult for the roads were being turned into a sea of mud under the tramping of many thousands of feet and at times the men had to struggle ankle deep. It was now that the real change began to show in the retreating troops, deterioration of arms and equipment under the trying circumstances was only to be expected, but the breakdown of discipline which spread from regiment to regiment in the leading columns was unforgivable. As each day passed it became worse and the rearguard were witness at first hand to its excesses as they followed in their wake. In the villages the Spanish shouted at the rearguard in disgust taking out their frustrations on them with shouts of 'Viva los Franceses'. As the last man left the village they would ring the bells as if to exorcise the evil spirit of the British but the French troops would prove to be even worse in their dealings with the inhabitants of these villages.

With all control lost in the advance divisions, the men at every opportunity would help themselves to the local wine and spirits which in turn led to looting, with the inevitable destruction of houses and shops in a never ending quest for more drink. The Spanish were not taking this lightly and in one of the burning villages the rearguard came upon a number of stragglers who had been stripped and attacked by the local peasants.

With the retreat now well under way Craufurd's brigade and the Reserve, the last troops in Sahagún, were ordered to leave. The Light Brigade were to form the final rearguard covering the immediate Reserve division,

Flat plains of León south of Sahagún

while the entire force were in turn covered by the cavalry. The whole of the rearguard was under the direct command of Sir John Moore and they retreated along the same road as taken by Hope's column.

After leaving Sahagún Craufurd's brigade pushed on all day without a halt and it was on this march that they passed an overturned commissariat waggon which had become stuck fast in the mud. They were surprised that it had been abandoned with no effort made to save any of its contents. This was a strange occurrence for the men at this stage of the retreat but one that was soon to become all too common a sight by the time they were to reach the transports. The true severity of the march, however, became all to apparent when a sergeant from the 91st Regiment fell dead from fatigue and no one stopped to offer him assistance. On the 25th December Rifleman Thomas Bulmer of No 9 Company 2nd 95th was listed as missing; the hardships of the campaign had started to take effect in the ranks of the Riflemen. The men were starving, having received no rations and what little they had originally carried in their haversacks had long gone.

By the 26th December, Baird's force had reached the Esla, which was now a torrent of raging floodwater and the only means of crossing it was by a ford at Valencia de Don Juan. At this point the enemy had not put any pressure on the retreating troops, for Napoleon was still fifty miles away, having halted on Christmas Day. Soult, however, was gaining on the rearguard, his cavalry having already made some minor contact with Paget's cavalry. The weather was so severe on the 26th that even though they set off early the 2nd 95th did not reach San Miguel until midnight the same day when they reported three Riflemen missing; Patrick Rignie No 7 Co, Cornelius Stephens No 8 Co and Robert Tinsdale No 10 Co. On the 27th they had another hard march to Castro Pipa, near to Castro Gonzalo.

Town of Mayorga

With the French cavalry rapidly gaining ground they were becoming a serious threat to the rearguard. Paget's cavalry, however, were invaluable in preventing the enemy from causing any real harm. An attack by the 10th Hussars under the command of Colonel Leigh on a body of the French cavalry being a prime example of their worth, breaking their line with hardly a casualty to themselves, while at the same time capturing around forty prisoners. The 18th Light Dragoons were equally successful making numerous charges against the enemy, one successful attack against a body of cavalry over one hundred strong. This was while Baird's infantry was still crossing the Esla at Valencia de Don Juan. The dragoons, only thirty-eight strong, broke through the French cavalry, killed twelve and captured another twenty.

The successful screening of the retreating British army by their cavalry led Napoleon into believing that their strength was more than double its actual size; when in truth the French cavalry actually outnumbered the British three to one. As a result, Baird's force was able to cross the River Esla without incident. Hope and Fraser's divisions, meanwhile, were being pressed by numbers of French light cavalry who had been able to slip through Paget's cavalry screen. The main defence of these divisions was down to General Craufurd's rearguard. It was inevitable that the French would get through somewhere, for the area covered by the retreat was too vast for Paget's cavalry to police thoroughly because of their lack of numbers. This put pressure on the troops crossing the Esla at Castro Gonzalo by way of the stone bridge.

Modern bridges over River Esla at Castro Gonzalo

By the 28th December the last of the stragglers from Hope's division had crossed and the area of the bridge was now under the immediate protection of Craufurd. For it had been planned that the engineers would blow the bridge in order to delay the advancing French a little longer to give the retreating army more time. It was here that two men of the 43rd Regiment displayed a fine example of courage in carrying out their duty as advance sentries, on rising ground approaching the bridge. Privates John Walton and Richard Jackson were in position on the enemy side of the river so as to be able to give ample warning to the regiments halted on the other side of the bridge should the enemy put in an appearance. However, what had not been allowed for was the deteriorating weather conditions which brought visibility down to only a short distance. The heavy rain also played its part in masking the approach of the French who were able to capture some women and baggage carts and come up close to the bridge undetected. This, therefore, aided the French in mounting a surprise attack on the bridge. Jackson at once in accordance with his orders made a dash for it to warn his regiment, while Walton stood his ground. The wet weather prevented them from firing the required warning shots into the enemy. Walton attempted to hold them off with the point of his bayonet. A group of French hussars immediately went riding after Jackson, firing at him at the same time, while the rest of their comrades confronted the resolute Walton. Jackson would always be second best in this uneven race and was soon overtaken by the hussars, who slashed away with their swords in every direction and in defending their blows he received between twelve and fourteen sabre wounds. Left for dead by his attackers he was still, however, able to crawl off and warn his regiment. Walton, meanwhile, was presenting much more of a challenge to the French hussars for he had managed to inflict injuries on them. They eventually, for some unknown reason rode off leaving him unharmed! Although he had received about twenty blows from their sabres not one had pierced his person. The condition of his knapsack, musket and bayonet, the latter almost bent double, bore witness to his uneven struggle.

Quartermaster Surtees who was approaching the bridge at this time with the Rifles' baggage carts, upon hearing the fire of the hussars' carbines made for the commanding officer of his battalion, Colonel Hamlet Wade, to report the closeness of the French. Colonel Wade did not believe his quartermaster, thinking he was in error, but there might have been a bit more to this for these two men were not on the best of terms. His mistake could have been costly for he failed to call the Riflemen to arms as a precaution. However, this was soon brought home to him with the arrival of General Craufurd, who having advanced to this position and not finding the Rifles at their posts ready to counter the French cavalry threat soon let his views be known. The French failed to take advantage of the success of their surprise attack and the rest of the night passed without incident.

The next morning the whole of Craufurd's brigade was assembled on the height above and in front of the bridge on the enemy side. The French were also formed up on the rising ground facing the British brigade. They also had a number of their cavalry in the plain where some minor skirmishing took place. Craufurd kept his brigade in position all day which eventually saw the last of the British cavalry safely over the river. Earlier all the houses and buildings in the surrounding area had been burned or destroyed so the French could not use the materials to repair it once the bridge had been blown. He continued to remain in this position to protect the engineers working on the bridge as they struggled to prepare for its destruction.

The masonry forming the main supports was too hard to place the charges at the required depth to be sure of success. The rain which continued to pour down was not helping, the sky gradually growing darker as both armies stood facing each other in total silence, ankle deep in mud, rain water streaming out of the muzzle of rifle and musket alike.

It was not until darkness fell that Craufurd was able to mobilise his force; not wishing to repeat the errors of the previous night he posted three companies of Riflemen from the 2nd Battalion and two from the 43rd as picquets on the hills overlooking the enemy. Under their cover he now started to withdraw the rest of his force over the Esla. Part of his infantry he posted behind a barricade which he constructed to give some degree of defence against any surprise attack from the enemy cavalry, while at the same time affording the engineers and working parties further security. The rain was still pouring down, Craufurd at the barricade in his sodden greatcoat watching the progress of the working parties. Now with darkness firmly set in he made his way up the hills to where his picquets of Riflemen were posted. He took with him a canteen of rum and a small cup and visited each picquet in turn giving the men a sip of spirit until it was all finished. At the same time warning them, 'When all is ready Riflemen, you will immediately get the word and pass over the bridge. Be careful and mind what you are about.' He then returned to the bridge to continue supervising in its destruction. The bridge, being of a very strong construction with several arches for supports, was taking longer than expected even though Craufurd had employed half his force in helping the engineers.

The French, meanwhile, were quite aware of what the British had in mind, they had been lined up against them during the day and were waiting for the slightest sign of weakness in the British Light Brigade's position to take advantage. Any attempt to withdraw by Craufurd during the day would have been catastrophic even if the bridge had been ready. He, therefore, had no choice, however uncomfortable it was for the men, but to remain in this stalemate position until the cover of darkness.

Once darkness fell the French were able to make their own plans and they made a number of attacks on the picquets Craufurd had immediately placed in position. Three squadrons of chasseurs charged them at one stage but they put up a strong resistance and forced them to retire. With the failure of the cavalry attack they tried again, this time on foot but the picquets were equal to their efforts and once more held them off. The French continued their attacks throughout the evening but more in the line of small skirmishes rather than a full scale onslaught, with which the defenders were quite capable of dealing.

Remains of the oldest bridge at Castro Gonzalo

At last when most of the bridge was finally blown up and the order was given for the picquets to cross, the men withdrew, coming down from the hills gradually so as not to alert the French. On reaching the bridge they had to cross in single file with the aid of planks placed across the broken arches. This was quite a precarious operation for tired, cold and wet men who had been lying out for hours in the pouring rain unable to move for fear of exposing their position to the enemy, for the river had swollen so much now that it was in danger of carrying the planks away. When the last man was safely over, the engineers blew the final charge which brought the central arch crashing into the river.

Meanwhile, Quartermaster Sergeant Surtees of the Rifles had more pressing matters on his mind than the activity at the bridge, namely the welfare of the men of his battalion and their desperate need for rations. He found a cart loaded with ration biscuit, which had been abandoned and proceeded to get it across the River Esla via a ford which he had located a little way downstream from the bridge. As a result he was able to distribute its contents to the Riflemen after they crossed the destroyed bridge. However meagre, they were glad to have something to put into their aching stomachs.

Whilst the rearguard had been holding back the French, the leading divisions had entered the town of Benavente, rested and were now leaving for Astorga. The Reserve and rearguard, having stalled the French, now marched the short distance to Benavente safe in the knowledge that for a short time they would be free from an imminent attack. Only the Reserve division remained in the town by the time the Light Brigades arrived. The Rifles were the very last troops, quartered in a convent along with the German Legion and the 10th and 15th Hussars. Their friends in the 15th seeing the plight of the Riflemen gave them some strong spirits to help revive them from the cold and wet; unfortunately their good intentions made a number of the men sick, the raw spirit reacting on their empty stomachs. The two days they had been at Castro Gonzalo they had received no rations. The blowing up of the bridge gained Moore's force twenty four hours respite from the French, roughly the time it took them to repair it. Though the troops under Craufurd's command destroyed all the possible bridge building materials in the surrounding area it had little effect on the French for they carried their own spare wood and bridge building materials with them.

Benavente, a walled town set in an extensive plain, had a magnificent Moorish-Gothic castle with very ornate turrets at its centre. The front of the castle which overlooked the plain was built on a series of Moorish arches supported by large columns while the streets of the town were narrow and rather gloomy. When the British troops first visited the town on their way up country the shopkeepers in their well stocked shops made the men pay exorbitant prices for any extra food or provisions they required. On their return nothing seemed to have changed which probably all added to fuel the black mood many of the men were already in, giving the troops of Hope and Fraser's divisions the excuse they needed in the initial destruction of the town.

The 52nd Regiment discovered this at first hand when they arrived in the town ahead of the Rifles, again frozen, starving and very wet. The officers could not obtain a single drop of wine for the men, no matter how much money they offered to the inhabitants, who after seeing the excesses of the British troops were in no mood to show them compassion or charity. They were told there was no wine for sale in the town and in most cases this was probably true. A sergeant, however, reported to Lieutenant Love of the 52nd that in an out house belonging to the convent in which they were billetted he had discovered a wall that had only recently been built. He thought that there might be wine concealed behind it. Lieutenant Love instantly confronted the friars and asked them for some wine offering prompt payment. The venerable father abbot constantly declared by a string of saints that there was not a drop to be had in the whole of the convent. Lieutenant Love, although a very young officer, was not deterred and after reconnoitring the premises, had a rope tied around his body. He was lowered through a sort of skylight into the outhouse, where the sergeant had found the fresh masonry, after peering through a crevice in a strongly barricaded door.

Once inside he was soon followed by two men of his company and with the aid of a log the trio then proceeded to batter down the newly built wall where enough wine was found to give every man in the company a generous allowance. The wine had been stored in a large vat and while it was being issued to the shivering drenched troops, the fat friar, who had been so adamant that there was no wine suddenly appeared through a trap door. He laughingly requested that at least he might have one drink before it was all consumed. One of the men then remarked, 'By Jove! when it was his, he was damn stingy about it; but now that it is ours, we will show him what British hospitality is, and give him his fill.' The men then lifted the friar and put him head first into the vat and were it not for the timely arrival of some officers he would have surely drowned.

Before the arrival of the Reserve division and the rearguard, mobs of drunken men from the divisions of Hope and Fraser were roaming the streets completely out of control, their officers and non-commissioned officers powerless to stop them wreaking havoc upon the inhabitants. Moore had witnessed their behaviour at first hand, both on the march from Sahagún and in Benavente and as a result wrote the following order:

'The misbehaviour of the troops in the column which marched by Valderas to this place exceeds what he could have believed of British soldiers. It is disgraceful to the officers; as it strongly marks their negligence and inattention. It is impossible for the general to explain to his army the motives for the movement he directs. The Commander of the forces can, however, assure the army that he has made none since he left Salamanca which he did not foresee, and was not judged prepared for; and as far as he is a judge, they have answered, the purposes for which they were intended. When it is proper to fight a battle he will do it; and he will choose the time and place he thinks fit; in the meantime he begs the officers and soldiers of the army to attend diligently to discharge their parts and to leave to him and to the General Officers the decision of measures which belong to them alone.'

Moore might just as well have not bothered for all the good it did, the men took no notice of their general's pleading and that night the troops continued in their quest for drink. When it could not be found they consumed the sacred wine of the convents. To make matters worse to keep warm and to dry their sodden clothes they built fires in most of the rooms of the convents and any other buildings in which they were quartered. Even when the rearguard arrived some of the men lit fires to gain comfort. As a result Captain Lloyd of the 43rd Regiment discovered a fire which threatened to destroy the area in which the cavalry had sheltered their horses and averted what could have been a catastrophe. Other fires, however, had broken out before their arrival, one of which was in the castle described earlier belonging to the Duchess of Ossuna.

Town of Valderas (sacked in the retreat)

Its ornate exterior was equally matched by its splendid interior. Originally the Duchess had fled with her daughters to Seville from what was thought the excesses of the French army, only to find, however, that on her return its inner beauty and priceless furnishings had been gutted and totally destroyed by the British!

Benavente was the advance depot for the stores of the commissariat and now that it was to be abandoned, rather than leave anything to the French, the divisions were told to help themselves to whatever they needed before continuing on the march. Piled up on the side of the road that led northwards out of the town were heaps of food and clothes. In the garden of a monastery, thousands of pairs of shoes, waggon-loads of biscuit, meat, shirts, blankets, stockings and belts were waiting to be turned into a massive bonfire.

Only Craufurd's troops remained in Benavente when the French cavalry started to ford the River Esla as the bridge at this time had not been repaired. The chasseurs of the Imperial Guard under the command of General Charles Lefebvre-Desnouettes had found the same ford as used by Quartermaster Surtees of the Rifles. As a result some five to six hundred French cavalry were now approaching from the river pushing the picquets of the 18th Light Dragoons before them. However, Lord Paget was waiting for them with his cavalry and as the French horsemen slowly advanced in line, charged down hill along with the cavalry of the King's German Legion. The French were able to repulse the first attack but a second succeeded in breaking through their line, but because Paget's force was too small to take advantage of their success, they had to retire. Paget retreated as far as Benavente itself, where he was then able to gather a force large enough to take on the French once more. The chasseurs continued to advance and were by now nearing the outskirts of the town. Paget had, meanwhile, concealed 450 troopers of the 10th Hussars and another 200 from the 18th Light Dragoons and King's German Legion in a natural fold of the ground. [1] These came charging out onto the unsuspecting French cavalry meeting them head on in a fierce sword fight. The British with their heavier swords soon gained advantage and in a short space of time the French were beaten, running for the safety of the river. Major Jesse of the King's German Legion gives a most graphic account of the cavalry clash, 'Men fell tumbling to the ground from their blood spattered horses, the sharpness of the British swords left a number of Frenchmen with their arms sliced clean off. One man fell to the ground with the whole of his head cut off horizontally from above the eyes, while others had their heads divided down to the chin.'

Lord Paget's cavalry continued after the retreating chasseurs who plunged into the Esla in a frantic attempt to escape the flashing swords of their pursuers. Not all of them were able to reach the ford by which they had first crossed and the river was too deep and the current was too strong to attempt to cross anywhere else. As a result some of the French cavalry had to return to the same bank of the river from which they had just fled. Here the British were waiting to make them prisoner. The French General Lefebvre-Desnouettes was amongst the latter, having also received a sabre wound to the forehead. The chasseurs on reaching what was thought to be the safety of their own side of the river promptly received a severe shelling from the British horse artillery who had quickly followed up the cavalry to the river. This added to the French defeat which left fifty-five dead or wounded on the battle field.

At dawn on the 29th, Craufurd's brigade marched out of Benavente, the Riflemen of the 2nd Battalion providing a guard for the captured French cavalry and their Commander Lefebvre-Desnouettes [2] of whom they had charge until handing him over at Astorga. Surtees described them as the Imperial Guard, the flower of Napoleon's army, being fine looking men, dressed in dark-green longcoats, with high bearskin caps and wearing moustaches. Napoleon is believed to have witnessed the defeat of his cavalry from the hills on the French side of the river.

---

[1] Interestingly Georges Blond on page 233 of his book *La Grande Armée* states that Lefebvre-Desnouettes with 1,500 cavalry was confronted by 5,000 British cavalry! [2] General Lefebvre-Desnouettes was eventually taken to Cheltenham, England where due to his high rank he was paraded at all the fashionable establishments. Ironically his origins were quite humble starting as a private soldier in the French army and his wife a washer woman to the regiment!

The Rifles now had a hard march before them in the region of thirty miles to the town of La Bañeza, one of their former camping places. The men without food, were starving and many were without boots or shoes. It can only be assumed that the stores which had been piled up for the divisions to help themselves had all been taken or destroyed by the time the rearguard reached Benavente. (Lieutenant Cox of the Rifles had to march the last ten miles in his bare feet.) On arriving at La Bañeza the officers and men were quartered in a convent as the rest of the town was crowded with the reserve troops. Here fatigue parties were busy throwing ammunition into the water to make it unserviceable, should it fall into the hands of the French. The condition of the Riflemen was starting to deteriorate and together with the march on the 29th resulted in the loss of eight men.

Arthur Malone	No 5 Company	missing
Alex Flint	No 8 Company	missing
William Dickenson	No 9 Company	missing
Thomas Fletcher	No 9 Company	missing
Donald McPhee	No 9 Company	missing
John Elliot	No 9 Company	died
James Douglas	No 10 Company	missing
John Lacey	No 10 Company	missing

After a cold, uncomfortable night the Rifles were awakened by the buglers sounding the parade ready for the march to Astorga. Lieutenant Cox, who could not envisage another march barefooted along the flinty Spanish roads acquired a pair of monk's sandals. No doubt a number of Riflemen had also taken the opportunity to improvise on their lack of footwear.

Soult, meanwhile, had helped to redress the balance a little for the defeat of the cavalry when on the 30th he attacked part of la Romana's army at Mansilla and captured more than half the force opposed to him plus two guns. The French were now able to cross the river making for León, which they reached and occupied on the 31st.

Moore originally asked la Romana to retreat over the Cantabrian Mountains into the Asturias but due to the change in his circumstances and the heavy snow blocking his way he made for Astorga. As a consequence his force now added to the congestion already on the road with the British and the local Spanish people trying to make for the safety of the coast.

Moore started to push the retreat hard now to put as much distance between his force and the French advance corps. The men already in bad humour, were now at their most rebellious. The criminal element in the ranks would not obey their officers which in turn influenced the good characters who soon followed suit. As a result the British army already resembled a completely defeated and spent force, with stragglers stretching for miles behind the main columns. The weather and terrain were also against them, it was becoming even colder and the snow was falling once more. The transport animals like their human masters struggled to keep up with the army. The horses pulling the guns were a most pitiful sight straining to move their heavy burdens, unable to keep their feet on the muddy, slippery roads into the mountains. Many collapsed with exhaustion where they remained unable to move no matter how much they were prodded or encouraged by their frustrated charges, death being their only release. The main priority, however, was to keep the supply carts and guns on the move. Waggons on which the women and children had been riding were the first to suffer and they had to join the men and proceed on foot, many woefully ill-equipped for such a journey.

On the 30th December the rearguard reached Astorga by which time the town was full of troops and every inch of shelter had already been taken up. To make matters worse the remnants of la Romana's army had already arrived in the town requiring shelter too. Though the British troops presented a sorry sight, their Spanish allies were in a worse condition, starving, barefoot, most without weapons, with their clothes in rags. But far worse was the fact that many were suffering from typhus fever. The worst cases, having already succumbed to the disease, lay unburied in the streets. Astorga now fell to the same treatment as Benavente, bands of British and Spanish soldiers roamed the streets. Food was in great demand but in short supply for only two days rations had been stored here and this was soon dispersed amongst the troops of both armies. A number of bullocks whose condition was suspect and did not look as if they would make the journey were killed and cut up. It was the usual story, however, once the troops found the wine cellars, the casks were brought up to the streets and the gutters were soon running with their contents.

The Riflemen of the rearguard, meanwhile, having left La Bañeza marched to another of their old camping grounds, the village of Zalada close to Astorga where they spent the night while the rest of the brigade continued on into Astorga. At least by staying in Zalada they were spared the stress of trying to find quarters. It was also while stationed here that the 2nd Battalion transferred their baggage from bullock carts to mules which made life much easier for Quartermaster Sergeant Surtees.

To move the army to Corunna Moore needed a large supply of food but the nearest stock pile was at Villafranca, a fifty mile march to the west. He had little option but to make for these supplies and in addition to his logistical problems there was still a small matter of the pursuing French army! His force could not hope to hold them off at Astorga, for the French could easily out manœuvre him by going north from León towards Villafranca or by going south along the mountain tracks between Benavente and Orense. Marching to Villafranca had to be his best and only option, at least he could be sure of enough supplies to continue the retreat. The Cantabrian Mountains situated behind Villafranca would also give him shelter making it harder for the French to inflict harm upon his disintegrating army, while at the same time giving him a choice of two embarkation points for the transports, Vigo or Corunna. To be sure that Vigo remained an option Sir John Moore altered part of his retreating formation by detaching the two Light Brigades of Alten and Craufurd with the sole purpose of securing the road from Orense to Vigo. Should Corunna be lost as an embarkation point he could still bring the army away at Vigo. At the same time it helped to release the pressure placed on the quartermaster general with two less brigades to supply, amounting to 3,000 men.

To attempt such an undertaking he needed a reliable and determined officer with the force to match. Moore had only two formations on which he could rely, the Light Brigade which was doing such a splendid job as rearguard, or the Reserve division. Moore gave the task of securing Vigo to General Craufurd and relied upon the Reserve division to cover the retreat as rearguard. By splitting his forces it was also to be hoped that part of the pursuing French troops would be forced to separate to enable them to follow both columns making the retreat a little easier for the main column.

Village of Celada (Formally Zalada)

The troops commenced their departure from Astorga on the 31st December having stripped the town of all its possessions and destroyed all that could be of service to the French. Most of the clothing had been given out to the first troops on arrival in Astorga who were not necessarily the most needy. This meant that most of the Reserve and the rearguard divisions missed out. All that remained was the destruction of the ammunition. The Rifles left Zalada and entered Astorga that same day where they remained for a couple of hours until the magazine was blown. At the same time a quantity of rum casks were also to be destroyed, the heads of which were staved in and the contents allowed to run into the street. For some of the men to see such precious liquid going to waste was too much and they scooped it up in their shakos, mud and all.

The Reserve division and the 15th Hussars now had the task of covering the retreat of Moore's force and on the 1st January the retreat began in earnest on the ice-covered roads winding into the mountains.

The Light Brigades' March to Vigo

The troops remaining at Astorga [1] were warned in the morning that the enemy was believed to be close to the town; consequently they were kept on the alert but the French failed to appear. The Rifles, now the only infantry left, finally evacuated the town to march the twenty miles to Foncevadon, which they reached that evening. Foncevadon was only a small village consisting of about five or six houses which meant that there was very little accommodation for the men. The battalion baggage contained a few tents and by adding these to the existing houses and outbuildings all the officers and men managed to spend the night sheltered from the severe cold, although two Riflemen were reported as missing on the 30th December: Thomas Clark from No 9 Company and William Miles from No 5 Company.

On the 1st January 1809, with the Light Brigades making for Vigo and Moore's divisions continuing along the main road to Corunna, the French finally reached Astorga. This was just after the last of the British cavalry had departed. Now that Napoleon's divisions were at Astorga he was at last able to concentrate the whole of his forces here, which numbered some 70,000 infantry, 10,000 cavalry and 200 pieces of artillery. The magnitude of his epic march across the snowy ridge of the Carpetinos after a two hundred mile march from Madrid to Astorga was lost because the British had escaped! From this day Moore would have to contend with the combined forces of the French instead of just their cavalry, for which up to this point he had been more than a match.

Napoleon made great capital out of the British dilemma which he described as cowardly for abandoning the Spanish, his propaganda machine working flat out to discredit them. It even reported the sacking of León when the nearest any British troops had come to it was about thirty miles! It was a shrewd move by the Emperor to try to cause as much discord for the British, as the people of the villages would be reluctant to help such so called allies. He was quite confident that it would only be a matter of time before his troops caught up with the British who they would finally crush and cast into the sea.

---

[1] Many authorities on the history of the Peninsular War state that the Light Brigades parted from Moore's main column at Astorga, when in fact it was not until after a day's march beyond Astorga that they left the main road to Corunna for Orense and Vigo.

How confident he was of achieving this is confirmed by his return to Paris leaving the task to Marshal Soult along with the redistribution of his forces in Spain, though circumstances were also proving difficult back home, for Austria was becoming the immediate danger now. At the same time Napoleon's personal life was undergoing some difficulties. (Later that same year he was divorced from the Empress Josephine.)

The Imperial Guard returned to Valladolid, Debelle's division made for Madrid and Bonnet's division took up the garrison duties at Santander, whilst Lapisse's division was sent south to the Douro. Junot's corps was reformed and part of it sent to join Soult whose force now numbered 25,000 infantry, 6,000 cavalry, with a further 16,000 men under Ney in support. Soult now pushed on after the British on a double front, his main body followed the route of Foncevadon and Ponferrada, while the second column took the road from Combarros and Bembibre.

Old road before Combarros

On the first day of the New Year, Craufurd and Alten's men found themselves heading into the mountains, with a difficult march before them. After a short time they halted and in the distance they could hear the sound of gun fire, coming from the direction of what would be Moore's rearguard. The French having reorganised themselves were putting in a concerted effort to press the British and it was now the turn of the Riflemen of the 1st Battalion, in action for the first time, to thwart the enemy.

The Light Brigades continued into the mountains and halted that night in a village, where upon arrival the commissary officer requested the local Alcalde to provide bread for the men for they were now in great need. He promised the officer he would set the bakers to work at once and told him that in a few hours the bread would be ready. However, he had no intention of complying with the request and though the officer and quartermasters called on him repeatedly they were met with all kinds of excuses as to the delay and told it would be coming shortly.

The next morning the brigades finally set off still without receiving any bread, the Alcalde's plan having succeeded; it is a wonder that Craufurd allowed this to happen but maybe at the time his mind was on other things? The Rifles were now acting as rearguard for both brigades and continued in this manner for the remainder of the march to Vigo. At the next halt they reported a further three men as missing: Terrance Higgins No 7 Company, Charles McCarthy and Thomas Rosten both of No 9 Company.

The hardship of these marches was beginning to tell on all, but none more so than in the ranks of their families. The wives of the Riflemen resembled a troop of travelling beggars, having acquired all manner of clothing in an attempt to keep warm, many wearing greatcoats taken from the dead which they wore buttoned up over their heads. Most of their lower garments were in rags which exposed their naked legs and feet to the elements. General Craufurd, however, was to be seen everywhere, riding at the head of the column one moment, then at the rear, with his ever watchful eye, encouraging the men while at the same time not allowing any slacking in the ranks. His mind was firmly set on getting the whole of his fighting force to the bridge over the River Miño and then as many as possible to Vigo and the transports. Craufurd could not afford to allow his brigades to fall into a rabble which would weaken the strength of his force as he might have to fight for the bridge. For at the end of the day, Moore's very existence could depend on Craufurd's success. Their was no way for the commanders to find out how each other's forces were progressing for intelligence gathering was hard at the best of times, in these conditions with a hostile enemy close by, impossible. The whole campaign had now turned into a game of chance; although the French were known to be in the rear of the British retreat, what was not known, was if they had managed to outflank them with other more mobile forces. They could already be marching into a trap. (It is easy to look at the campaign and the position Moore found himself in through modern day eyes and with hindsight, as some military authors have done, condemn him, when the logistics of the campaign, its terrain and severe weather conditions have to be taken into account as a whole. Only then can we appreciate what a task the commanders of these two forces had.)

There was, however, no hope or help for those who dropped out unable to continue, even with the threats of Craufurd ringing in their ears, men still fell to the ground. Craufurd though could have made life more bearable for the men by having them discard their heavy and useless knapsacks. This is probably the only fault that could be levelled at him throughout the whole retreat. Many more would have survived the march if they had not been carrying this unnecessary burden. Most of the men's clothing and equipment had already become unserviceable and most of them were without any form of footwear. The officers were no better off than their men; washing and shaving had long been dispensed with.

Conditions for the men at best were horrendous, but for their women, many dragging exhausted children along behind them, to keep up with the column was an impossible task. For one Rifleman's wife this can be magnified a thousand times, for Mrs. M'Guire was heavily pregnant and could not keep up with her husband's company and finally, unable to go any further slumped to the ground at the side of the road. Rifleman M'Guire was allowed to remain with his wife and as the company moved off his comrades looked back in pity, many believing that they had little chance of seeing them both again. However, Mrs. M'Guire was made of sterner stuff, being a strong, hardy Irish woman and after lying for a short time in a deep snow gave birth to a healthy son.

JAMES DANN

At the next halt the men of M'Guire's company were both surprised and delighted to see them coming along the road with the baby wrapped up in Mrs. M'Guire's arms to protect him from the bitter cold. This little trio eventually survived the hardships of the retreat and reached England safe and sound, a credit to female endurance. The sight of Mrs. M'Guire must have been an inspiration to all around her and no doubt many gained strength from the example she set.

There were probably many more such instances of the hardships that went unrecorded on the retreat but many believed their general was an inspiration to their own personal survival. Craufurd was mounted as were the captains of companies but many of the latter eventually ended up on foot like their lieutenants. Craufurd, ever sensitive to the hardships of his men, could often be found walking along in the ranks, an act which was not lost on them. The baggage animals of the column were also in dire stress and like the men had very little to eat. Once they fell to the ground there was very little chance of getting them mobile again. The French had no chance of losing their quarry even in the dark for the road was strewn with the dead and dying animals, men, women and children who lay amidst all the discarded trappings of an army in flight. Those who fell dead were now a source of survival to the living who soon made use of any clothing or equipment that could be pressed into service. Footwear was the item of which they were most in need; anything that could be used to relieve frozen, blistered, bare, cut feet was a welcome blessing.

Once darkness fell Craufurd would halt the column in the nearest village to try and gain as much shelter from the elements as possible, though it was practically impossible to get any provisions from the local inhabitants; those who remained were also starving. Most of the villages were buried in snow and the men had to feel with long poles for the doors to gain access to the houses. Nearly all were empty anyway, the inhabitants having fled taking what food they had with them. The only consolation for the Light Brigades was that the French had not chosen to follow them for their target remained Moore's fleeing army, though Craufurd's force was not to know this at the time, the threat always hanging over them.

Craufurd on nearing his objective pushed the troops hard but at the same time kept his iron discipline over them, not allowing any to stray from the column. He was often to be found amongst a group of Riflemen, scolding them for something or other, 'You think that because you are Riflemen, you may do whatever you think proper, but I will teach you the difference before I have done with you.'[1] Then he would go off with the Riflemen trailing him like a faithful pack of hounds.

---

[1] From *Rifleman Benjamin Harris*.

He eventually had to exert his authority after seeing two Riflemen straying from the column and resorted to make an example of them. Craufurd at once halted the retreat and ordered a drum-head court martial of the culprits at which they were sentenced to one hundred lashes a piece. Whilst the trial was taking place he dismounted and stood in the middle of the brigade close to a company of the Rifles. Rifleman Daniel Howard muttered to his comrades, 'Damn his eyes, he would do better to try and get us something to eat and drink than harass us in this way.' Craufurd, however, overheard this dissent and not wishing it to spread to the rest of the brigade, turning around grabbed the rifle out of the hands of Rifleman Ben Jagger and knocked him to the ground with the butt end. 'It was not I who spoke' said Jagger protesting his innocence to the general as he got up shaking his head. 'You should not knock me about.' 'I heard you, Sir,' was Craufurd's reply 'I will court martial you as well.' At this moment Dan Howard stepped from the ranks saying, 'Ben Jagger never said a word, I am the man who spoke.' 'Very well,' returned Craufurd, 'Then I'll try you Sir.' At which Howard was found guilty and sentenced to three hundred lashes, it was getting too dark to carry out the punishment and Craufurd ordered the brigade to advance. This particular night was one of intense cold for a severe frost descended upon the marching column. Craufurd was marching in the ranks having dismounted. Next morning as it became light it looked as if the whole brigade had aged overnight for their eyebrows, hair and beards were white with frost! The general now called a halt and ordered a punishment square to be formed and had the three Riflemen brought forward, then he addressed the brigade, 'Although I should obtain the goodwill neither of the officers nor the men of the brigade hereby so doing, I am resolved to punish these three men, according to the sentence awarded, even though the French might be close on our tails. Begin with Daniel Howard.' Because the Rifles did not have halberts Howard was taken to a slender tree close by. 'Don't trouble yourselves about tying me up,' he said to the buglers, folding his arms. 'I'll take my punishment like a man!' Howard then received the whole of the three hundred lashes in front of the brigade. When it was over his wife stepped from amongst the onlookers and covered him with his greatcoat. Craufurd then gave the order to march. Howard's wife, another hardy Irish woman, carried her husband's jacket, knapsack and pouch, for his lacerated back could not bear the weight of these items against his skin.

After a short march he halted the brigade once more and ordered the other two Riflemen to be brought out to receive their punishment. Colonel Hamlet Wade, the commanding officer of the Rifles stepped forward and lowering his sword, requested that he would forgive these men, as they were both good soldiers having fought in the battles in Portugal. 'I order you Sir,' said Craufurd, 'To do your duty. These men shall be punished.' Colonel Wade about turned and fell back to the front of the Rifles. One of the Riflemen, Armstrong started to unstrap his knapsack to prepare for the lash, Craufurd turned and walked up to one side of the square and said. 'In consequence of the intercession of your Colonel, I will allow you to draw lots and the winner shall escape.' The sergeant major, one Robert Ferguson of the Rifles, plucked two pieces of grass from the frozen ground for the two men to choose. Armstrong's companion drew the short straw and was tied to a tree. The buglers now started to lay on the lash, but when the bugle major had counted out seventy-five strokes, the general allowed him to be taken down and join his company.

Craufurd now called for his horse and mounted for the first time since the court martial the night before. But, before ordering the march he addressed the brigade saying, 'I give you all notice, that I will halt the brigade again the very first moment I perceive any man disobeying my orders, and try him by court martial on the spot.' This was not only confined to the men but also to the officers, for a little while later he caught an officer riding on the back of a man across a stream so that he would remain dry for the rest of the march. Craufurd plunged into the stream and in a frightful rage ordered the man to drop his charge. He then ordered the officer to return to the bank and wade through it again. The officers of the commissariat were also singled out at times for his special attention and in one incident he threatened to hang them if the provisions were not brought up.

This treatment might seem harsh but it was necessary, especially when the returns for those missing in the Rifle companies for the 2nd January are considered: John Clark, James Lambeth, John Lincoln, all of No 1 Company; John Coulter, John Gray, James Hughes, Edward Hunt, Thomas Pilkington, Thomas Port, James Richards, Henry Roberts, all of No 7 Company; Daniel Kearney, Patrick Kerrigan, Patrick Wall, Drummer Joseph Weatherall, Thomas Burke, all of No 9 Company; Joseph Arms, Patrick Flanagan, Ambrose Hughes, James O'Neil, John Sullivan, George Wilson and Alexander Yuil, all returned as missing, except Joseph Arms who is listed as dead. However, he was at Waterloo where he was wounded so it is safe to say he was also missing.

One day's march was much like the next on the retreat, but by the 3rd January only one man was reported missing, Joseph Siddown of No 7 Company. A few days earlier he had been allowed with his wife to continue ahead of the Rifles for he was in very poor health. The Rifles of the rearguard eventually passed them at the side of the road lying in the snow, huddled in each other's arms. The men were unable to give them any assistance and could only pray that their end came swiftly. It was a case of every man for himself which was understandable, for helping a comrade could be their own undoing. There was, however, one exception to this rule in the Rifles, in the case of Rifleman Patrick McLauchlin, a good humoured Irishman.

He was always in high spirits and kept the men amused in the most trying of times. It was from him that the men learned of their true destination at the beginning of the retreat, which McLauchlin had gained from Lieutenant Dudley Hill. On the retreat McLauchlin collapsed screaming in agony, wracked with acute rheumatism, his comrades rallied to his aid and got him to his feet. Even in his agony he still had them laughing and it was in this manner that he was able to reach the transports and England. (Rifleman Harris in his book states that McLauchlin was left behind and never reached England, although he was not listed as missing. A couple of months after reaching England he transferred into the 1st Battalion. This was probably why Harris thought he never returned for as we know Harris was one of the last to board the transports and with the aid of his comrades McLauchlin must have reached the transports before him.)

Craufurd was most anxious to gain his objective and gathered together a force of some three hundred of the fittest men from the two brigades whom he sent on 4th January by double forced marches to secure the bridge, over the Miño, which they reached unopposed. The two Light Brigades finally reached the bridge on 7th January and on 8th January Craufurd called a halt. The immediate pressure was now off Craufurd and his force for he knew Sir John could retreat via his position should the need arise. With this in mind he could afford to allow the men to rest which also gave the stragglers time to catch up with the column. Many of the men after regaining some of their strength now put this short halt to some use as most of them were filthy and their clothes were in rags. It was a luxury to be able to remove their clothing and attempt to wash it in the swollen river, their uniforms having been worn continuously since the beginning of the retreat, while their knapsacks had been on their backs for some days without being able to remove them. The men received some provisions here and the Rifles were also able to report the loss of only one man, Henry Henderson of No 9 Company on 8th January, which was welcome news after the severe loss of twenty three men reported on the 2nd.

With the Light Brigades halted and recovering at Orense we will now return to the Reserve division covering Moore's retreat on Corunna.

The British columns moved into the mountains with the rearguard struggling in their wake. The weather had changed once again, the wind dropped and the snow turned to sleet, then rain, which in turn made the mountain tracks into seas of mud. By the end of New Year's Day the rearguard reached the town of Bembibre. It had been a miserable place before the British arrived but by the time the divisions of Baird, Hope and Fraser had passed through it was a thousand times worse. The town's main function was the storage of wine which was brought down from the surrounding hills to be placed in underground vats. There was now neither a house nor a store that had not been broken into, all the windows and doors had been smashed in by the men in their search for food and wine. A large number of the culprits responsible for this orgy of wanton destruction and plunder still remained in the town. The divisions had left behind more than a thousand stragglers who were lying in the streets too drunk to move. This was not confined only to the men, for the women and children were also lying about equally in a drunken stupor, with wine pouring from their mouths and noses which likened them to gunshot victims. The women amongst this sorry horde were receiving the attentions of a number of soldiers who were joined by Spanish muleteers and were in no condition to resist them even if they wanted to.

When the rearguard finally entered the town they did their best to get them moving by prodding them with the point of their bayonets and in some cases by a sharp kick. The 95th spent most of this day dragging them out of the houses and cellars and into the streets in an effort to get these drunkards on the road, to follow in the wake of the retreating army. The 15th Hussars, meanwhile, were being employed in burning a quantity of officers' baggage and regimental stores to prevent it falling into the hands of the French.

One company of the Rifles had been left at the village of Cubilos, which was also to be the quarters for some of the 15th Hussars, whose horses were suffering terribly for the want of shoes. When they first arrived they were ordered to form up in the centre of the village while their quartermasters made arrangements for their shelter for the night. A sudden discharge of small arms fire sent a shower of musket ball into the walls and roofs of the houses just behind them. The Rifle company turned out and attacked the French for this unexpected attack. The hussars at once despatched a strong patrol to aid the Riflemen and the French were soon sent packing.

Eventually the rearguard could do no more and had to leave the town, for the picquets and hussars were starting to fall back through the streets with the French close on their heels. Those men and women still lying helplessly in the puddles of mud and wine now fell prey to the French dragoons who slashed left and right at their prostrate bodies as they charged through the streets. The instant shock and screams brought a number of them to their feet in panic, which made them even easier targets for the horsemen. Many were killed with a single fatal blow while a few lucky ones did manage to escape, suffering horrific wounds. The dragoons did spare some of the women from immediate death and now they became the objects of amusement and fun for them, but mercifully most were in no condition to know what was happening before they too fell to the same fate as their friends.

A picquet of the 15th Hussars rescued a man caught up in the French cavalry attack who had been trying to advance through the woods to keep clear of the main road. He was brought to the officer in charge and they could see by the light of the fire that he was in quite a sorry state. He had pulled his shirt up over his head to keep the frosty air from his dreadful wounds. When the covering was removed his face was a most shocking sight. It was impossible to distinguish a single feature of his face, the flesh of his cheeks hung loose at each side of his head, his nose had been slit, while his ears had also been cut off. Besides his head wounds he had also received many more to various parts of his body. It amazed the hussars that he had been able to escape, having lost so much blood. They tried to relieve his suffering by giving him some warm wine for he was unable to swallow any solid food.

Moore, in a desperate attempt to try to stem the flow of stragglers who, as each day passed reduced the effective strength of his army, had some of the survivors of this massacre paraded before the regiments. It was hoped that the sight of these wretches would shock them into keeping up with the main army. While Moore was employing these shock tactics in the rear divisions the advanced troops had reached Villafranca on the 1st January. It was thought by many of the troops and a number of senior officers that a stand might be held here, food, stores and ammunition were well stock-piled while the town had a natural defence with the Cantabrian Mountains behind. However, discipline had all but gone from the army except in the Guards and the rearguard who were having a hard time pushing the stragglers before them while at the same time attempting to keep the French at bay.

With Moore's force concentrated at Villafranca a riot broke out on the 2nd of January, which carried on into the night, the men then breaking into all the houses and shops. They plundered everything they could lay their hands on, even the churches fell to their greed and wanton destruction, their behaviour was unforgivable. It did not stop here for the commissariat's stores were the next target, barrels of salt, meat and fish, waggons loaded with biscuit, badly needed clothes, ammunition and the medical supplies all suffered the same fate. What could not be used, eaten or drunk was destroyed; while the rearguard of the Reserve, fighting for the survival of these very same troops, were desperately in need of these supplies and ammunition. Anything that could not be taken by an individual was left lying in the streets, broken or trodden into the muddy puddles of wine, the latter the main cause for the self-destruction of Moore's army.

Any chance of the hoped for stand was lost with the actions of the advanced troops. Sir John at this point was still with the rearguard and as a result missed the worst excesses of the men. When he entered Villafranca the streets were ample evidence of what had gone before; he at once issued an order for the army to parade in the streets of the Plaza Major the following morning. With the men lined up, a soldier from the cavalry was dragged into the Plaza, tied to a tree and shot for plundering a house and striking an officer. An example to the troops on parade who were then ordered to march past his corpse. Moore then returned to the area around Cacabelos and the rearguard who were making for this village. This was to give them a personal speech to instill a sense of duty into their ranks, for some members of the Reserve had also been reported as emulating the deed of the advanced corps. If the rearguard faltered then all would be lost, for the indisciplined rabble of an army in their front would be no match for the French troops only too willing to exact a swift and fleeting revenge for their humiliating expulsion from Portugal.

Cacabelos

While Moore was making for Cacabelos, Paget had already made his displeasure known to the troops under his command. As they neared the village he halted them in a field close to the road. Here he had them formed up in column in order to give them a stern warning as to their future conduct. When Moore arrived with his staff, Sir John at once addressed the men reminding them of their past conduct and in an almost pleading speech, hoped that they would all do their duty in the remaining days of the retreat. The 1st Battalion together with the 15th Hussars were taking up a position some three to four miles away on the Bembibre road where they had orders to keep a watchful eye for the advancing French cavalry.

It was almost dark by the time Moore had finished, Paget then reiterated his own feelings and informed the men that they were not allowed to seek quarters in the village. They were to camp out on the open ground in the immediate area, no man was to enter the village unless accompanied by a non-commissioned officer and then only with a specific duty to perform. Paget, well aware of the bad characters amongst his force after witnessing their behaviour at Bembibre (a number of whom were still missing) and to prevent a repeat of this, ordered a number of patrols to be assembled from the various regiments. Their task was to make regular visits to the village throughout the night to deter any would-be plunderers. Even after taking these measures a number of men still thought the risk worth taking. The attraction of so much illicit liquor only a short distance away proved too great. A number of stragglers from Bembibre had also reached the village by this time and it was soon under attack from them and groups of determined men from the Reserve division. The locked houses in no time had their doors smashed in and access was now gained to the cellars and the wine was plundered. As a result the regimental patrols made numerous arrests because of the crass stupidity and craving for drink of the men.

Moore had already decided that Cacabelos was a strong enough position to mount a suitable defence and delay the French long enough to allow his main force to destroy the remaining stores and provisions at Villafranca, then continue their retreat on Corunna. It was vital for the force to gain the far side of the Corunna road where it met the road from Forencava. Until this was achieved his force would always be open to the threat of an outflanking movement by the enemy.

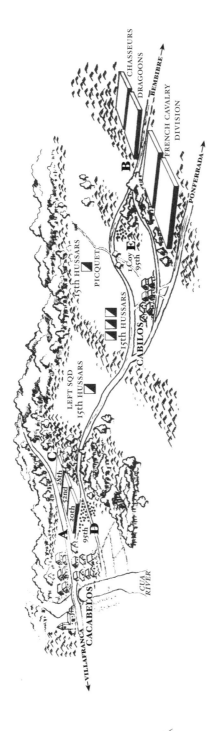

ACTION AT CACABELOS
3rd January 1809

The high ground between **A** and **B** masked the British position from the French cavalry division who, as a result, made a more cautious advance on the British. Paget's punishment parade took place at **A** under cover of the hills at **C**. Once the French reached **E** they were able to see how small the force was opposed to them, for the main body of the 1st Bn 95th Rifles had by this time retired to **D**. The regiments of the Reserve eventually crossed the bridge to take up their positions on the ground beyond the church, leaving only the two remaining Rifle companies and hussars to fall back through the village, with the 28th Light company formed up at the bridge. The Rifle companies formed across the road close to **A**, from which it is easy to see how the French were able to get in rear of them via the road from Cabilos. GC/RC

The village of Cacabelos was situated in a valley some six miles east of Villafranca on the main road, where a tributary of the River Sil, the Cua, wound its way close to the village. Though not very wide it was quite deep at this time of year, crossed by a small stone bridge flanked by a number of vineyards. These in turn were enclosed by hedges and walls running parallel with the stream. The high ground on the Villafranca side gradually rose from the bridge for about five hundred yards to its crest where it gave a commanding view of Cacabelos and the surrounding area. From this vantage point Moore and Paget could conduct an ideal defence while at the same time observe any outflanking movements by the French.

On the morning of 3rd January, Paget had the men of his Reserve who had been caught in any criminal act during the night, brought before the regiments of the division. These had been ordered to form up in a hollow square under the cover of a low hill. The men were now tried by drumhead court martial and sentenced to a varying number of lashes. Like General Craufurd, Paget was determined to make an example of these men, even though firing could now be heard coming from the direction of his rearguard. The punishment parade continued; nothing could deter Paget, not even the advancing French army! Once each man had been tried and given his sentence he was brought forward, stripped to the waist and tied to a triangle formed by the halberts belonging to the sergeants. The drummers then beat out the number of strokes while the buglers laid on the lash. After every twenty five strokes the regimental surgeons would inspect the man's blood soaked back, for it had been known for the flesh of a man's back to be stripped so severely that the spine was exposed! The allotted punishment having been received, the man was untied and returned to the ranks only to be replaced by the next one. It was in this manner that the punishment parade continued throughout the morning and because of the large number of miscreants involved, took rather a long time.

The French first made an appearance between nine and ten o'clock in the morning when they advanced to within about a mile of the British rearguard position, held by the 95th and 15th Hussars. Finally they halted on top of rising ground in three lines. The Rifles now moved into position and were soon making contact with the enemy cavalry. In an attempt to encourage his men an officer of the French chasseurs, mounted on a fine grey horse, rode along the front of the cavalry lines. Occasionally he would gallop forward in a gesture to intimidate a member of the hussars to meet him in single combat. The hussars, however, held their ground and left it to the Rifles to dampen his ardour, who after taking a couple of well aimed shots had the satisfaction of seeing his horse fall dead under him, thus putting an end to his display. A little later a farrier of the 22nd Chasseurs was brought into the rearguard lines with a rifle ball in his thigh. The chasseur made it plain to his captors that their good fortune would soon be short lived and that they should treat him well, for opposed to them was a division of cavalry under the command of General Colbert and two infantry divisions were expected to arrive within a couple of hours.

Armed with this information General Slade who was in command of the British cavalry now had a ready excuse to leave the action. He headed back to the Reserve division where he made his report to Paget, explaining the troop movements of the enemy, who by this time were pushing back the Rifle picquets and cavalry vedettes. Paget showed his displeasure at receiving such a report from his senior cavalry officer with a sarcastic reply which intimated that his place was with the 15th Hussars! Rather than save face and his honour by returning to the rearguard Slade actually continued towards Villafranca where he joined the 10th Hussars! Paget, however, would not be swayed from his course of action and relied on his outposts to hold back the French. Finally at about one o'clock the rearguard could hold the French no longer. Colonel Beckwith ordered the companies of Norcott and O'Hare to act as rearguard together with a troop of hussars to cover the withdrawal of the rest of his Riflemen and the cavalry, who now doubled back to the division.

Beckwith's Riflemen joined the division at a critical stage in the parade, for only two men remained to be punished, their sentence being death. Both of these men were bound and a rope placed around the neck, with one end thrown over the branch of a tree. Four soldiers lifted them to shoulder height and were ready to release them on the command of Paget, who now turned to the troops on parade saying, 'If I spare the lives of these two men will you promise to reform?' Not a sound came from the ranks, at which Paget repeated his question. Again all was quiet, except for the firing which was becoming louder as the rearguard were continually pushed back. Beckwith whispered to his men, 'Say yes!' A few Riflemen said 'Yes,' which was gradually picked up by the others, then by the division. The silence having been broken the condemned men were released to the cheers of their comrades.

Paget now ordered the division to fall back on Cacabelos. The 52nd had been ordered to double in advance of the rest of the division and to cross the bridge where they were to line the opposite bank, until the rest of the division arrived with the guns. The 20th, 28th and 91st along with the Royal Horse Artillery now crossed over leaving Beckwith's Riflemen to cover them on the road leading down to the village. Paget detached the light company of the 28th who he had formed up in the road at the entrance to the bridge, to cover the withdrawal of the Riflemen and hussars. Paget now with the greater part of his force on the Villafranca side of the stream made provision for its defence by extending the 20th to his right, along the bank of the stream behind the vineyard walls. The battery of horse artillery he ordered to continue along the Villafranca road to a position which overlooked a small dip in the land at the side of the road which was large enough to conceal it from the enemy. The light company of the 28th, when recalled, were to proceed to a point just below the guns where they were to form up allowing the guns to fire over their heads. On the left of the position the 52nd formed in extended order with their right resting on the road close to the bridge. The 28th was split into two wings, with the left wing behind and to the left of the guns for their protection, while the right wing was posted on the extreme left, but in rear of the 52nd with the 91st held in reserve.

The French cavalry had been advancing steadily after the retreating outposts with a band playing at their head. Finally they reached a high point in the road which overlooked the retreating Riflemen and hussars. They were surprised to see the small body of troops who were actually opposed to them and at once attacked.

Moore at this point was on the enemy side of the stream, with General Paget and his staff a little in advance of the village. Had the French been aware of the prize that was only a short distance away, they may have made a concerted effort to capture what would have been the most important part of the British high command. The manner in which the hussars and Riflemen came bursting onto the scene and rushing towards the village, startled Moore and his staff making them all too aware of how perilous their position was and in no time they were galloping towards the river. As they came thundering down through the village they passed Beckwith's Riflemen who were also making for the bridge. Moore shouted a warning to them that the French were attacking the village.

The French cavalry came swiftly onto the retreating Riflemen of Norcott and O'Hare's companies, enabling them to overtake those labouring to reach the village, taking them prisoner. Once the companies reached the main street of the village, Norcott and O'Hare ordered a halt and had the men turn to face the enemy cavalry. The Rifles were then formed in line across the whole width of the street but before they could fire they had to open up their ranks to allow the last of the British cavalry to pass through. Once reformed they set about pouring their deadly fire into the pursuing horsemen. Needless to say there were soon a number of empty saddles! The sheer number of French cavalry was now too much for the two Rifle companies and as some horsemen had gained access to the rest of the village through the side streets, they were able to threaten them from the rear. Once amongst the Riflemen they soon put their swords to good use and a number of Riflemen fell with severe head wounds or were trampled on by their horses. To save them from further casualties Norcott and O'Hare ordered them to take shelter in the nearest houses and fire from the windows. With the 15th Hussars now on hand a bloody combat took place, the severity of which can be envisaged when a French chasseur was decapitated by a single blow from the sword of a British hussar.

With the cavalry locked in mortal combat the Riflemen now made good their escape. The men from the two companies came running out of the village and headed for the bridge, which Beckwith's Riflemen were still crossing. The British hussars were also close on their heels with the enemy in hot pursuit. There was no time for ceremony and the 15th Hussars thundered onto the bridge scattering the Riflemen and in no time at all the area was choked with men and horses. Some Riflemen had been drinking and were a little the worse for wear, having helped themselves during the previous night's actions to the wine found in the houses. In their panic to cross the bridge they commenced firing their rifles in all directions and their comrades were in danger of being shot by their own men. To avoid the chaos at the bridge some Riflemen jumped into the river and swam to safety. The light company of the 28th faced by this surge of men and horses had their formation severely disrupted and it was not until most of the men had cleared their immediate front that they were able to send a crashing volley into the enemy horsemen. This blank range fire brought the pursuing cavalry to a halt and as a result they retreated through the village, where they were able to capture a number of Riflemen who were still trapped in the houses, along with a few hussars.

The French cavalry was now joined by an even larger body of their own cavalry under the command of General Colbert who had in fact requested infantry support from Marshal Soult. He responded by sending more cavalry, possibly the quickest way to reinforce the general as the infantry were already on the march and it was only a matter of time before they would reach his position. With the immediate danger from the French horsemen over, the light company and the remaining Riflemen were able to cross the bridge in safety.

At the height of the confusion at the bridge the battalion buglers of the 28th, situated on the opposite bank, had been ordered to sound the recall to their light company, in an attempt to save them from what appeared to be immediate destruction, but it was impossible for them to obey. They would have only made matters worse on the bridge by trying to cross. By disobeying this order they actually eased the situation which enabled the remaining troops to cross without any further loss.

Once on the opposite bank the Riflemen took possession of the vineyards and positioned themselves behind the walls flanking the road. The light company, meanwhile, made their way up the road towards the guns, while the hussars continued until they reached the town of Villafranca, taking no further part in the action.

The cavalry from the initial attack moved out of the village to regain their formation close to the main road, where they joined with the 3rd Hussars under Colbert. From this position Colbert could see that the road was now clear right up to the crest of the hill where on the road a thin red line of British infantry, the light company of the 28th, presented any sort of resistance. The massed cavalry now came charging down from the road to the village. This distance of about one hundred yards was devoid of cover and they presented a perfect target for the guns of the Royal Horse Artillery on the heights, who until this point had been concealed from the view of the enemy. The guns were now pushed out onto the Villafranca road from where they poured a severe fire of grape shot into the advancing horsemen. This caused a number of casualties in their ranks, but their bravery kept them going and they soon reached the village, then charged over the bridge. However, they were met by the flanking fire of the Rifles, from as little as two yards in some places and as they continued on their way, the 52nd fired into their opposite flank. Those who survived the rifle and musket fire now continued towards the guns and light company of the 28th Regiment. These resolute men having already seen what their fire could do now waited for the right moment to send a crashing volley into the depleted ranks of the French horsemen, which had a devastating effect to their front ranks causing the whole body to halt. They were no match for the troops opposed to them. The only option was to about turn and retreat down the hill to the bridge and face the flanking rifle and musket fire again.

The French hussars on finally reaching the village were able to reform with the dragoons, who had arrived under the command of La Houssaye. He had already crossed the river at a ford a little further downstream from the bridge. Once on the opposite bank he ordered them to dismount and engage the Rifle picquets who were the closest British troops at this point. Two infantry divisions finally arrived at about four o'clock, under the command of General Merle who at once sent some 1,000 voltigeurs to join with La Houssaye's dismounted men. The voltigeurs were brought down on the back of the horses of the dragoons and in no time were also engaged with the Riflemen. This was on the right of the British position. While the voltigeurs skirmished with the Riflemen the dragoons stood behind their horses using them as both a rest and protection. When the dragoons had originally crossed the stream they had been opposed to only the picquets of the Rifles. Now that the voltigeurs had put in an appearance, one wing of the battalion was ordered from the cover of the vineyard walls to confront this new threat in support of the picquets.

It was around this time that Moore ordered the withdrawal of the 52nd and 20th Regiments to the summit of the hill, leaving only a picquet from each regiment at the bridge. Moore's concern was that if the enemy crossed the river on his left the 52nd would come under attack from both flanks. The skirmishing between the two bodies of sharp shooters continued for about an hour but by now the light was beginning to fade, for once darkness fell the action would come to a close. The arrival of more French infantry gave the enemy hope of completing a victory. As a result of this far superior force the Riflemen were pushed back and the buglers sounded for their advance companies to fall back on the rest of the battalion, where they extended along the walls of the vineyards once more. It was at this time that some of the 52nd were sent to help the outnumbered Riflemen and strengthen the British right.

From his position on a hill overlooking the river, General Merle had seen the withdrawal of the 20th and 52nd Regiments, which made the British left flank vulnerable to attack. He, therefore, sent a column of infantry to his right to cross the river and attack this position. By this movement he hoped to threaten the British on both flanks. With this column marching down to the river Moore and Paget could see what the French general had in mind and to counter this they ordered the full force of the six horse artillery guns to be brought to bear on this column. This soon had the desired effect, for the devastation the exploding shrapnel caused in their ranks halted the column after which the French infantry turned and fled, to the cheering of the 95th and 52nd who sent a rifle and musketry fire after them. With the break up of the French right attack the left now started to fall back and it amused the Riflemen to see the voltigeurs race to their mounted comrades, the dragoons and jump up behind them to make good their escape. Once again the Riflemen sent a couple of well aimed shots after them to help speed them on their way.

Rifleman Thomas Plunket made a couple of memorable shots in this action for he advanced from the cover of the vineyard walls and lying on his back in the snow, wrapped the loose sling of his rifle around his foot. From this well known rifle shooting position, used to make a steadier and accurate shot, he killed General Colbert whose orderly trumpeter, upon seeing his general fall, charged to his aid. Plunket reloaded and with the next shot, the trumpeter also fell dead close to his general. The French cavalry incensed at seeing their general killed, raced after the retreating Plunket, who just managed to reach the safety of his cheering comrades as the horsemen charged with their swords drawn ready to dispatch the impudent Rifleman.

JAMES DANN

It was practically dark by now and the firing gradually ceased, leaving both armies counting the cost of the day's actions which amounted to about two hundred casualties on both sides. From the Rifles' point of view this was severe as they had the most casualties and missing men, having been in action from the beginning to the end of this affair. Captain Latham Bennett was mortally wounded fighting with his men at the bridge, whilst Lieutenant Charles Eeles was also wounded in the general action. Two sergeants and seventeen Riflemen were killed while four sergeants and forty four other ranks were taken prisoner. No return was made of the numbers wounded though eight men were listed as missing and unaccounted for.

Casualties
Captain Latham Bennett died of wounds 11/1/09 and Lieutenant Charles Eeles was wounded.

No 1 Company
Died: Riflemen Thomas Phillips, Joseph Rhodes, John Stott.

Missing: Sergeant Ishmael Cooke POW, Corporals George Crookshanks, John Winterbottom, Riflemen Joseph Adkins, Henry Barbrook, Charles Cassody, Zacharia Dent, Robert Ewen, William Harry, John Johnson, Archibald Lacky, James Lee, Witherington Lee, Donald McIntire, Joseph Moore, Hugh Paisley (POW), Peter Phoss, Richard Rice, John Richards, James Ridley, James Ross, Joseph Sipson, Daniel Smith, Patrick Stanton, John Sturges, George Sweeney, Charles Turner, Benjamin Tuttle.

No 2 Company
Died: Riflemen James Darrett, killed, John McDonough.

Missing: Corporal James McKenzie, Bugler John Harvey, Riflemen Robert Boyd, Robert Briggs, Andrew Clarke, John Cope, Laurence Dooly, Richard Fanning, Thomas Hill, George Pitt, William Swan, William Thornton.

No 3 Company
Died: Rifleman William Cleaver KIA.

Missing: Riflemen Isaac Fiddler, Laurence Kinchlow, William Livemore, John Piper.

No 4 Company
Missing: Bugler Patrick Mitchell, Riflemen Joseph Betson, Edward Williams, Brooks Wright.

No 6 Company
Died: Sergeant Mathew Alison KIA.

Missing: Buglers Brien McGrath, Brien Tierney, Riflemen George Tomkins, William Townsend.

No 7 Company
Died: Rifleman Adam Ross KIA.

No 8 Company
Missing: Riflemen Joseph Billings, James Curran.

No 9 Company
Died: Riflemen William Burroughs, Lauchiston Curry, James Esky KIA, William Reynolds KIA, Richard Woods KIA,

Missing: Riflemen William Edmonds, Edward Evans, Jonathan Underton.

Though the general action ceased when darkness fell, the division was still kept on the alert, which for the Rifles meant holding their positions lined along the walls of the vineyards and along the riverbanks. The order was then given to make for Villafranca but to move off with the minimum amount of noise. In order to achieve this the wheels of the artillery guns and equipment were wrapped in sacking padded out with grass or any other materials that would make their movement along the hard frozen road as quiet as possible. Once these regiments had moved off the Rifles remained in position until about ten o'clock that same evening before they received the order to follow. The battalion moved off leaving only a picquet to annoy the enemy should they venture onto the British position under the cover of darkness.

The delaying tactics by Moore and Paget's Reserve in holding Cacabelos had been without doubt a success, for the advanced divisions had been able to make reasonable progress towards Lugo. In fact, the closest troops to the Reserve, should they have been in need of assistance, was Sir David Baird's division, who were at Nogales some forty miles away. At Villafranca only the commissariat officers and their men remained, who were destroying the last of the stores and supplies.

To the regiments of the Reserve approaching Villafranca it looked as if the whole town was on fire, but as they gradually drew nearer it became clear that it was only the fires of massive piles of food, stores and equipment tended by the commissariat troops. What annoyed the men on reaching the town, was that although they were starving and in great need of the very same stores, the commissariat officers had placed a guard over the stockpiles waiting to be burned. For these brave men it was too much to be denied even the basic necessity, biscuit! To these desperate men this must have seemed so unjust, for they were fighting for the very existence of the men to their front who had taken whatever they wanted with no thought for anyone but themselves. The temptation was too great for a number of them and as they passed, they plunged their swords and bayonets into the fires, pulling out chunks of half burnt salt meat. The Reserve marched through the town without a halt, for they had an eighteen mile march ahead of them to Herrerias in the severe cold along a road knee deep in snow. They arrived at the town a couple of hours before daylight on the morning of the 4th January. Those with the pilfered meat now enjoyed a very welcome meal which they shared with their comrades. Having halted after their exhausting, forced march the fatigued men hoped for a well earned rest, but as soon as it became light the buglers sounded the assembly and they were ordered to move off again.

Mountainous terrain towards As Nogales

In the daylight, the Reserve were able to see at first hand the devastation happening in the columns of the advanced divisions. From Villafranca the road to Corunna twisted its way through the Cantabrian Mountains until it reached the plains of Lugo. Every mile of the way bore testimony to the condition of the troops, horses, camp followers and equipment of the army. Even the snow on the road was red with the blood of thousands of tramping bare feet, too numb from the cold to be noticed. Even the poor horses had blood oozing from their unshod feet, while at the same time there lay dead men, women, children and horses by the side of the road. The suffering of the horses could have been avoided but once they became lame their riders had no choice but to shoot them. Moore had originally ordered the farriers' carts to be abandoned, as far back as the withdrawal from Benavente. As a result, the vital tools and equipment to shoe the horses was no longer available, a decision that was to prove costly. The destruction of the horses was made all the more ludicrous when at Herrerias it was found that there were a number of forges in the town with enough equipment to shoe most of these poor animals.

Blakeney of the 28th gives a graphic description of a scene he witnessed on this march which highlights the conditions prior to their arrival.

'After marching about seven or eight miles out of Herrerias, seeing a group of soldiers lying in the snow, I immediately went forward to rouse them up and send them on to join their regiments. The group lay close to the roadside, on my coming up a sad spectacle presented itself. Through exhaustion, depravity, or a mixture of both, three men, a woman and a child all lay dead, forming a kind of circle, their heads turned inwards. In the centre were still the remains of a pool of rum, made by the breaking of a case of that spirit. The unfortunate people must have sucked more of that liquor than their constitutions could support. Intoxication was followed by sleep, from which they awoke no more, they were frozen to death.'

The Riflemen, meanwhile, had force marched through the night in the most trying of conditions, some of it through vineyards to join the division. It was here that Bugler William Green fell into a dry well about six feet deep but before he could right himself another two Riflemen fell into the same well landing on top of him. All three had to shout to their comrades to come and get them out. Luckily Green was only badly bruised, but his sword was broken in the fall. In the darkness he also lost the lock cap to his rifle and both his forage cap and shako. The Rifles eventually arrived at Curtro just before dawn. The picquets who had been left behind at Cacabelos by this time were also on the retreat, for the French had finally pressed them and found that the position had been abandoned. These Riflemen now had the unenviable task of having to double after their comrades while at the same time engaging the enemy cavalry and voltigeurs, for the dragoons continued to carry the voltigeurs with them which added to their own fire power and made life difficult for the Riflemen. However, they were equal to the task and the French were never allowed to get the better of them. The constant probing attacks from enemy cavalry patrols on the Riflemen were beginning to have some effect for they were almost exhausted. The small number of men who made up the rearguard picquet did receive some casualties in these skirmishes, but under the cover of darkness these were kept to a minimum. Not only did they have the problem of the enemy and the bad weather but also the number of stragglers still on the road whom the Riflemen did their best to protect and keep on the move.

Just after Blakeney's encounter with the dead soldiers he was joined on the road by Captain Latham Bennett of the Rifles, who was bent double over the saddle of his horse. The Rifles' officer was in a very bad way and in severe pain. The wound he had received at Cacabelos, a musket ball in the groin was bleeding profusely. Blakeney helped him to the best of his ability by padding out his wound with a silk handkerchief, but their was little or no hope for the dying officer. Although he was making his way to Corunna, sadly he died of his wounds on the 11th January.

With the officers and men of the Reserve division in a similar plight to the horses of the cavalry, the condition of their footwear was becoming a serious problem. However, providence seems to have taken a hand in coming to their aid, for just as it was getting dark and a couple of miles from Nogales the division came upon a convoy of carts. They were originally destined for the troops of la Romana's army but in fact were heading in the direction of the enemy when they were abandoned. The carts were full of much needed clothing, shoes and equipment. The men at once helped themselves to the contents, much against the wishes of their officers, which made no sense to the men for they would have been taken by the French if they had not happened on them first! The priority was to replace the damaged footwear, the more wily amongst them took extra pairs which they later sold. Acquiring new trousers was also a most welcome bonus. The rearguard also benefited from these stores but for most of the men the relief was short lived as after a few miles the soles fell off leaving the upper leather laced around their ankles. Their stockinged feet were soon cut to pieces and the men cursed the makers of this footwear which had been made and supplied in England! The men continued on into Nogales where they halted long enough to rest and regain a little of their strength. The march was resumed on the morning of the 5th January when one man, Rifleman William Giffen was listed as missing.

From Herrerias to Nogales the division completed a forced march of some thirty six miles through mountainous country in very severe weather conditions. For the Riflemen of the rearguard and their supports this meant even more difficult marches. Having repulsed an enemy attack they then had to double after the retreating division, only to halt and take cover to be confronted by the enemy once more, ready to repeat the process all over again. For the whole distance the Riflemen kept the French cavalry patrols from harming the retreating British army. By evening they finally reached Constantino, where a bridge crossed a river at a most difficult part of the road. On the enemy side, a hill overlooked the river and had the French taken possession of it before the Reserve had time to cross they would have been able to cause much devastation. Moore, who had remained with the Reserve throughout the march, ordered a battery of the horse artillery to be posted on the hill, which he protected with a battalion of Riflemen. From this position they were able to keep the enemy back long enough to allow the Reserve to get across the narrow bridge without mishap. Their mission accomplished the artillery limbered up and followed them with the Riflemen doubling behind. This was achieved without the loss of a single man. The French seeing the guns and Riflemen retire came rushing up to the crest of the hill, but it was too late. What could have been a serious situation with drastic consequences was avoided by Moore's use of his guns and the resolute Riflemen.

With the artillery following on after the rest of the division the Riflemen kept their vigil from the opposite bank, Paget's troops made for Lugo and the Riflemen guarded the bridge. Their presence was enough to prevent the French from attempting a crossing. The Riflemen remained in this position until just after dark when they finally moved off to join the division.

Holding back the French at the bridge had gained Moore the valuable time he needed to allow the whole of his army to concentrate on Lugo. Sir John had originally sent orders to Sir David Baird when he was still at Nogales, to halt his division at Lugo, with instructions to inform Generals Hope and Fraser to do the same with their divisions. Fraser, however, did not receive the order in time because the dragoon who was sent to relay the order got drunk on the way and he had already started with his division along a track to Compostela. He finally returned to Lugo with his force, the men tired and hungry and having lost some four hundred stragglers on this unnecessary march.

The Riflemen accomplished the march to Lugo with the loss of only one man, Thomas Poole of No 9 Company who was listed as missing. The women belonging to the battalion, however, had difficulty in keeping up with their men and as a result a group of them fell into the hands of the enemy cavalry. The French horsemen took no pity on these poor wretched women who they took in turn to rape and once finished with them returned them to the Rifles' lines. In the town, the Guards were cooking and relaxing with their belts hanging on the bushes close by, asking the passing Riflemen if they had seen the French! (This to men who had been fighting the enemy for the best part of the retreat.) The Riflemen replied 'Yes and so will you soon, you had better get prepared ready to meet them' and although the Guardsmen could not believe that the enemy were so near, soon heard firing coming from that direction.

Treated to twenty fours hours rest, quartered on the inhabitants of the town, the Riflemen received rations of bread, meat and wine. For once the outposts were provided by the regiments of the other divisions, thus enabling the men of the Reserve to get a good night's sleep and regain some of their strength.

With the Rifleman and regiments of the Reserve division taking a well earned rest in and around the convents of Lugo, we will now return to the Rifles of the 2nd Battalion under the command of General Robert Craufurd, who we left earlier at Orense, resting from their forced march, having succeeded in securing Sir John Moore an alternative embarkation point.

For the two days the men were halted at Orense they were able to attend to their own personal needs, or just generally rest from their exertions of the retreat. Another benefit was that many stragglers were able to catch up and rejoin their respective regiments. Craufurd finally gave the order to continue the retreat and the brigades moved out of Orense on the 9th January. The men, now in much better shape after resting, crossed the Miño and marched towards the town of Ribadavia which was at the confluence of the Rivers Avia and Miño. Both rivers were now very swollen after the heavy rain and melting snow, which added to the torrent of water by the hour.

For Quartermaster Sergeant Surtees of the Rifles, the task of keeping up with his battalion was one long struggle. The baggage animals in his care also carried the spare ammunition and they had fallen well behind the main body of whom they had lost sight. Upon approaching Ribadavia the road into the town was indistinguishable from the surrounding area, for the river at this point had overflowed into the fields. Without a guide to see him safely across and the fact that it was nearly midnight, Surtees' task was made all the more impossible. He could not risk an attempt at crossing for fear of losing his precious cargo. Should any of the baggage animals fall into the river or have to wade too deeply through the flood water the gun powder for the men would be rendered useless.

The quartermaster, therefore, decided to take his mules into the mountains to try to approach the town from a different direction, in the hope that he would find a much safer crossing place. The poor baggage animals now had to struggle up the steep and rugged paths, slipping and sliding on the wet, muddy surfaces. One incline was so steep that all the casks of ammunition slid off a mule's back and rolled down into a ravine. Surtees now had the added problem of going down into the ravine in the dark with some of his men to retrieve the missing casks. After much searching they were finally found and reunited with the mule. In spite of all his efforts to keep the ammunition dry it was later found that much of the powder carried in the casks was damp owing to the constant rainfall, thus rendering it unusable to the Riflemen. [1]

---

[1] From this it is safe to assume that either Craufurd's undertaking to cover the powder casks with the ox hides was a failure, or that Harris and his party only worked on the powder casks for the brigade and not the Rifle Battalion which would be against all logic?

Surtees finally managed to get to the town via this mountain track without further mishap. However, upon arrival his party was informed of an accident that had happened earlier to part of his battalion. When the Rifles arrived in the town they had been allotted quarters in a convent to which two companies were allocated an upper corridor. Under the combined weight of men and equipment it collapsed at the time when most of the men were sleeping. This resulted in a number of them being injured, some receiving broken limbs in the fall.

It took another three days of hard marching for the brigades of Craufurd and Alten to finally reach Vigo. As the men came up to the last range of hills which overlooked the bay, they were elated to see three ships awaiting them in the harbour, while the transports could be seen in full sail making for the open sea and Corunna. Tired legs and aching feet now gained an inner strength to complete this final march to the harbour, which they reached on the 12th January. The men embarked onto the allotted ships to carry them safely back to England, in order that a number of stragglers could catch up and be taken on board the sailing was delayed for several hours. Rifleman Harris was in fact amongst the very last to be taken on board when a ship's boat returned to collect him from the shore.

A number of men and their women arrived too late to reach the boats to return to England and with heavy hearts had to witness the ships leaving in the distance. Some of these, however, did manage to make their way back to Portugal while others found it safer to join local bands of guerrillas. In these final marches the Rifles reported five more men as missing: Rifleman Henry Henderson No 8 Company on the 8th January, Drummer [2] Jeremiah Morgan, Rifleman John Brown both of No 3 Company and Rifleman Robert Wynn of No 1 Company all listed on 9th, with Rifleman William Hallaghan of No 8 Company on 10th. Rifleman William Bruckely of No 9 Company was also reported as missing in Spain but no date given.

With Craufurd's brigades safely on their way back to England we can once again return to Sir John Moore's force at Lugo. The regiments of the divisions were left in no doubt now that a battle was expected with the French. Morale was at its highest since the advance on Benavente. It was hard to believe that these were the same troops on the retreat of a couple of days previous.

---

[2] The term Drummer often occurs in rolls and reports for the 95th Rifles mainly because many of the printed forms still refer to Drummers and Fifers. Even as late as Waterloo rolls have been seen with the title of Drummer for the Rifles. The Rifles did have a band which would have included at least one or two Drummers in their ranks, but these men were listed under the rank of Private, Riflemen. Buglers were introduced into the 'Experimental Rifle Corps' in 1800 when the regiment was first raised by transfers from a number of line regiments. Each detachment included one Drummer, who was to be trained in the use of the bugle, so that he could use it to give all the commands and new movements.

Besides the lifting of their spirits by the prospect of battle, the troops were also set an example of what dedicated soldiers could achieve in the most trying of circumstances with the arrival of the Reserve division. This was further highlighted with the arrival of three fresh battalions between Villafranca and Lugo. These battalions had originally been left by Baird at Astorga when he first moved up country. The divisions now regained much of their discipline and everywhere men could be seen checking their arms and equipment to be in a state of readiness for when the French made their attack. As we have previously seen the French were soon onto the battle field, though at this stage they were lacking in numbers. It was only their cavalry patrols that had been pressing the rearguard who now sent back a report to Soult, telling him that the British had finally halted and were preparing to give battle.

The French gradually arrived in strength and on the 7th, took up position just opposite the rearguard of the Reserve regiments. They immediately set about attacking the outposts in an effort to test out the British troop displacements. The outposts, however, were equal to their attack and were able to repulse them. This did not deter the French for they made a similar attack on the 8th, which again the outposts repulsed. Soult finally arrived at the head of a force of some ten to twelve thousand men at mid-day. To find out for himself the intentions of the British, he ordered four guns and some cavalry to advance with him and to fire on them. The fire was returned with a salvo from fifteen artillery pieces forcing the French marshal into a hasty retreat. Soult, however, was left in no doubt as to the British intentions and this was more than just a rearguard action he was facing. It was not until the 8th that the British troops were finally in place ready to offer battle to the enemy but Soult had no plans to attack until he was sure he had a numerical advantage over them. He sent dispatches to Heudelet and Ney to hasten to his cause and further ordered that Ney, who was at Villafranca, send a division via the road from Val des Orues to Orense. Ney, however, made only a token gesture in reply to this order by sending some cavalry as far as the Syl valley. Soult's artillery had finally arrived along with a mass of stragglers; it was not only the British who were having problems keeping together on the march.

The British army waited all day on the 8th for the French to make their move, but to no avail, for Soult was preparing to engage them on the following day. His force now numbered 17,000 infantry, and 4,000 cavalry with 50 artillery pieces (Napier).

The British commander though frustrated at the French delay chose to retire on Corunna that same night, for he had little to gain in engaging the French even if it had ended in victory in his favour. He would still at some point have to make for Corunna to reach the transports to embark his army, while the French commander was in a position to receive further reinforcements at any time. For Moore to keep his troops at Lugo he would also require further food, ammunition and equipment which was stock piled in Corunna.

The order to retire was given reluctantly, being met with much disapproval from the men, but was eventually achieved under the cover of darkness. Once again the Reserve was to cover the withdrawal and remained in position at Lugo to create the impression that the whole of Moore's army was still there. They managed this by keeping the camp fires of the army well stoked up even though the weather was making it rather difficult as the rain and sleet was falling once more in very heavy showers. The freezing rain drenched the men to the skin and the cold numbed them to the bone. Finally, it was their turn to fall back and they retired on Betanzos. On the 9th the Rifles reported another three men missing; Riflemen Henry Michael, John Corder and John Burk.

Though initially only three men had been reported missing on the 9th by the Rifles, an incident which happened prior to leaving Lugo involved another Rifleman who was added to the missing at Corunna. In the ranks of Captain Norcott's No 1 Co was Thomas Baxter, an habitual drunkard, who at the time of leaving Lugo was so full of red port wine he was incapable of marching. Colonel Beckwith was so incensed at having to leave one of his men in such a state that he ordered the bugle major to cut all the buttons off his uniform. He did not want the French to recognise what an honourable regiment he belonged to when captured. Baxter was at one time an excellent scholar, his qualifications had eventually raised him to the position of an attorney. This later as a soldier enabled him to rise from the ranks to corporal and sergeant on a number of occasions, only to be reduced in disgrace because of his fondness for drink, and ultimately caused his downfall. Also left at Lugo that night were a number of Spanish guns which could not be taken, their gunners having previously spiked them so they could not be of any use to the French.

It was about fourteen English leagues to Corunna from Lugo and the Reserve division, though setting off last, actually got ahead of the other divisions who all managed to get lost in the dark. So instead of being the rearguard they were actually the advance guard! As a result, the Reserve had to keep halting to allow the regiments of the other divisions to pass through them as they eventually came up, while at the same time placing them in a difficult position for every time they halted they had to make sure that the body of troops to their rear was not the advance guard of the French! The conditions did not help, for the heavy black clouds made it a very dark night, which gave way to a tremendous downpour of freezing cold rain. General Paget, meanwhile, had given specific orders to his division that no man was to leave the ranks or the road under any circumstances.

On the morning of the 9th January the last of the lost divisions finally came up and the army was once again reunited. After a halt of a couple of hours the whole army moved off, with the Reserve once again in their rightful position as rearguard.

Moore called a halt on the night of the 9th, but instead of keeping the troops under strict orders as Paget had done, a number of the leading regiments allowed their men to seek shelter in the nearest houses, which was a mistake for again the men were able to take advantage of what wine or spirit remained in these dwellings. As a result many were in no condition to move off on the morning of the 10th, while some of the more stubborn elements of the soldiery refused to move at all now that they were comfortable. Once again it was left to the Reserve to move them on; much of their patience had gone by this time and they treated these men more harshly than they had previously, by kicking, prodding with the sword or bayonet, or hitting them with the butt end of their firearms; much to no avail and a number were left behind. The whole army was now marching to Betanzos where it halted for the night with the rearguard some distance from the town. This march had resulted in more losses than at any other time during the retreat. The road from Lugo was choked with stragglers which made the Reserve division's task of covering the retreat most difficult.

The French outposts, seeing the British fires gradually die down, reported this fact to their officers and at once their cavalry was on the move. They finally caught up with a mass of drunken stragglers on the 10th, but these men had lost none of their soldierly instincts and in fact formed themselves into a large defensive pack. It was in this formation that they were able to defend themselves quite well. Sergeant Newman of the 43rd Regiment actually gathered together a group of these men at one point and was able to inflict a number of casualties onto the advancing French. General Paget had the Reserve division formed up in a strong position ready to attack the French cavalry patrols but refrained from going to their aid, for they were defending themselves quite admirably and at the same time he was not prepared to lose a single good man of his division to save any of these drunkards, who had only themselves to blame for the position they were now in.

In the end the French decided to leave this now organised rabble alone, due to their strong formations and especially as the Reserve was close at hand in a strong position. This mob, therefore, was eventually able to reach Paget's division without any further loss. The general now halted them and would not allow any of them to continue until they had been thoroughly searched by the picquets of his division, who confiscated whatever money they found for it was quite plain that this could only have been obtained by criminal activity! The money now taken from these miserable wretches was piled up at the side of the road and soon amounted to an unbelievable sum. The men doing the searching were surprised at the different types of plunder the men had managed to conceal about them or had hidden in their haversacks; brass candle sticks which had been bent double, bundles of common knives, copper saucepans hammered flat, every sort of domestic utensil one could think of. Many of these men actually laboured with this plunder which in many cases exceeded the regulation weight they were required to carry. Some fifteen hundred stragglers eventually passed through the lines of the Reserve division to their regiments. Now under escort from the Reserve they reached Betanzos. The money that had been stock piled at the road side was shared out between the men of the Reserve as a fitting reward for their service and bravery on the retreat.

With the Reserve halted for the night they were delighted to receive a large quantity of supplies brought out by the commissary from the stores at Corunna and for once the men were able to rest on full stomachs. Captain O'Hare's company who had been on outlying picquet that evening were surprised in the morning to find a red coated soldier and a woman in the distance making their way along the road towards their position. When the couple finally arrived the Riflemen asked them why they were so far behind the division, for the private was actually a member of the 91st Regiment and from their own division.

He told them that his wife had been taken in labour about twelve o'clock the previous night in an outhouse of some buildings, where she had been attended by the regimental surgeon and delivered of a healthy child. The surgeon, his work completed told the private to stay with his wife and allow himself to be taken by the French, to which he agreed. However, having rested for some time and just a little before dawn, his wife said they should carry on after the army. She did not want her man to be put into a French prison, while having seen what they had done to other women on the march she was in no condition to be used by the enemy soldiers! Having now reached the safety of the Rifles' picquet, with the wife standing before the Riflemen without any shoes or stockings and the baby wrapped in her apron and shawl, their hardship had all been worth while. The Rifles now gave them some of their food, for they had been issued with three day's rations of bread and pork. The couple then carried on towards Corunna. They had only been gone about a half hour when the French cavalry came in sight at the full trot causing the picquet to fall back on the bridge at Betanzos.

Moore marched the army out of Betanzos on the morning of the 11th January for its final advance to Corunna, with Paget's division covering them as usual. The Reserve was followed closely by the light cavalry of Franceschi's division, though at a safe distance, until they reached the bridge on the other side of Betanzos. Here, an engineer and his party were waiting for the last of the Reserve to come up and cross so that they could blow the bridge. Once they were all over Paget ordered the 28th Regiment to form up and protect the demolition party. Finally all was ready and the train was lit. After the explosion, to the dismay of the engineer officer it was found that only half of the supporting arches had been destroyed. General Paget asked the engineer how long it would take to complete the task and was told that it would be no more than twenty minutes, for only one of the barrels of powder had ignited. It would now just be a matter of checking and setting a new train. With the engineers preparing for a second explosion, Paget ordered the grenadier and light companies of the 28th to cross the bridge again where they were to form a protective screen for the working parties. Once on the other side the two companies moved through the nearest streets and were immediately engaged by a large body of French dragoons. As a result, Lieutenant Blakeney of the light company was caught out in the open with only a light cavalry sword for protection. An officer of the dragoons was soon upon the dismounted Blakeney and about to deliver a fatal blow when Private Oats of his company sent a musket ball crashing into the Frenchman's head at close range which killed him instantly. Blakeney's first thought after this lucky escape, however, was not to thank Oats but to avail himself of the dead dragoon's green cloak, which would be more than welcome in the cold weather!

The two companies now had to combine to pour volley fire into the enemy cavalry, which was joined by a severe rifle fire from the Riflemen who had now lined the opposite bank and hedges of the river. This finally drove the dragoons back through the streets of Betanzos, where they were joined by their infantry, who had come charging into the village. The remaining companies of the 28th, formed up opposite the bridge, had also joined in the fight adding their fire to that of their light and grenadier companies with the 20th, 52nd and 91st Regiments to their rear. Paget was required to show a strong presence here and keep the French on the other side of the river for as long as possible, to allow Sir John Moore to get his army safely across the bridge at El Burgo which was about eight to ten miles from Betanzos. With the bridge still not blown and the French infantry now well established in large numbers in the houses opposite, Paget had no option but to recall the two 28th advance companies.

The intense fire coming from the British side of the river was causing severe casualties in the enemy ranks, too many for the French to contemplate a full scale attack. So instead their sharpshooters established themselves in the houses at the end of the bridge and returned an accurate fire. Paget, receiving word that Moore had crossed at El Burgo, now ordered the division to follow the main army. Moore's divisions were at last marching as an organised body, the colonels placed at the head of their regiments while the captains and lieutenants were ordered to march on the flanks. No man was allowed to leave the ranks until a regular halt was called. The main body of Moore's force eventually arrived at Corunna in the evening of the 11th, more like soldiers.

Battle of Corunna

Present bridge at El Burgo

The French immediately crossed the bridge once the rearguard moved off and were soon pressing them once more. That same evening Paget's force finally reached the village of El Burgo, which was about four miles from Corunna. The bridge here across the Mero had also been ordered to be blown. When the last of the rearguard was over, which consisted of the light company of the 28th Regiment and Captain Cameron's company of the 95th, the officer of engineers lit the train. This was in all probability the same officer who had the failure at Betanzos. But this time it would seem he was determined that it would be a success for he placed more than enough powder to complete the task! The two main centre arches were totally destroyed, sending large pieces of masonry through the air. A man of the light company was killed instantly in the blast and another four were badly injured and had to be taken to Corunna. The Riflemen must have been faster runners than the 28th, for they seem to have escaped any injury from the explosion.

With the bridge blown, it now only required a small rearguard to hold this position and the Reserve was able to continue on towards Corunna following the rest of the army. Major Norcott was left with two companies of the Rifles in the town while the remaining companies continued with the Reserve, who were all cantoned on the high road to Corunna. The exception was Captain Cameron's company which was posted in a house at the end of the bridge, while the 28th Regiment's Light company occupied another house also at the end of the bridge but on the other side of the road. From here they were both able to defend the bridge and send out patrols to report on the enemy movements from the safety of the bank on the British side of the river. The French did not put in an appearance that night, but at first light the next morning the rearguard found them lining the opposite bank.

Behind them and only a short distance away there was a small village, where the enemy was amassing its troops. Possibly on the orders of the ever vigilant Paget the British horse artillery suddenly appeared and promptly sent a couple of rounds into the village. This caused such confusion that it compelled the advanced force to pull back from the bridge. This last movement allowed Captain Cameron to send one of his best marksmen onto the bridge. From here the Rifleman was able to establish himself securely behind some of the broken masonry, which he piled up on what was left of the British side of the bridge. His advanced position was safe from enemy attack being protected by the gap blown in the centre of the bridge.

This proved a clever and successful move by Cameron, for the Rifleman was able to take some fourteen shots at the enemy. Each one found a target which either killed or wounded a member of the French force and only ceased when he ran out of ammunition, even though he called for fresh supplies to be brought to him. The French were trying to rid themselves of this deadly threat by giving him plenty of attention, which prevented his comrades from reaching his position. Though he was safe, it was too dangerous for any of them to cross the open ground. With the two companies laying down a heavy covering fire he managed to run back to the safety of the houses at the end of the bridge, which he reached unharmed; though a number of shots were fired at him, they all missed.

That night under cover of darkness the French returned the compliment by placing a number of their own sharpshooters on their part of the bridge, which left the opposing armies only a short bridge span from each other. The two rearguard companies, though protected by the houses, were still in a dangerous position and whenever they presented a target to the French, a shower of lead balls would greet them. As a result, the Riflemen and their comrades in the light company had to spend most of their time crawling around on all fours to escape injury!

In the house where the 28th were posted they found a quantity of potatoes in the cellar and in an outhouse a number of chickens. That night with the contents of the find consigned to the cooking pot, the officers of this company invited Captain Cameron over for dinner, which he was loath to turn down. However, there was the small problem of getting across the open ground to their house. At the allotted time, Lieutenant Blakeney shouted over to Cameron that they would make a target for the French voltigeurs to aim at.

Once three shots rang out in response to this, the Rifles' captain was to race across to their house, as this seemed to be the regular pattern established by the enemy marksmen. Blakeney now placed his shako on the end of a sword and moved it in range of a window in a way which made it look as if a head was attached to it. Instantly three shots rang out and Cameron raced across the street. Just as he reached the safety of the doorway a fourth shot rang out and a ball passed through the skirt of his greatcoat, luckily without injuring the gallant Cameron. The officers now enjoyed a happy evening squatting in a corner of a room in what was thought to be the safest part of the house, attended by their servants, who had to crawl across the floor pushing the plates before them!

The rearguard remained at the bridge until the evening of the 13th, when Paget ordered them to evacuate their position immediately and without the need of organised formations. This was a strange request for men who had been used to such strict discipline, but just as the last of the men ran from the bridge it became quite clear as to why their general was anxious for them to retire. The French had finally brought up their guns and formed a strong battery within range of the town on which they now sent a destructive fire. The houses which had been held by the rearguard were soon reduced to rubble and the town was also treated to an equally destructive onslaught. The rearguard now joined the Reserve and they all made for Corunna.

Four men of the Rifles were reported as missing during this period, Riflemen John Lees, Richard Ball, George Fletcher and Thomas Wilsey, while Captain Bennett died on the 11th from the wounds he had received at Cacabelos.

The exertions of the Riflemen with their constant doubling and skirmishing were starting to take effect once more, again many were without shoes. Though their initial hunger had been satisfied to a small degree with the rations received at the beginning of their halt at and around El Burgo, their clothing was in rags. The officers were no exception and had suffered just as much as the men, some of whom were in such a poor condition that they had to be carried on mules.

Napier, in his History of the Peninsular War pays a fitting tribute to the men of the rearguard at this point;

'For twelve days these hardy warriors had covered the retreat, during which time they had traversed eighty miles of road in two marches, passed several nights under arms in the snow of the mountains, were seven times engaged with the enemy, and now assembled at the outposts, having fewer men missing, including those who had fallen in battle, than any other division of the army; an admirable instance of the value of good discipline.'

The Reserve finally took up a position with the army along the heights about two miles in front of Corunna and within sight of the city. The Rifles arrived on the 12th and as the enemy had not put in an appearance began to light a number of fires on which to cook the meat that had just been issued. They now took off their belts and began sponging out their rifles, servicing their weapons while their was still time before the expected battle. A fresh supply of ammunition was also issued to them, many of the men also took off their jackets in an attempt to rid themselves of the vermin that had travelled with them over the last two weeks of the retreat. Many men were sporting heavy growths of beard and as they had been ordered to throw away their knapsacks some days ago they now had no means of removing them.

Around nine o'clock on the morning of the 13th, Moore had the two main British magazines destroyed, containing some twelve thousand barrels of gunpowder (Verner). These magazines were situated on the heights of Penasquedo about three miles from Corunna. Even at this distance nearly every window in the city was shattered by the blasts. Besides startling the British army it also had a frightening effect on the inhabitants of Corunna, many of whom, only half dressed, came rushing out into the streets, where they fell onto their knees and began to pray. Some of the troops in the city thought they had been shelled by the French, but on looking beyond the British line they could see the cause of their concern, an immense column of black smoke billowing into the sky. At the scene of the blasts a number of men employed in the destruction of the ammunition had been killed or injured, for the power and might of the explosions had been far beyond what had been expected.

By this time Moore had already commenced strengthening the landward side of Corunna at the expense of the defences on the seaward side. Meanwhile, the French had repaired the bridge at El Burgo, sufficient to allow two divisions of infantry and one of cavalry to cross on the morning of the 14th. It may be noted, however, that Merle's horse artillery and troops had come up and attacked the rearguard on the 11th, their main force of cavalry having crossed the Mero on the 12th further upstream, while the bridge was being repaired.

The same afternoon that the explosions took place, the transports finally sailed into the harbour and Moore immediately began to embark his forces. The first to be put on board were the sick, wounded, dismounted cavalry and baggage, which amounted to about 2,000 men, along with the remaining women. This reduction, when added to the losses on the march of about 5,000 either killed, died or prisoners in the hands of the enemy, added to the 3,500 detached with the Light Brigades at Vigo, meant that Moore was left with an effective strength of about 15,000 infantry and 200 artillery, with which to confront Soult. (Record of services Lt. Gen. G. Cookson R. A. (War Office) and 'Royal Military Calendar,' ii., 179.) The best of the horses were selected to go on board which now left Moore with no cavalry support. [1]

The poor animals that remained were ordered to be destroyed and thrown into the sea. This was a most harrowing duty and many of the men were reduced to tears having to kill what had become trusted friends who had carried them safely for many weeks of the retreat and in a number of cases through the hazard of battle. Some fifty pieces of artillery had also been man handled onto the ships by the ever willing sailors, leaving only eight British and four Spanish guns to defend Moore's position.

Delaborde's division had arrived in force by the 15th and took up position immediately on the extreme right of Soult's line and that same morning the Rifles were ordered to advance to a position about a half mile in front of the Reserve. The reason for this move was so that they could take possession of commanding ground to the right of Lord William Bentinck's brigade, positioned close to the village of Elvina. Soult's army gradually gained in strength, marching onto the heights in full view of the British force, which continued throughout the night. At the head of each regiment a band played them onto the position and even in the dark their arrival was noticeable by the cheers and shouts which came from thousands of Frenchmen already in position. The whole of their army believing it was only a matter of time before they inflicted a most severe defeat on the British army, who had no choice now but to fight.

---

[1] The horse artillery and the waggon train had shipped all their horses which were worth bringing away, while the officers of the cavalry were allowed to take all their horses, but the troop-horses were limited. The 7th and 10th Hussars embarked ninety, the 15th thirty, while the 18th and 3rd Germans did not embark a single horse! As a result many fine animals were destroyed to prevent the French benefiting from their services. (Gordon)

When the Royal Navy and the transport ships arrived in the harbour the officers and men on board could see quite plainly the two armies drawn up ready for battle. The British were positioned on the lower ridge of hills nearest the sea, while the French were represented by the dark mass of men along the skyline overlooking the whole battlefield. Crew members were concerned for the well being of their friends in the army, whom they had brought out to Spain and Portugal at the beginning of the campaign. Even when it became dark it was still possible to distinguish the battle positions of the two armies, for the hills were amassed with lines of camp fires, which would suddenly flare up as fresh wood was put on them. In one of the ships in the harbour was a naval officer who had friends amongst some of the Rifles' officers. He was Basil Hall, who was lucky enough to be allowed on shore on the 16th, the morning of the battle, one of the very few naval men to do so. The sailors, meanwhile, had worked hard throughout that night and the next day to get Moore's baggage and the sick embarked along with the horses and guns. It did, however, amuse some sailors to see one officer's servant struggling to get on board with a huge violin cello which had accompanied his master all the way from Lisbon!

Back at the Rifles' position those not on duty now settled down for a night out in the open, close to their regimental camp fires which sent numerous dancing shadows flickering across their sleeping forms. The officers were also sleeping out in the open like their men; Colonel Beckwith and Adjutant Stewart lay wrapped in their boat cloaks not far from where Rifleman William Green was resting. Earlier a group of Riflemen, with the welfare of these two officers in mind, scattered some chopped straw over them in an attempt to shield them from the bitter cold. As the day dawned on Sunday the 16th, with the Riflemen preparing for the coming day, William Green observed Adjutant Stewart rise and brush the straw from his trousers, shocked at catching a large louse. 'You're not surprised are you Mr Stewart?' said Colonel Beckwith, 'I am,' replied the Adjutant. 'Well I have plenty about me,' returned the Colonel, 'and I bet there is not a man in the whole of the army that is wholly free of them.' Beckwith, by now standing next to Stewart, placed his telescope to his eye and looking towards the enemy position said, 'Though we are under orders for embarkation mark my word for it, we shall have something to do in another shape, for I see Soult is preparing for an attack.' (Green)

Mr Hall and the ship's Purser, Oughton landed in the harbour that same morning and were hoping to see a battle at first hand. They at once set off through the streets of the city, which they thought were in a shocking state of disorder. They then continued along the coast road, which actually cut across the position of both armies. The morning was quite fine and the officers found the scene one of amazing tranquillity, with the soldiers lying scattered about in their rags of uniforms, many sporting weeks of growth on their weather beaten faces. As soap and water had also been somewhat of a luxury, combined with the smoke and grime from numerous campfires and the discharges from rifles and muskets, the dirt was ingrained into their skin all adding to their appearance. With muskets piled, many men lay stretched on the ground fast asleep, their hands clasped behind their heads while their faces were covered by what remained of a cap. At the same time their officers stood around in little groups just watching the men about them. It seemed strange to these two naval officers to see the soldiers looking so relaxed, whilst an odd sort of silence hung over the whole area especially when considering how many thousands of men were confined to it. Hall and Oughton were actually on the left of the British position at this time and in the middle of Sir John Hope's division. They then moved off to the right through the ranks of sleeping men, piled muskets and camp equipage in search of the Rifles, whom they finally found on the extreme right of the line. Here, Hall was reunited with his officer friends, finding them fit and well. In fact the Rifles' officers were all in high spirits, better than any the two naval men had encountered so far that day. They were laughing and full of fun when they arrived, for the regimental cooks were in the process of cutting up a large wild pig. This had originally been disturbed by a French picquet, near the village of Elvina. The frightened animal then ran into the Rifles' lines in an effort to make good its escape. Here it was chased and finally caught by the men, who soon despatched it with their sword bayonets.

The Rifles' officers tried to entice their visitors to stay and share in their good fortune but they could not, for they had been given strict orders to return to their ship before nightfall. Being some distance from Corunna they now had to start back. Before leaving, however, still hoping to see a battle, the two naval men asked the Riflemen what chance they thought they had of seeing an engagement that day. To which they just shrugged their shoulders saying, 'we have already had enough of fighting and there is no earthly advantage to be gained, even by victory. While a reverse would be a very serious, perhaps desperate, affair; and therefore we have but one wish, which is, to get snugly on board the ships and be off from such a rascally country, and such a dastardly, procrastinating, pompous set of useless allies as the Spaniards!' 'Nevertheless,' said the naval officers, 'you could no doubt still make a good show if you were put to it.' 'I don't know that,' replied one of the Riflemen, 'look at the men, they are worn out, and disheartened, if they are not sleeping or eating whatever they can get hold of, they are looking at the vessels and thinking of home. Like us indeed, they are wishing for anything but an attack from those confounded fellows over the way.'[2]

---

[2] Though the Rifles' officer said his men were not in any condition to fight, this was probably said more tongue in cheek for the Riflemen were soon to prove their worth. GC/RC

From this reply it is quite clear that the Rifles had little love for their allies, but the people of Corunna were different and, therefore, should not be judged in the same way as their fellow countrymen whom the Riflemen had seen at first hand. The inhabitants of Corunna were in fact preparing to defend the city and cover the British withdrawal, knowing that once they had gone the French would take out their revenge on them.

The naval officers now left their Rifle friends to enjoy their meal and set off the way they came to reach the road leading back into Corunna, but they had not gone far when the French opened up with a severe cannonade. This was from a large battery of eight and twelve pounder guns which had been constructed unobserved. These guns were now able to rake the whole of the British right, including the Rifles' camp from which the two naval officers had just left! The whole of the British line now jumped up as one, grabbing their muskets and rifles, moving instinctively into their battle formations. The calm and quiet of the British position had now turned to one of animation, from which there rose a steady humming sound, followed by bugles sounding the alarm and the shouted commands of officers and non-commissioned officers, all accompanied by the rhythmic click of bayonets being fitted onto thousands of muskets.

Moore had put his divisions in place on the first day they arrived at Corunna, General Hope's division formed the left of his line, Hill's brigade consisting of the 5th and 14th Regiments forming his first line, with their left against the sea, with the 32nd and 2nd Regiments in reserve. In rear of these was Catlin Craufurd's brigade, consisting of the 92nd, 71st and 35th Regiments. The El Burgo to Corunna coast road ran along the right of this division which separated it from General Baird's, who continued the line from the Corunna road along the base of the Monte Mero to a position just short of, but in rear of, the village of Elvina. The three brigades forming this division had Leith on the left, with the 76th in line, its left against the Corunna road in continuation with Hope's division, the 51st on their right also in line, with the 59th forming their reserve. Manningham's brigade formed the centre, with the 81st and 1st Regiments in line and the 25th in reserve. The right brigade, Bentinck's, had the 42nd, 50th and 4th Regiments in line, with the 1st Guards brigade about a quarter of a mile to their rear, close to the village of Eiris. To the right of Bentinck's brigade about three quarters of a mile away were the heights of San Christobal, which was separated from them by the Monelos stream, which flowed down to the sea. After leaving the British left, the Corunna road continued down towards the city with the sea to its right, skirting the heights of Santa Lucia. At a point where it crossed the Monelos stream near Oza, Moore had placed Paget's Reserve division with the 95th, 52nd and 28th Regiments as his first line with the 91st and 20th Regiments in reserve.

From here they could protect the road leading into Corunna, keeping it open for the army to retreat along should the need arise. To the right of Paget's brigades, along part of the Santa Margarita Heights, were formed the regiments of Fraser's 3rd division. Their position protected the right of Moore's army against any possible attack which could come sweeping down from the San Christobal Heights.

The Riflemen had been lining up waiting for their daily issue of wine when the first cannon ball came bounding towards them. The buglers at once sounded the alarm and then the advance resulting in the camp kettles being hastily packed away. The order was then given, 'Rifles move to the front in extended files in chain order.' For the French had sent out in front of their main army a screen of skirmishers some three thousand strong to attack the whole of the British line of picquets. The 52nd Regiment were on outlying picquet at this time for the Reserve division and were being driven back. The bugles now sounded for the Rifles to advance in double quick time to attack these advancing light troops, with whom they were soon engaged in this part of the field. The Riflemen were able to hold the French skirmishers back long enough to allow the rest of the division to get into order. Poor William Green in O'Hare's company was suffering at this time from the flux and was in a bad way. Having advanced with his company the effects of his malady were such that he needed instant relief. The French, meanwhile, pressed the Rifles hard and they were forced to give way a little, causing their companies to fall back which left Green out in the middle of the two opposing skirmish lines. The French seeing this Rifleman isolated from his comrades, were not going to let such an opportunity pass and peppered the ground around the unfortunate Riflemen with their shots, but without hitting him![3] Green was in such a bad way that he did not care and a fatal shot would have put him out of his misery. However, he was eventually able to get back to his company without injury, possibly not without receiving some jibes from his comrades.

The area around the Reserve brigade's position was criss-crossed as was most of the battlefield by numerous stone walls, roads, hedges and trees. In a number of places the roads had been cut through the hills, giving them steep banks which were from eight to ten feet deep. Combined with the walls the fields were dissected into several individual battlefields, making ideal cover for the Riflemen who loop-holed the walls. As a result they were able to send a telling fire into the enemy skirmishers, while being well protected themselves. Their abundance of fresh powder and ball, when combined with the excellent cover, meant the French light troops were no match for Moore's Riflemen,

---

3 It would be hard to believe that the French could miss such a good target caught out in the open, when the shots were falling in such numbers all around Green. It is more likely that the French seeing the Rifleman's predicament had some fun at his expense! GC/RC

who in their short history had made skirmishing into an art form in which they excelled. Behind the skirmishers facing the British line, which now occupied the village of Elvina, came the packed ranks of the French infantry in three columns, all heading for the British.

The first of these columns was directed against Baird's right hand brigade, the second made for his centre and Manningham's regiments, while the third attacked Hope's division from the direction of the village of Palavia Abaxo. The only real threat to Moore's line at this point, however, was against Baird's right hand brigade. Soult's main objective was to turn the British right flank and if successful, get behind Moore's army in an effort to cut him off from the harbour and the safety of the transports. Moore, therefore, ordered General Paget to advance with his Reserve division and attack the French left to counter Soult's movements, turning defence into attack! At the same time he needed to put pressure on the great French battery, which was causing havoc on the right of his line and also many casualties. To ensure the success of this movement Moore ordered Fraser's division to support Paget. Soult's cavalry, meanwhile, had come around from the French left into the valley between the village of Elvina and the San Christobal heights. Because of the nature of the ground with its maze of stone walls and roads they were unable to operate in their conventional role. This meant they were no threat to the Riflemen in their loose formations, who at any sign of an attack could take shelter behind the nearest cover knowing that a powerful charge would be impossible and the numbers opposed to them would be easily dealt with.

The first column of Soult's infantry on nearing the village of Elvina split into two wings, the right engaged Baird's front line, while the left ascended the valley to pressure Baird's flank. Baird ordered his flanking battalion the 4th Regiment, to pull back but to remain in line so that they formed a right angle with his other regiments. From this position they were able to pour a concentrated fire into the flank of this wing of the French column. The 50th and 42nd Regiments, meanwhile, moved out of the line and attacked the wing at Elvina and as this area was also intersected by walls and hollow roads the fighting was fierce and much hand to hand combat took place. The terrain again was not suitable for the French mode of fighting in which they excelled, massed ranks or columns could not produce any impact when they were constantly broken up to negotiate obstacles. Baird's two regiments in consequence were able to force the French back with severe loss. The 50th established themselves in the village and eventually pushed the French some distance beyond it. Moore ordered up a battalion of the 1st Guards to bridge the gap in the line made by the forward movement of the 50th and 42nd Regiments. Seeing the Guards advance into the line the 42nd, who were almost out of ammunition mistakenly retired towards the line, except for their grenadier company. The French having received reinforcements renewed their attack. Moore came up at this point and after a few appropriate words ordered the 42nd back to the village to confront the enemy with their bayonets.

Finally at about five o'clock, with Lord William Bentinck's brigade receiving severe casualties from the great battery and the muskets of the French infantry, Paget's Riflemen started to make some progress. The general having sent Colonel Beckwith with the whole of his battalion of Riflemen down into the valley in extended order to engage the enemy horsemen. Restricted in their formations they began to fall back some distance until their Commander, La Houssaye ordered them to dismount and act as tirailleurs! Deployed along the lower slopes of the San Christobal they opened up with a half hearted fire against the advancing Riflemen. Beckwith's men took full advantage of the ground and soon put the cavalry to flight, who were no match for such skilled skirmishers, backed by four first class supporting regiments in the 52nd and 28th followed by the 91st and 20th.

The Riflemen out in advance now with the 52nd pushed on right up to the position of the great battery where the Riflemen set about attacking the guns in a most determined manner. Their attack was so severe that Soult was in danger of losing all the guns in this part of the field. The French commander seeing this danger sent two battalions of voltigeurs immediately out from his second line, who moved out so swiftly that their superiority in numbers forced the Riflemen to retreat a short distance from the guns. For some considerable time these two bodies of light troops blasted away at each other in a heavy fire fight, which eventually ended in favour of the Riflemen who inflicted a severe loss on the enemy skirmishers. At the same time they were able to capture seven officers and one hundred and fifty-six men, who were sent to England as prisoners of war.

With the Rifles heavily engaged on the high ground to the right of the village of Elvina, they were within sight of General Coote Manningham's brigade who, as the founder of the regiment, no doubt looked on with pride as his young regiment engaged the enemy skirmishers! It is ironic that he never commanded the regiment in battle or even in a skirmish, yet his first sight of them in action was to be at Corunna, his last engagement. Sadly on returning to England, Manningham's constitution was so poor from years of service that he died in the August of that same year. The regiment he founded, however, continued to flourish and cover itself in glory, a lasting memorial to his memory.

Shortly after Moore gave the order to the 42nd to continue the fight at Elvina, he received a mortal blow from a cannon ball which knocked him from his horse. The ball carried away the general's left shoulder, leaving his arm hanging by the exposed tendons. General Baird had also been struck by a cannon ball a little earlier, which resulted in the amputation of the arm from the shoulder. As a result the command of the army devolved to General Hope. Moore though lying mortally wounded, sat up and asked how the battle was going and after being assured it was with the British, allowed himself to be carried from the battlefield. He was gently placed in a blanket but his sword still at his side became tangled up in the process and entered the wound. When an officer attempted to remove it Moore asked for it to remain so it could leave the field of honour with him. Men of the 42nd Highlanders carried Moore down into Corunna, where he was placed in the house he had used as his headquarters. Surrounded by his friends, servants and staff he constantly requested news of the battle. There is no doubt that had Moore not become a casualty he would have ordered a counter attack on the French centre who, beaten in every part of the field, were falling back in confusion. With the British gaining ground and advancing rapidly, Ferguson's division of fresh troops could have been brought up into the main line, completing the victory over the French army from which they would have found it hard to recover. The British would then have been able to embark at their leisure.

Under the command of Colonel Nicholls some companies from the 14th Regiment in Hope's division carried the village of Palavia Abaxo which General Foy had been defending. With the loss of the village the French defeat was now complete. By the time it was dark the British line had advanced way beyond the original position they held in the morning. With the last of the daylight went any chance of following up on the retreating French and devoid of cavalry, Hope made it his priority to embark the army. General Hope knew it had been Moore's wish to return his army safely to England and used the darkness and confusion in the ranks of the enemy to withdraw his force to Corunna and onto the transports.

For the Rifles this meant another night out in the open, sleeping on the battlefield by the light of their camp fires. The picquets kept the fires burning, while at the same time making as much noise and movement as possible in an effort to make it sound as if the whole of the British army remained in position. The wounded were also being removed from the battlefield, groups of men from a number of regiments holding lighted torches were wandering over the position which all helped to create an illusion of a strong force being present. An attempt was also made to count the cost of the day's victory. The Rifles had been in constant action from the beginning of the day right up to the point of victory and as a result had received their fair share of casualties. At the height of the action Lieutenant Noble was killed defending a position with his company behind one of the numerous walls on the battlefield. Major Norcott came up to the Riflemen who were not asleep and offered two dollars to any man who could find Lieutenant Noble's body and to bring back the dead officer's sword, sash and watch, after having first covered him with stones. Norcott was in a most distressed state at the loss of Noble, for he was his brother-in-law, having married his sister. However, the night was too dark and the walls too many that the men could not find the place where the lieutenant had been killed.

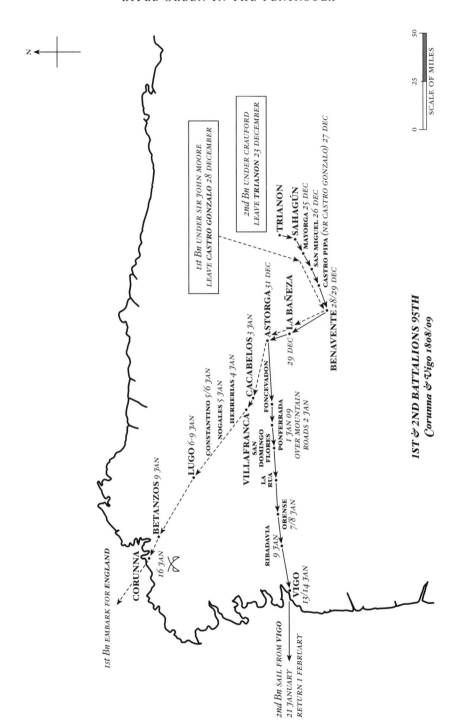

1st & 2ND BATTALIONS 95TH
Corunna & Vigo 1808/09

1st Bn UNDER SIR JOHN MOORE
LEAVE CASTRO GONZALO 28 DECEMBER

2nd Bn UNDER CRAUFORD
LEAVE TRIANON 23 DECEMBER

TRIANON
SAHAGÚN
MAYORGA 25 DEC
SAN MIGUEL 26 DEC
CASTRO PIPA (NR CASTRO GONZALO) 27 DEC

ASTORGA 31 DEC
LA BAÑEZA
29 DEC
BENAVENTE 28/29 DEC

CACABELOS 3 JAN
FONCEVADON
VILLAFRANCA
SAN
DOMINGO
FLORES
PONFERRADA
1 JAN 09
OVER MOUNTAIN
ROADS 2 JAN

HERRERIAS 4 JAN
NOGALES 5 JAN
CONSTANTINO 5/6 JAN
LUGO 6-9 JAN

BETANZOS 9 JAN

CORUNNA

16 JAN

LA
RUA
ORENSE
7/8 JAN

RIBADAVIA
9 JAN

VIGO
13/14 JAN

1st Bn EMBARK FOR ENGLAND

2nd Bn SAIL FROM VIGO
21 JANUARY
RETURN 1 FEBRUARY

N

0   25   50
SCALE OF MILES

The official casualties for the 1st Battalion 95th Rifles:

Lieutenant Charles Noble, 1 sergeant, 10 rank and file killed,
8 rank and file taken prisoner
Lieutenant Eeles, 1 sergeant, 33 rank and file landed in England wounded

List of casualties we have been able to extract from the paylists:

Listed as killed in action:

Lieutenant	Charles Noble
Sergeants	John Mann
	John Steele
Rifleman	Miles Capstick

Listed as wounded missing:

Riflemen	Thomas Allen
	Thomas Billings
	James Hickey
	William Stafford

Listed as missing:

Riflemen	James Allen	Riflemen	Duncan McDonald
	Christopher Bath		George Page
	John Baldwin		Thomas Phillips
	Archibald Bell		Daniel Ryan
	Andrew Carr		John Reeves
	Patrick Dwyre		Samuel Robb
	Abraham Fincham		Samuel Sudbury
	William Fuller		John Spencer
	Andrew Ingles		George Smith
	Philip Larner		Thomas Taylor
	John Long		William Townsend
	Thomas Lancaster		John Turner
	John M' Kelly		John Walton
	Nicholas Malabar		Isaac Young

(As was Thomas Baxter, but we know he was left at Lugo.)

Rifleman	Thomas Allen rejoined from prisoner of war 30th May 1814.
Rifleman	Christopher Bath rejoined from prisoner of war 13th May 1814.
Rifleman	William Stokes rejoined from prisoner of war 10th May 1814.

It was not until about five o'clock on the morning of the 17th that the Rifles finally received the order to move into Corunna, the last regiment in fact to leave the battlefield! With the camp fires now dying down it became quite apparent to the French that the British had made their way into Corunna and the transports. With their artillery still intact they were able to bring their guns up to a point of advantage over looking the shipping in the harbour. On reaching Corunna the Rifles marched over the drawbridge into the city, where the 23rd Regiment had the duty of organising their embarkation. Moving through the streets on their way to the harbour they encountered a number of horses still galloping around in a crazed condition, these poor animals were probably all too aware of the fate that awaited them.

Extract from Lieutenant-General John Hope's Official Despatch:

'The enemy, finding himself foiled in every attempt to force the right of the position, endeavoured by numbers to turn it a judicious and well-timed movement, which was made by Major-General Paget with the Reserve (20th, 28th, 52nd, 91st, and 95th Regiments) which corps had moved out of its cantonments to support the right of the army, by a vigorous attack defeated this intention. The Major-General having pushed forward the 95th and 1st Battalion 52nd Regiments, drove the enemy before him, and in his rapid and judicious advance threatened the left of the enemy's position.'

Extract from Hope's General Orders:

'To Major-General the Honourable E. Paget, who, by a judicious movement of the reserve, effectually contributed to check the progress of the enemy on the height, and to the 1st Battalion 52nd and 95th Regiments, which were thereby engaged, the greatest praise is justly due.'

BATTLE OF CORRUNA
16th January 1809

SCALE OF MILES

The Army Returns to England

General Hill's division remained in Corunna to embark the wounded while Beresford's brigade was ordered to hold the citadel until the 18th. Moore, the architect of the British retreat and victory over the French, died from his wounds on the evening of the 16th. Unlike the hero Nelson, however, he was laid to rest on Spanish soil in a grave dug in one of the bastions of the city.

Castillo de San Antonio at Corunna harbour

Most of the troops were already on board the transports by the time the Rifles reached the city for their embarkation. There had been much confusion when conveying the troops on the evening of the 16/17th, originally each regiment had been allotted a specific ship. The darkness of the night combined with a heavy mist meant that the sailors rowing the men from shore to ship deposited their cargoes on the first transport they came upon. As a result they were full of troops mixed up from the different regiments. The Rifles fared no better than the rest when it came to their boarding.

Rifleman William Green awoke on the morning of the 18th and when mustering to receive his rations found there were sixty one rank and file on board from twenty nine different regiments, all under the command of a sergeant of the 95th Rifles, who, as there were no officers present, was the most senior rank.

The French, meanwhile, on the 17th, having discovered the withdrawal of the British and their picquets, immediately sent a gun battery to the heights behind the Castillo de San Diego. From here they shelled the transports in the bay. This lasted for about an hour and caused very little damage. It did, however, cause panic and confusion amongst the masters of the transports, with a result that several immediately ordered their cables to be cut. This added further to the confusion as seven vessels ran aground, four of which were refloated. The troops from the grounded ships were transferred to other transports. The ships which remained aground were destroyed by setting them on fire. The only casualties of this affair were nine men from the Royal Waggon Train who were drowned when their boat overturned.

The fleet now moved out of the harbour and into open water, with the whole of Moore's army on board, with the exception of Beresford's brigade who finally embarked on the 18th after securing the last of the wounded on board and handing the defence of the city over to the Spaniards.

Though now safe from the French, there was a new danger to be faced, for the elements were against Moore's army reaching England's shore. Shortly after gaining the open sea, the fleet was hit by a severe south-westerly gale, which scattered the ships far and wide, causing many of the vessels to remain at sea for many weeks. Two ships carrying the 7th Hussars and the King's German Legion were sent crashing onto the rocks of the Cornish coast, with the loss of 273 men! As a result the army was landed along the south coast of England at a variety of ports. Rifleman Green's ship arrived off Spithead on the 3rd February, taking eighteen days to reach British soil.

The 2nd Battalion 95th under Craufurd who we left embarking at Vigo, suffered the same fate as the rest of the fleet even though they put to sea some days earlier. Many of Craufurd's Riflemen on boarding their transports just slumped to the deck and slept where they lay, that is until the storm hit. As soon as they awoke they were ordered below decks, so that the hatches could be battened down ready to face the severity of the storm. It was just as well, for a particularly large wave hit the ship throwing it onto its side. The men were ordered to move onto the opposite side of the ship in an attempt to add their weight to try and right it. However, both the troops and ship remained in this perilous position throughout the whole of the storm until it finally righted itself when the gale subsided.

Back in England news soon spread of the return of Sir John Moore's army. Friends, relations, wives, children and mothers all mingled with the curious to witness the arrival of the troops. They were shocked at the picture they presented; almost all were without shoes, faces caked in grime and many framed with flowing beards, clothes and accoutrements were torn and ragged, with bits of cloth wrapped around many a head; weapons were rusted in the hands of those who still had them; while many were only able to shuffle up the beaches and many more had become blind all adding to the sorry spectacle.

One spectator, Sir Marc Isambard Brunel was so shocked at the condition of the troops that he set out to find the cause of their deterioration. His investigations were to eventually have a far reaching effect on the British army, for he found that as many casualties had been caused by shoddy footwear as from action with the enemy. Having obtained a couple of pairs of the offending footwear he took them to his workplace where he cut them up and examined them. It soon became quite clear why the footwear broke down after very little use. Between the inner and outer soles, the manufacturers had filled the gap with a layer of clay to add weight to them. However, once they became wet, such as when the troops were landed on a beach or marching along very wet and muddy roads, the clay just disintegrated. Brunel, seeing the need for quality footwear and the ready market in the British army invented a machine to mass produce shoes and boots. The original sub-standard footwear could not be blamed on the Government, for they had provided adequate funding to be made available. They had, however, been at the mercy of shoddy manufacturers.

Brunel's footwear was a success, this in the days when shoes and boots were produced as single items! The day of the left and right boot was still to come. Regrettably, the superior footwear produced by Brunel was not taken up by the army until as late as 1812.

For the battle of Corunna there were no official losses published, possibly due to political pressure? Losses were estimated at about 800 for the allies, with an exaggerated figure of 3,000 for the French; although their losses were in fact far more numerous than the British.

With the Rifles now back in England those Riflemen fit and able enough to march returned to their barracks at Hythe. Here they burnt their clothing on huge fires on the barrack square along with the vermin of which they were at last glad to be rid. The hardships of the campaign are confirmed by the long list of men confined to the general and regimental hospitals. Many lessons, however, were learnt from this ordeal and as a result the French army in Portugal and Spain would again be faced by their old adversary, Wellington. The Peninsular War would now take on a completely different perspective.

Men listed as having died on their return to England:

Corporals	James Moss	disembarked 20.02.1809	died 23.03.1809
	William Sutherland	disembarked 24.01.1809	died 19.02.1809
Bugler	Richard Watts		died 24.01.1809
Riflemen	James Alderton	disembarked 24.01.1809	
	Joseph Benidge	disembarked 02.02.1809	died 21.02.1809
	James Bens	disembarked 02.02.1809	died 16.02.1809
	John Biddle	disembarked 15.02.1809	died 18.02.1809
	David Browne	disembarked 01.02.1809	died 14.02.1809
	Richard Chambers	*Plymouth	died* 13.03.1809
	John Champane	disembarked 02.02.1809	died 01.03.1809
	William Chapman	disembarked 01.02.1809	died 06.02.1809
	John Charms	disembarked 27.01.1809	died 04.03.1809
	Samuel Clarke		died 24.01.1809
	John Cox	disembarked 02.02.1809	died 19.02.1809
	Brice Dixon		died 21.01.1809
	John Farrel	*depot Hythe	died* 15.03.1809
	Samuel Gaston	disembarked 03.02.1809	died 16.02.1809
	David Griffith	disembarked 27.01.1809	died same day
	John Gunn	disembarked 27.01.1809	died 31.01.1809
	Joseph Hall		died 24.01.1809
	Richard Jessop	disembarked 27.01.1809	died 31.01.1809
	William Jessop	disembarked 27.01.1809	died 02.02.1809
	Uriah Kemp	disembarked 02.02.1809	died 28.02.1809
	William Kirkman	disembarked 02.02.1809	died 17.03.1809
	Joseph Loddington	disembarked 28.01.1809	died 18.02.1809
	Duncan McKenzie	disembarked 24.01.1809	died 16.03.1809
	Roderick McNash	disembarked ?	died 06.02.1809
	John Margrates	disembarked 24.01.1809	died 02.03.1809
	Francis Meadon	*Plymouth after returning	died* 12.03.1809
	Thomas Middleton	disembarked 24.01.1809	died 30.01.1809
	Adam Miller	disembarked 19.02.1809	died 25.02.1809
	James Moffat	disembarked 25.01.1809	died same day
	Job Moore	disembarked 19.02.1809	died 06.03.1809
	William Newton	disembarked 19.02.1809	died 02.03.1809
	Richard Palmer	disembarked 01.02.1809	died 14.02.1809
	William Patrick	disembarked 26.01.1809	died 07.02.1809
	Robert Pearson		died 24.01.1809
	John Robinson	disembarked 02.02.1809	died 08.03.1809
	Benjamin Sanderson	disembarked 27.01.1809	died 18.02.1809
	Joseph Scott	*depot Hythe	died* 04.03.1809
	William Shepherd	disembarked 25.01.1809	died 30.01.1809
	James Smith	disembarked 01.02.1809	died 06.02.1809
	Joseph Stratton		died 23.01.1809
	George Thistlewood	disembarked 20.02.1809	died 03.03.1809
	William Turner (1st)	disembarked 27.01.1809	died 06.02.1809
	Thomas Whittle	disembarked 19.02.1809	died 16.03.1809
	Joseph Wilkinson	disembarked 28.01.1809	died 01.02.1809

All the above men returned to England on different transports as can be confirmed by the dates on landing. Some of these men would have died from wounds but at this stage it is not possible to separate them from those who died of hardship. Besides the men listed we have also been able to compile a short list of further casualties in the campaign but with no detail as to when they were wounded:

Sergeants	James Farmer	wounded forehead
	William Hall	wounded in the head
	John Reid	wounded ankle
Corporals	Duncan Campbell	sabre wound
	Philip Larner	gunshot wound left leg
Riflemen	Humphry Allen	wounded
	Martin Hart	wounded
	Israel Harvey	sabre wound to the head
	James Neasmith	wounded left knee

The following men are all listed as being sick on returning to England, again there is no way to distinguish those who were wounded:

No 1 Company

Riflemen	John Anderson	at Plymouth
	John Coward	at Plymouth
	James Goff	at Plymouth
	Stephen Hall	at Plymouth
	Samuel Hutton	at Plymouth
	Thomas Jones	at Plymouth
	William Law	at Plymouth
	Philip Lees	Regimental Hospital
	Mick Markie	at Plymouth
	Solomon Wilkes	at Plymouth
	William Wilkinson	at Plymouth

No 2 Company

Sergeant	Thomas Burroughs	at Plymouth
Riflemen	Humphrey Allan	at Plymouth
	John Anderson	at Plymouth
	Isaac Bradbury	Regimental Hospital
	James Browne	at Plymouth
	William Browne	at Plymouth
	John Daves	at Plymouth
	John Goodman	at Plymouth
	John Kendall (1st)	Regimental Hospital
	James Lush	at Plymouth
	Andrew Lockhard	at Plymouth
	Peter Septon	at Plymouth
	John Sykes	died onboard ship 18.01.1809
	Thomas Waghorn	at Plymouth

No 3 Company

Sergeant	John Solomon	at Plymouth
Bugler	Thomas Grant	at Plymouth
Riflemen	Patrick Beahan	at Plymouth
	Thomas Canning	at Plymouth
	James Chambers	at Plymouth
	Joseph Dier	at Plymouth
	Thomas Farrant	at Plymouth
	John Greenwood	at Plymouth
	Thomas Hall	at Plymouth
	Thomas Jinkins	at Plymouth
	Samuel Keen	at Plymouth
	William Mathews	at Plymouth
	Samuel Price	at Plymouth
	Samuel Sewell	at Plymouth
	Joseph Watts	at Plymouth
	Oliver Wheland	at Plymouth

No 4 Company

Corporal	Charles Masling	at Plymouth
Riflemen	Archibald Bell	at Plymouth
	William Burgess	at Plymouth
	Thomas Hamstead	at Plymouth
	Francis Holmes	at Plymouth
	John Loddington	at Plymouth
	John Martin	at Plymouth
	John Naughton	at Plymouth
	Thomas Porter	at Plymouth
	Walter Prior	at Plymouth
	Samuel Skilmore	at Plymouth
	John Webster	at Plymouth
	William Wheatley	at Plymouth

No 5 Company

Bugler	William Hall	at Plymouth
Riflemen	Henry Benham	at Plymouth
	Thomas Bunton	at Plymouth
	Thomas Daly	at Plymouth
	Joseph Davy	at Plymouth
	Henry Eldridge	at Plymouth
	William King	at Plymouth
	Joseph Morgan	at Plymouth
	Benjamin Slaughter [1] (p. 173)	at Plymouth
	Thomas Taylor	at Plymouth
	Edward Teagan	at Plymouth

No 6 Company

Corporal	John Cleland	at Plymouth
Riflemen	David Ade	at Plymouth
	George Archer	at Plymouth
	William Bacon	at Plymouth
	John Bellow	at Plymouth
	George Bradford	at Plymouth
	James Cavenagh	at Plymouth
	Joseph Cowan	at Plymouth
	William Dalton	at Plymouth
	Edward Evans	at Plymouth
	William Hanes	at Plymouth
	Charles Hughes	at Plymouth
	John McAllister	at Plymouth
	James McMaster	at Plymouth
	John Marlow	at Plymouth
	Patrick Moran	at Plymouth
	Thomas Mason	at Plymouth
	Richard Rouse	at Plymouth
	James Shoebridge	at Plymouth
	Thomas Wright	at Plymouth

No 7 Company

Riflemen	John Browne	at Plymouth
	Donald Campbell	at Plymouth
	William Campbell	at Plymouth
	Richard Chambers	at Plymouth
	Robert Gilcrist	at Plymouth
	David Harsall	at Plymouth
	Henry Jacons	at Plymouth
	Donald McGregor	at Plymouth
	Kenneth McKenzie	at Plymouth
	James Roulstone	at Plymouth
	Francis Young	at Plymouth
	Thomas Young	at Plymouth

No 8 Company

Sergeants	James McLaulin	at Plymouth
	Thomas Walker	at Plymouth
Corporal	Abraham Fotheringham	at Plymouth

Riflemen	Thomas Blubber	at Plymouth
	Thomas Bowen	at Plymouth
	John Hewley	at Plymouth
	James Humbly	at Plymouth
	Patrick Mahony	at Plymouth
	Patrick Meath	at Plymouth
	Benjamin Pring	at Plymouth
	William Tuttle	at Plymouth
	Thomas Warby	at Plymouth
	John Wicks	at Plymouth
	William Wicks	at Plymouth

No 9 Company

Sergeants	Thomas Griffiths	at Plymouth
	William Hipkiss	at Plymouth
Corporal	William Kennedy	at Plymouth
Riflemen	John Bedwell	at Plymouth
	William Browne	at Plymouth
	George Jones	at Plymouth
	William Kellam	at Plymouth
	William Lincoln	at Plymouth
	Francis Meaden	at Plymouth
	William Meaden	at Plymouth
	William Mills	at Plymouth
	John Molloy	at Plymouth
	James Raeburn	at Plymouth
	George Saunders	at Plymouth
	William Sharpe	at Plymouth
	Jasper Stoddard	at Plymouth
	David Walsh	at Plymouth
	Ellis Williams	at Plymouth

In addition to these casualties the Rifles also had Assistant Surgeon W P Turner severely wounded at the Battle of Corunna.

---

1 (From p. 171) Benjamin Slaughter is unique amongst the Rifles' medalists. As well as receiving the Military General Service medal with clasps Corunna and Badajos, he also received the Waterloo Medal. He was also amongst the few survivors to have taken part in the battle of Copenhagen in 1801. As such he was also entitled to the Naval General Service Medal clasp Copenhagen. Why he did not receive this is not known for only two Riflemen survived to claim this medal yet Slaughter was still alive having made his claim for the MGS. One can only assume that he did not know of his entitlement. When claiming his MGS the board would have checked out his claim for the two clasps and his service papers would confirm the entitlement to the Naval medal. By not receiving this the Rifles and Slaughter were denied a unique medal combination.

PART TWO
Military General Service Medal 1793-1814

The veterans of the Peninsular War had to wait thirty four years for their services to King and Country to be recognised with a lasting memento to the hardships and severe fighting they undertook to overthrow the might of Napoleon. Unlike, however, those serving at Waterloo who received a medal the following year for a campaign that lasted only three days. This was a bone of contention with many old soldiers, who had either been discharged before Waterloo or who went to America, where they took part in the severe fighting at New Orleans, which was not rewarded with any form of recognition. Some of these older Riflemen on being posted to France, when meeting with young soldiers displaying their medals would take exception to this and rip the medals from their coats.

MGS Medal showing clasps for Roleia, Vimiera and Corunna

As a result many Riflemen who fought with great distinction and honour in defeating the French in the famous battles of Portugal, Spain and France never lived to receive their reward of the Military General Service Medal. As an example it is worth noting that Rifleman Michael Norton who joined the Rifles in 1805 was entitled to a fifteen clasp MGS including Talavera, had he lived long enough to claim it. He was present at Waterloo and this was his only medal!

It was not until 1847 that a medal was finally sanctioned to redress the balance and commemorate the actions in the Peninsula, France and the Colonies. This was to be issued to all claimants who served in any of a selected number of actions from 1793 to 1814 though no clasp was awarded before 1801. The medal was eventually issued in 1848, but not to next of kin. Many veterans failed to claim their medal, simply because they did not know of their existence, which seems odd, especially when a number of Indian Warriors and Foreign troops who had been in the British service managed to apply for the medal? However, some 25,000 medals were eventually struck and issued and as a result, with such a large demand there are some noticeable differences in the die designs. The medal was impressed in capitals with the recipients name and regiment and rank for corporals and above. Therefore, no genuine medal would have been engraved, although a couple of medals have been seen that have had the odd letter engraved to correct an obvious error at a later stage.

Officially the 95th Foot Rifles received 691 medals, with one man receiving fourteen battle clasps to his medal. The first clasp the regiment was entitled to was for Roleia, fought on the 17th August 1808. The regiment was present at seventeen of the actions authorised by a clasp, from the total of twenty-nine clasps sanctioned.

However, some Riflemen of the 95th were issued one or more of the remaining clasps for service with another regiment at the time of the action.

The rarest clasp to the regiment is for Talavera, which will be covered in volume two. In volume one the medal roll covers the clasps ROLEIA, VIMIERA and CORUNNA. It will be noticed that the spelling of these honours differs from that shown in the history, this was due to an error by a clerk at the War Office and as a result the medals and colours displayed by the regiments of the British army are all shown or spelt incorrectly.

Many collectors of these MGS medals have relied on the medal roll compiled by Lieut-Colonel Kingsley Foster of the Royal Northumberland Fusiliers and more lately that of Tony Mullen. We have consulted both of these rolls when researching the 95th claimants as well as a third roll compiled for Lt Colonel Frederick S. S. Brind of the 17th Regt. Foot. This latter roll was compiled in the late 1890's and is in four separate sections probably more in line with its original format. This is most helpful when researching an individual recipient in a way that neither of the other two rolls can. The officers are listed separately and the men under three separate headings; Pensioners, Direct Applicants and Non-Pensioners. It is quite obvious from this that a man found under one of these headings points the researcher in a certain direction for further study, eliminating unnecessary time searching through the whole roll of categories.

We have been able to take the findings in the three rolls mentioned a step further, having concentrated all our research into one regiment which would have been a monumental task in a general work. As a result our in depth knowledge and research into the 95th Rifles has unearthed some interesting results, via the muster and paylists rolls and pension lists for the regiment. From the very outset of our research into the Military General Service Medal Roll for the 95th it was quite clear that it contained several errors! Some of the major ones we believe are down to the Royal Mint, who produced and issued the medals.

All Military General Service Medals are impressed in the same style of small seriffed capitals and the inscription on the medal has three distinct styles shown for the naming of the regiment;

Style one:
J. TATT SERJT. 95TH FOOT, RIFLES.
W. HALL SJT. 95TH FOOT, RIFLES.
THOS. EGGERTON CORPL. 95TH FOOT, RIFLES.
CHARLES ALLEN, 95TH FOOT, RIFLES.
THOS ROBINSON, 95TH FOOT, RIFLES.
J. CROOKS, 95TH FOOT, RIFLES.

Style two:
J. AUSTIN LIEUT. 95TH FOOT.
W. MARSHALL QR ME SERJT 95TH FOOT.
J. FARMER SERJT 95TH FOOT.
J. MURPHY CORPL 95TH FOOT.
JAMES STILLWELL, 95TH FOOT.
THOS COLESTON 95TH FOOT.
R. HAINES, 95TH FOOT.

Style three:
J. MIDDLETON CAPT 95TH RIFLES.
W. FARMER LIEUT, 95TH RIFLES.
J. N. GOSSETT LIEUT 95TH RIFLES.

MGS Clasp ROLEIA Battle of Roliça 17th August 1808

Excluding the skirmish on the 15th August at Obidos, Roliça was the first battle to be fought against the French in the Peninsula. The clasp for Roliça is a 2nd Battalion award and only four companies of the 2nd Battalion 95th were present at this combat. We find that 40 clasps were awarded to the Rifles; 36 to the 2nd Battalion and 4 to the 1st Battalion. This figure excludes Captain John Kent who was serving with the 50th Foot at Roliça but includes Lieutenant John Molloy who is entitled to an 8 and not 6 clasp MGS medal. Lists which show him as a 6 clasp MGS omit his Roliça and Vimeiro entitlement which the paylists confirm. In addition to the 36 2nd Battalion men entitled to the clasp we have found a further 26 2nd Battalion men entitled but not awarded the clasp making a total of 62.

The 4 we have excluded are:

1	Subaltern William Humbley	1st Battalion 95th
2	Rifleman William Rind	1st Battalion 95th
3	Rifleman Benjamin Pring	In Baird's force from Corunna and in 1st Battalion 95th
4	Rifleman John Tatt/Tait	In Baird's force from Corunna and in 1st Battalion 95th

Both Humbley and Rind, strictly speaking, are not entitled to the Roliça clasp being in the 1st Battalion. They did not land in Portugal until two to three days after the battle. However, the situation can be altered if evidence can be produced to show that they arrived in Portugal in advance of the 1st Battalion and were present at the battle.

1st Clasp Roliça 17th August 1808

Reference: 1st Bn WO 12 9522 25 June-24 September 1808
              2nd Bn WO 12 9579 25 June-24 September 1808

2nd Bn   Capt. J. Crampton No. 1 Co., Capt. J. Creagh No. 2 Co.
         Capt. J. Leach No. 3 Co. and Capt. H. R. Pakenham No. 4 Co.

In the following lists, the number before 'MGS' denotes the number of official clasps awarded to that individual.

1	Sub	John Cox	10 MGS	Ensign in 2nd Bn
2	Capt	William Cox	7 MGS	Lieutenant in 2nd Bn
3	Lieut	Dudley Hill	4 MGS	Lieutenant in 2nd Bn, Wounded 17th Aug
4	Sub	William Humbley	12 MGS	Ensign in 1st Bn Not entitled to clasp
-	Capt	John Kent	5 MGS	In the 50th Foot at Roliça
5	Capt	Jonathan Leach	12 MGS	Captain of No 3 Co 2nd Bn
6	Lieut	John Molloy	8 MGS	Ensign in 2nd Bn
7	Capt Hon	Hercules Pakenham	2 MGS	Captain of No 4 Co 2nd Bn
8	R'man	David Beattie	9 MGS	Rifleman No 4 Co 2nd Bn (Beety) Wounded 17th Aug
9	R'man	Joseph Bell	8 MGS	Rifleman No 3 Co 2nd Bn (On paylist as Joseph Bull)
10	Sgt	Joseph Bowley	10 MGS	Corporal No 3 Co 2nd Bn
11	R'man	James Cavanagh	2 MGS	Rifleman No 1 Co 2nd Bn (Cavinough)
12	R'man	Benjamin Harris	3 MGS	Rifleman No 3 Co 2nd Bn (Rifleman Harris)
13	Sgt	Robert Hayes	2 MGS	Corporal No 1 Co 2nd Bn
14	Sgt	Joseph Hindle	14 MGS	Rifleman No 3 Co 2nd Bn 'Missing 21st Aug' Joined from French prison 6th Sept
15	R'man	Thomas Kelly	10 MGS	Rifleman No 4 Co 2nd Bn
16	Sgt	John Lowe	8 MGS	Rifleman No 3 Co 2nd Bn
17	Sgt	Michael Malone	5 MGS	Rifleman No 4 Co 2nd Bn (On paylist as Nicholas Malone)
18	R'man	John McKitchie	2 MGS	Corporal No 2 Co 2nd Bn
19	Sgt	Charles McPherson	6 MGS	Sergeant No 1 Co 2nd Bn
20	Bug Maj	James Mitchell	8 MGS	Rifleman No 2 Co 2nd Bn
21	R'man	Nicholas Myers	6 MGS	Rifleman No 2 Co 2nd Bn
22	R'man	John O'Brian	3 MGS	Rifleman No 2 Co 2nd Bn
23	R'man	Thomas Osborne	4 MGS	Rifleman No 4 Co 2nd Bn 1st Bn 25th Aug but in 2nd Bn at Corunna
24	R'man	Joseph Piers	8 MGS	Rifleman No 3 Co 2nd Bn (Perrs) (Sick on board ship)
25	R'man	William Prestage	5 MGS	Rifleman No 2 Co 2nd Bn (Duty)
26	R'man	Peter Price	10 MGS	Rifleman No 2 Co 2nd Bn (Sick on board ship)
27	R'man	Benjamin Pring	11 MGS	Not on 1st or 2nd Bn paylist with Baird's force from Corunna, not entitled.
28	R'man	William Rind	3 MGS	Rifleman No 5 Co 1st Bn, not entitled.
29	Sgt	Edward Rochford	2 MGS	Corporal No 4 Co 2nd Bn
30	R'man	George Smith	3 MGS	Rifleman No 4 Co 2nd Bn (Duty)
31	R'man	John Smith	2 MGS	1 Rifleman No 2 Co 2nd Bn (Duty) 2 Rifleman No 1 Co 2nd Bn
		3 on 2nd Bn paylist		(Wounded 17th Aug) MGS man 3 Rifleman No 4 Co 2nd Bn
32	R'man	Thomas Smith	11 MGS	Rifleman No 2 Co 2nd Bn (Duty)

33	R'man	Daniel Stott	2 MGS	Rifleman No 2 Co 2nd Bn (Wounded 17th Aug, Sick General Hospital)
34	R'man	Jonathan Stubbs	10 MGS	Rifleman No 1 Co 2nd Bn
35	R'man	John Tatt	6 MGS	Not on 1st or 2nd paylist with Baird's force from Corunna, not entitled.
36	Sgt Maj	John Thompson	5 MGS	Sergeant No 4 Co 2nd Bn
37	R'man	Peter Ware	3 MGS	Rifleman No 2 Co 2nd Bn (Wear)
38	Sgt	John Wheeler	1 MGS	Corporal to Rifleman No 4 Co 2nd Bn
39	Bugler	Maurice Wildes	6 MGS	Bugler No 1 Co 2nd Bn (Wilds)
40	R'man	David Wylie	6 MGS	Rifleman No 1 Co 2nd Bn (Wiely)

Additional names of MGS men not awarded the clasp for Roliça

1	R'man	Joseph Arms	11 MGS	Rifleman No 1 Co 2nd Bn
2	R'man	James Barrett	2 MGS	Rifleman No 1 Co 2nd Bn
3	Sgt	Stephen Bedford	6 MGS	Rifleman No 2 Co 2nd Bn
4	R'man	Richard Broom	4 MGS	Rifleman No 2 Co 2nd Bn
5	Sgt	Patrick Brown	3 MGS	Sergeant No 2 Co 2nd Bn (Wounded 17th Aug, Sick absent)
6	R'man	Neil Cameron	8 MGS	Rifleman No 4 Co 2nd Bn
7	R'man	Michael Connor	1 MGS	Rifleman No 2 Co 2nd Bn
8	R'man	James Crooks	6 MGS	Rifleman No 4 Co 2nd Bn
9	R'man	Robert Deacon	5 MGS	Rifleman No 2 Co 2nd Bn
10	R'man	Edward Donaghoe	3 MGS	Rifleman No 3 Co 2nd Bn (Duty)
11	R'man	Michael Fagan	3 MGS	Rifleman No 4 Co 2nd Bn
12	R'man	Edward Farmer	5 MGS	Rifleman No 3 Co 2nd Bn
13	R'man	John Gallagher	2 MGS	Rifleman No 3 Co 2nd Bn
14	Sgt	William Grant	1 MGS	Corporal No 3 Co 2nd Bn
15	R'man	Christopher Grimes	8 MGS	Rifleman No 2 Co 2nd Bn (From General Hosp 6th July, Sick on board transport)
16	R'man	William McKay	5 MGS	Rifleman No 4 Co 2nd Bn
17	R'man	John Maher	5 MGS	Rifleman No 1 Co 2nd Bn (Duty)
18	R'man	Arthur Malone	2 MGS	Rifleman No 4 Co 2nd Bn
19	R'man	James Mason 2 on 2nd Bn paylist	3 MGS	1 Rifleman No 1 Co 2nd Bn MGS man 2 Rifleman No 4 Co 2nd Bn (Duty)
20	R'man	Daniel Milton	6 MGS	Rifleman No 2 Co 2nd Bn
21	Sgt	John Moran 3 on 2nd Bn paylist	11 MGS	1 Rifleman No 2 Co 2nd Bn MGS man 2 Rifleman No 1 Co 2nd Bn (Duty) 3 Rifleman No 4 Co 2nd Bn (Duty)
22	R'man	Anthony Mullins	3 MGS	Rifleman No 2 Co 2nd Bn
23	R'man	James O'Neil	7 MGS	Rifleman No 2 Co 2nd Bn
24	R'man	William Phillips	1 MGS	Rifleman No 3 Co 2nd Bn (Wounded 17th Aug, Sick General Hosp)
25	R'man	William Rhodes	9 MGS	Rifleman No 2 Co 2nd Bn
26	R'man	Bartholomew Rogers	1 MGS	Rifleman No 3 Co 2nd Bn (Rodgers)

MGS Clasp VIMIERA Battle of Vimeiro 21st August 1808

The second clasp to be awarded to the Rifles for the battle of Vimeiro where both 1st and 2nd Battalions were present. Two companies from the 1st Battalion and four from the 2nd Battalion. Again, excluding Captain John Kent still with the 50th Foot and Riflemen Charles Murphy with the 71st but including Lieutenant John Molloy, the Rifles were awarded 105 clasps.

In addition to the 37 1st Battalion and 54 2nd Battalion men entitled to the clasp we have found 8 1st Battalion and 8 2nd Battalion men entitled but not awarded the clasp making a total of 107.

We have excluded the following 14 MGS men awarded the Vimeiro clasp:

1	Rifleman	James Buckler	
2	Rifleman	James Cairns	
3	Sergeant	James Farmer	
4	Rifleman	David Hughes	Sir David Baird's force, not present at Vimeiro
5	Rifleman	Benjamin Pring	
6	Rifleman	William Shaughnessy	
7	Rifleman	John Tatt/Tait	
8	Rifleman	Tuttle Betts	
9	Sergeant	Andrew Carr	
10	Rifleman	James Coleman	Sir John Moore's force, not present at Vimeiro
11	Rifleman	James Cooke	
12	Rifleman	Israel Harvey	
13	C/Sgt	James Davison	Not on 1st or 2nd Battalion paylist for Vimeiro. In England with 2nd Bn at Falmouth Harbour
14	Sgt	John Norton	Not on 1st or 2nd Battalion paylist for Vimeiro. In 2nd Battalion 'Recruiting at Glasgow'

2nd Clasp Vimiera 21st August 1808

Reference: 1st Bn WO 12 9522 25 June-24 September 1808
2nd Bn WO 12 9579 25 June-24 September 1808

1st Bn Capt S. Ramadge No 4 Co and Capt A. Cameron No 5 Co
2nd Bn Capt J. Crampton No 1 Co, Capt J. Creagh No 2 Co
Capt J. Leach No 3 Co and Capt H. Pakenham No 4 Co

1	Capt	Alexander Cameron	5 MGS	Captain of No 5 Co 1st Bn
2	Sub	John Cox	10 MGS	Ensign in 2nd Bn
3	Capt	William Cox	7 MGS	Lieutenant in 2nd Bn
4	Lieut	Dudley Hill	4 MGS	Lieutenant in 2nd Bn
5	Sub	William Humbley	12 MGS	Ensign in 1st Bn
-	Capt	John Kent	5 MGS	In the 50th Foot at Vimiera
6	Capt	Jonathan Leach	12 MGS	Captain of No 3 Co 2nd Bn
7	Lieut	John Molloy	8 MGS	Ensign in 2nd Bn
8	Capt Hon	Hercules Pakenham	2 MGS	Captain of No 4 Co 2nd Bn
9	Capt	Smith Ramadge	2 MGS	Captain of No 4 Co 1st Bn
10	Sgt	James Anderson	9 MGS	Rifleman No 5 Co 1st Bn
11	R'man	Joseph Arms	11 MGS	Rifleman No 1 Co 2nd Bn
12	R'man	James Barrett	2 MGS	Rifleman No 1 Co 2nd Bn
13	R'man	David Beattie	9 MGS	Rifleman No 4 Co 2nd Bn (Beety)
14	Sgt	Stephen Bedford	6 MGS	Rifleman No 2 Co 2nd Bn
15	R'man	John Bell	11 MGS	Rifleman No 5 Co 1st Bn
16	R'man	Joseph Bell	8 MGS	Rifleman No 3 Co 2nd Bn (On paylist as Joseph Bull)
17	R'man	Tuttle Betts	3 MGS	Rifleman No 3 Co 1st Bn (Not 4 or 5 Co) With Moore's force, not entitled
18	Sgt	Joseph Bowley	10 MGS	Corporal No 3 Co 2nd Bn
19	Sgt	Patrick Brown	3 MGS	Sergeant No 2 Co 2nd Bn (See Roliça list)
20	R'man	James Bryce	9 MGS	Rifleman No 5 Co 1st Bn
21	R'man	James Buckler	6 MGS	Not on 1st or 2nd Bn paylist With Baird's force, not entitled
22	R'man	William Buckley	7 MGS	Rifleman No 4 Co 1st Bn
23	R'man	James Byford	5 MGS	Rifleman No 4 Co 1st Bn
24	R'man	James Cairns	12 MGS	Not on 1st or 2nd Bn paylist With Baird's force, not entitled.
25	R'man	Neil Cameron	8 MGS	Rifleman No 4 Co 2nd Bn
26	Sgt	Andrew Carr	11 MGS	Rifleman No 3 Co 1st Bn (Not 4 or 5 Co) With Moore's force, not entitled.
27	R'man	James Cavanagh	2 MGS	Rifleman No 1 Co 2nd Bn
28	R'man	James Coleman	12 MGS	Rifleman No 3 Co 1st Bn (Not 4 or 5 Co) With Moore's force, not entitled
29	R'man	Patrick Connell	2 MGS	Rifleman No 4 Co 1st Bn
30	R'man	Michael Connor	1 MGS	Rifleman No 2 Co 2nd Bn
31	R'man	James Cooke	13 MGS	Rifleman No 2 Co 1st Bn (Not 4 or 5 Co) With Moore's force, not entitled
32	Sgt	Joseph Cowan	9 MGS	Rifleman No 4 Co 1st Bn
33	R'man	James Crooks	6 MGS	Rifleman No 4 Co 2nd Bn
34	C/Sgt	James Davison	7 MGS	Not on 1st or 2nd Bn paylists, not entitled
35	R'man	George Dempster		Rifleman No 4 Co 1st Bn
36	R'man	Edward Donaghoe	3 MGS	Rifleman No 3 Co 2nd Bn (Duty) (Donahoo)
37	R'man	George Dunlop	3 MGS	Rifleman No 5 Co 1st Bn

38	Sgt	Alexander Eason	13 MGS	Rifleman No 4 Co 1st Bn
39	R'man	Michael Fagan	3 MGS	Rifleman No 4 Co 2nd Bn
40	R'man	Edward Farmer	5 MGS	Rifleman No 3 Co 2nd Bn
41	Sgt	James Farmer	9 MGS	Not on 1st or 2nd Bn paylist
				With Baird's force, not entitled
42	Sgt	Hugh Fraser	1 MGS	Sergeant No 4 Co 1st Bn
43	R'man	James Fraser	7 MGS	1 Rifleman No 4 Co 1st Bn MGS man
		2 on 1st Bn paylist		2 Rifleman No 5 Co 1st Bn
44	R'man	Joseph Fuller	6 MGS	Rifleman No 5 Co 1st Bn
45	R'man	Robert Gilchrist	9 MGS	Rifleman No 5 Co 1st Bn
46	Corp	William Gillis	6 MGS	Rifleman No 5 Co 1st Bn
47	Sgt	William Grant	1 MGS	Corporal No 3 Co 2nd Bn
48	R'man	Christopher Grimes	8 MGS	Rifleman No 2 Co 2nd Bn
49	R'man	Benjamin Harris	3 MGS	Rifleman No 3 Co 2nd Bn
50	R'man	Israel Harvey	8 MGS	Rifleman No 2 Co 1st Bn (Not 4 or 5 Co)
				With Moore's force, not entitled
51	Sgt	Robert Hayes	2 MGS	Corporal No 1 Co 2nd Bn (Promoted
				to Sergeant on the 22nd August)
52	Sgt	Joseph Hindle	14 MGS	Rifleman No 3 Co 2nd Bn
53	R'man	David Hughes	6 MGS	Not on 1st or 2nd Bn paylist
				With Baird's force, not entitled
54	R'man	Patrick Hussey	10 MGS	Rifleman No 4 Co 1st Bn
55	R'man	Charles Jones	7 MGS	Rifleman No 4 Co 1st Bn
56	R'man	George Kay	3 MGS	Rifleman No 5 Co 1st Bn
57	R'man	Thomas Kelly	10 MGS	Rifleman No 4 Co 2nd Bn
58	R'man	Thomas Laurison	9 MGS	Rifleman No 4 Co 1st Bn
59	R'man	David Law	11 MGS	Rifleman No 4 Co 1st Bn
60	Sgt	John Lowe	8 MGS	Rifleman No 3 Co 2nd Bn
61	R'man	John Maher	5 MGS	Rifleman No 1 Co 2nd Bn (Duty)
62	R'man	Arthur Malone	2 MGS	Rifleman No 4 Co 2nd Bn (Duty)
63	Sgt	Michael Malone	5 MGS	Rifleman No 4 Co 2nd Bn
				(On paylist as Nicholas Malone)
64	R'man	James Mason	3 MGS	1 Rifleman No 1 Co 2nd Bn MGS man
		2 on 2nd Bn paylist		2 Rifleman No 4 Co 2nd Bn (Duty)
65	R'man	John McKitchie	2 MGS	Corporal No 2 Co 2nd Bn
66	Sgt	Charles McPherson	6 MGS	Sergeant No 1 Co 2nd Bn
67	R'man	Alexander McRae	8/9 MGS	Rifleman No 5 Co 1st Bn
68	R'man	Daniel Milton	6 MGS	Rifleman No 2 Co 2nd Bn
69	Bug Maj	James Mitchell	8 MGS	Rifleman No 2 Co 2nd Bn
70	Sgt	John Moran	11 MGS	1 Rifleman No 2 Co 2nd Bn
				(Morran) MGS man
		3 on 2nd Bn paylist		2 Rifleman No 1 Co 2nd Bn
				(Duty) (Moren)
				3 Rifleman No 4 Co 2nd Bn
				(Duty) (Mooran)

-	R'man	Charles Murphy	6 MGS	Not on 1st or 2nd Bn paylist
				In 71st Foot at Vimeiro
71	R'man	Nicholas Myers	6 MGS	Rifleman No 2 Co 2nd Bn
72	R'man	James Neasmith	2 MGS	Rifleman No 5 Co 1st Bn
73	Sgt	John Norton	9 MGS	Not on 1st or 2nd Bn paylists, not entitled
74	R'man	John O'Brian	3 MGS	Rifleman No 2 Co 2nd Bn
75	R'man	Thomas Osborne	4 MGS	Rifleman No 4 Co 2nd Bn (To 1st Bn
				25th Aug but in 2nd Bn at Corunna)
76	R'man	John Palmer	12 MGS	Rifleman No 5 Co 1st Bn
77	R'man	William Phillips	1 MGS	Rifleman No 3 Co 2nd Bn
78	R'man	Joseph Piers	8 MGS	Rifleman No 3 Co 2nd Bn
79	R'man	William Prestage	5 MGS	Rifleman No 2 Co 2nd Bn
80	R'man	Peter Price	10 MGS	Rifleman No 2 Co 2nd Bn
81	R'man	Benjamin Pring	11 MGS	Not on 1st or 2nd Bn paylist
				With Baird's force, not entitled
82	Sgt	John Reakes	10 MGS	Corporal No 4 Co 1st Bn
83	R'man	William Rind	3 MGS	Rifleman No 5 Co 1st Bn
84	Sgt	Edward Rochford	2 MGS	Corporal No 4 Co 2nd Bn
85	R'man	Bartholomew Rogers	1 MGS	Rifleman No 3 Co 2 Bn (Rodgers)
86	Sgt	Charles Ross	7 MGS	Corporal No 5 Co 1st Bn
87	R'man	Richard Rouse	8 MGS	Rifleman No 4 Co 1st Bn
88	R'man	James Russell	4 MGS	Rifleman No 5 Co 1st Bn
89	R'man	William Shaughnessy	3 MGS	Not on 1st or 2nd Bn paylist
				With Baird's force, not entitled
90	R'man	James Shields	2 MGS	Rifleman No 4 Co 1st Bn
91	R'man	George Smith	3 MGS	Rifleman No 4 Co 2nd Bn (Duty)
92	R'man	John Smith	2 MGS	1 Rifleman No 2 Co 2nd Bn (Duty)
		3 on 2nd Bn paylist		2 Rifleman No 1 Co 2nd Bn MGS man
				3 Rifleman No 4 Co 2nd Bn
				Killed 21st August
93	R'man	Thomas Smith	11 MGS	Rifleman No 2 Co 2nd Bn (Duty)
94	R'man	John Smyth	12 MGS	1 Rifleman No 4 Co 1st Bn
		2 on 1st Bn paylist		(Smith) MGS man
				2 Rifleman No 5 Co 1st Bn (Smith)
95	R'man	James Steele	6 MGS	Rifleman No 4 Co 1st Bn
96	R'man	Daniel Stott	2 MGS	Rifleman No 2 Co 2nd Bn
97	R'man	Jonathan Stubbs	10 MGS	Rifleman No 1 Co 2nd Bn
98	R'man	George Sutherland	9 MGS	Rifleman No 5 Co 1st Bn
99	R'man	John Symington	11 MGS	Rifleman No 5 Co 1st Bn
100	R'man	John Tatt	6 MGS	Not on 1st or 2nd Bn paylist
				With Baird's force, not entitled
101	R'man	John Thomas	4 MGS	Rifleman No 4 Co 1st Bn
102	Sgt Maj	John Thompson	5 MGS	Sergeant No 4 Co 2nd Bn
103	R'man	Peter Ware	3 MGS	Rifleman No 2 Co 2nd Bn (Wear)
104	Bugler	Maurice Wildes	6 MGS	Bugler No 3 Co 2nd Bn (Wilds)
105	R'man	David Wylie	6 MGS	Rifleman No 1 Co 2nd Bn (Wiely)

Additional names of MGS men not awarded the clasp for Vimeiro

1	R'man	John Baldwin	4 MGS	Rifleman No 4 Co 1st Bn
2	R'man	Archibald Bell	1 MGS	Rifleman No 5 Co 1st Bn
3	Corp	George Law	12 MGS	Rifleman No 4 Co 1st Bn
4	Sgt	John McDonald	7 MGS	Sergeant No 5 Co 1st Bn
5	R'man	Hugh McLeod	6 MGS	Rifleman No 5 Co 1st Bn
6	R'man	James Rawledge	7 MGS	Rifleman No 4 Co 1st Bn
7	R'man	James Rolestone	4 MGS	Rifleman No 5 Co 1st Bn
8	R'man	William Wright	10 MGS	Rifleman No 4 Co 1st Bn
9	R'man	Richard Broom	4 MGS	Rifleman No 2 Co 2nd Bn
10	R'man	Robert Deacon	5 MGS	Rifleman No 2 Co 2nd Bn
11	R'man	John Gallagher	2 MGS	Rifleman No 3 Co 2nd Bn
12	R'man	William McKay	5 MGS	Rifleman No 4 Co 2nd Bn
13	R'man	Anthony Mullins	3 MGS	Rifleman No 2 Co 2nd Bn
14	R'man	James O'Neil	7 MGS	Rifleman No 2 Co 2nd Bn
15	R'man	William Rhodes	9 MGS	Rifleman No 2 Co 2nd Bn
16	Sgt	John Wheeler	1 MGS	Corporal No 4 Co 2nd Bn

MGS Clasp CORUNNA Battle of La Coruña 16th January 1809

Corunna is the third clasp to be awarded to the Rifles. Officially a total of 192 clasps were issued although this figure excludes Captain William Booth. On this occasion it should be a 1st Battalion clasp as they marched to Corunna and fought the battle there on the 16th January 1809. The 2nd Battalion, however, marched to Vigo and so they are not entitled to the clasp. From the list it can be seen that 51 2nd Battalion have been awarded the clasp. Strangely a further 29 2nd Battalion men who marched to Vigo did not receive the clasp. No doubt the 2nd Battalion men felt that they were entitled to the clasp as they had covered the retreat for nearly half the distance between Sahagún and Corunna.

We have 195 names for Corunna, 140 1st Battalion, 51 2nd Battalion men, A. E. Gregory ADC to Coote Manningham, William Rind now in the 91st Foot, Charles Murphy in 71st Foot and William Boyd not in the paylists. By subtracting Rind, Murphy and Boyd from this number we arrive at 192 clasps.

As a 1st Battalion clasp we have:

140   1st Battalion men ENTITLED and given the clasp
plus 10   1st Battalion men entitled but NOT given the clasp
total 150

As a 2nd Battalion clasp we have:

51   2nd Battalion men NOT entitled but given the clasp
plus 29   2nd Battalion men NOT entitled and not given the clasp
total 80

3rd Clasp Corunna 16th January 1809

Reference: 1st Bn WO 12 9522 25 December-20 February 1809
                 2nd Bn WO 12 9580 24 December-3 February 1809

1st Bn	Capt A. Norcott	No 1 Co
	Capt J. Ross	No 2 Co
	Capt P. O'Hare	No 3 Co
	Capt C. Beckwith	No 4 Co
	Capt Hon H. Pakenham	No 5 Co
	Capt S. Ramadge	No 6 Co
	Capt A. Cameron	No 7 Co
	Capt G. Miller	No 8 Co
	Capt G. Elder	No 9 Co
2nd Bn	Capt L. Gray	No 1 Co
	Capt J. Creagh	No 2 Co
	Capt J. Crampton	No 3 Co
	Lieut M. Pratt	No 5 Co
	Capt J. Leach	No 7 Co
	Capt T. Drake	No 8 Co
	Capt J. Jenkins	No 9 Co
	Capt D. Cadoux	No 10 Co

The following dates in parenthesis denote the disembarkation in England.

1	Capt	William Booth	4 MGS	Lieut 2nd Bn
2	Lieut	John Budgen	8 MGS	2nd Lieut No 4 Co 1st Bn [2nd Feb]
3	Capt	Alexander Cameron	5 MGS	Captain of No 7 Co 1st Bn [2nd Feb]
4	Lieut	A.E.Gregory	1 MGS	ADC to Maj Gen Coote Manningham
5	Lieut	William Hallen	6 MGS	Lieut No 8 Co 1st Bn [2nd Feb]
6	Sub	William Humbley	12 MGS	2nd Lieut No 6 Co 1st Bn [26th Jan]
7	Asst Surg	William Jones	12 MGS	Assist Surgeon to 1st Bn [28th Jan]
8	Capt	Smith Ramadge	2 MGS	Captain No 6 Co 1st Bn [27th Jan]
9	Lieut	Harry Smith	12 MGS	Lieut No 3 Co 1st Bn [19th Feb]
10	Lieut	Thomas Smith	10 MGS	2nd Lieut No 9 Co 1st Bn [2nd Feb]
11	R'man	Charles Allen	5 MGS	Rifleman No 9 Co 1st Bn [19th Feb]
12	Sgt	James Anderson	9 MGS	Rifleman No 7 Co 1st Bn [2nd Feb]
13	R'man	Joseph Arms	11 MGS	1 Rifleman No 10 Co 2nd Bn
		2 on 2nd Bn paylist		'Died 2nd Feb'
				2 Rifleman No 3 Co 2nd Bn, MGS man
14	Corp	Andrew Ash	8 MGS	Rifleman No 4 Co 1st Bn [20th Feb]
15	R'man	James Ashworth	7 MGS	Rifleman No 8 Co 1st Bn [19th Feb]
16	R'man	John Baldwin	4 MGS	Rifleman No 6 Co 1st Bn
				'Missing 16th Jan'
17	R'man	Jacob Barlow	5 MGS	Rifleman No 3 Co 1st Bn [17th Feb]

18	R'man	Archibald Bell	1 MGS	1 Rifleman No 4 Co 1st Bn [26th Jan]
		2 on 1st Bn paylist		'Sick at Plymouth'
				2 Rifleman No 7 Co 1st Bn
				'Missing 16th Jan' MGS man
19	R'man	John Bell	11 MGS	1 Rifleman No 4 Co 1st Bn [2nd Feb]
		2 on 1st Bn paylist		2 Rifleman No 7 Co 1st Bn [2nd Feb]
				MGS man
20	R'man	Henry Berry	11 MGS	Rifleman No 4 Co 1st Bn [24th Jan]
21	R'man	William Berry	11 MGS	Rifleman No 4 Co 1st Bn [2nd Feb]
22	R'man	Tuttle Betts	3 MGS	Rifleman No 3 Co 1st Bn [20th Feb]
				'To Corporal 13th Jan'
23	R'man	John Bidwell	8 MGS	Rifleman No 9 Co 1st Bn [28th Jan]
				'Sick at Plymouth' (Bedwell)
24	R'man	Thomas Bloomfield	3 MGS	Rifleman No 8 Co 2nd Bn
25	R'man	Edward Bolton	2 MGS	Rifleman No 1 Co 1st Bn [5th Feb]
26	R'man	Edward Bowen	7 MGS	Rifleman No 9 Co 1st Bn [19th Feb]
27	Sgt	Joseph Bowley	10 MGS	Corporal No 7 Co 2nd Bn
				'Sick General Hospital Portsmouth'
28	R'man	William Boyd	4 MGS	Not on 1st or 2nd Bn paylist, In 2nd Bn
				'Sick absent at Hillsea' Not entitled
29	R'man	Richard Broom	4 MGS	Rifleman No 2 Co 2nd Bn
30	R'man	James Bryce	9 MGS	Rifleman No 7 Co 1st Bn [19th Feb]
31	R'man	James Buckler	6 MGS	Rifleman No 1 Co 2nd Bn
32	R'man	William Buckley	7 MGS	Rifleman No 6 Co 1st Bn [19th Feb]
33	R'man	David Burnet	6 MGS	Rifleman No 4 Co 1st Bn [2nd Feb]
34	R'man	John Burr	8 MGS	Rifleman No 5 Co 1st Bn [19th Feb]
35	R'man	John Burrows	8 MGS	Rifleman No 8 Co 1st Bn [2nd Feb]
36	R'man	James Byford	5 MGS	Rifleman No 6 Co 1st Bn [19th Feb]
37	R'man	James Cairns	12 MGS	Corporal No 9 Co 2nd Bn
38	R'man	Neil Cameron	8 MGS	Rifleman No 5 Co 2nd Bn
				'Sick General Hospital Famasa'
39	R'man	Thomas Canning	6 MGS	Rifleman No 3 Co 1st Bn [17th Feb]
				'Sick at Plymouth'
40	Bugler	William Carden	11 MGS	Rifleman No 9 Co 1st Bn [2nd Feb]
				(Carder)
41	R'man	Andrew Carr	1 MGS	Rifleman No 8 Co 1st Bn 'Missing
				16th Jan'
42	Sgt	Andrew Carr	11 MGS	Rifleman No 3 Co 1st Bn [20th Feb]
43	R'man	Patrick Casey	3 MGS	Rifleman No 1 Co 2nd Bn
				'General Hospital Portsmouth 3rd Feb'
44	R'man	Robert Claxton	7 MGS	Rifleman No 9 Co 1st Bn [14th Feb]
45	R'man	James Coleman	12 MGS	Rifleman No 3 Co 1st Bn [19th Feb]
46	R'man	Patrick Connell	2 MGS	Rifleman No 6 Co 1st Bn [19th Feb]
47	R'man	Owen Connelly	12 MGS	Rifleman No 6 Co 1st Bn [2nd Feb]
48	R'man	Thomas Connelly	2 MGS	1 Rifleman No 3 Co 2nd Bn Louth,
				Dundalk, Tobacconist. MGS man

		2 on 2nd Bn paylist		2 Rifleman No 8 Co 2nd Bn
				Roscommon, Taylor 'Regimental Hosp'
49	R'man	John Connor	1 MGS	Rifleman No 1 Co 1st Bn [2nd Feb]
50	R'man	John Conway	7 MGS	Rifleman No 2 Co 1st Bn [11th Feb]
51	R'man	James Cooke	13 MGS	Corporal No 2 Co 1st Bn [2nd Feb]
				(Cook)
52	R'man	Edward Cope	7 MGS	Rifleman No 10 Co 2nd Bn
53	Sgt	Joseph Cowan	9 MGS	Rifleman No 6 Co 1st Bn [24th Jan]
				'Sick at Portsmouth'
54	R'man	John Cox	1 MGS	1 Rifleman No 1 Co 1st Bn [2nd Feb]
				Ayr, Cumnock, Weaver.
		3 on 1st Bn paylist		2 Rifleman No 2 Co 1st Bn
				'Died 19th Feb'
				3 Rifleman No 8 Co 1st Bn [2nd Feb]
				Hampshire, Kingston, Labourer.
		1 on 2nd Bn paylist		4 Rifleman No 9 Co 2nd Bn Whittlesey,
				Cambridge, Labourer. MGS man
55	R'man	Daniel Crozier	1 MGS	Rifleman No 8 Co 2nd Bn
				(Daniel Crousier)
56	R'man	Thomas Daly	3 MGS	Rifleman No 5 Co 1st Bn [3rd Feb]
				'Sick at Plymouth'
57	R'man	George Dempster	9 MGS	Rifleman No 6 Co 1st Bn [2nd Feb]
58	Sgt	Tobias Digby	9 MGS	Rifleman No 5 Co 1st Bn [19th Feb]
59	R'man	Terence Dillon	1 MGS	Rifleman No 8 Co 2nd Bn
60	R'man	John Druce	1 MGS	Rifleman No 8 Co 1st Bn [2nd Feb]
61	R'man	James Duncan	1 MGS	1 Rifleman No 1 Co 2nd Bn Shoemaker
		2 on 2nd Bn paylist		2 Rifleman No 2 Co 2nd Bn Stonecutter
				'Sick Bellem Portugal'
62	R'man	George Dunlop	3 MGS	Rifleman No 7 Co 1st Bn [2nd Feb]
63	Sgt	Alexander Eason	13 MGS	Corporal No 6 Co 1st Bn [2nd Feb]
64	R'man	Thomas Eastwood	6 MGS	Rifleman No 2 Co 1st Bn [1st Feb]
65	R'man	Henry Eldridge	6 MGS	Rifleman No 5 Co 1st Bn [20th Jan]
				'Sick at Plymouth'
66	R'man	Bartholomew Fairhurst	10 MGS	No 4 Co 1st Bn [2nd Feb]
67	R'man	John Farlin	5 MGS	Rifleman No 5 Co 1st Bn [27th Jan]
				(Farlane)
68	Sgt	James Farmer	9 MGS	Rifleman No 8 Co 1st Bn [2nd Feb]
69	Corp	John Fisher	1 MGS	Rifleman No 4 Co 1st Bn [17th Feb]
70	R'man	James Fitzgerald	5 MGS	Rifleman No 4 or 9 Co 1st Bn [2nd Feb]
				(as John Fitzgerald)
71	R'man	James Fraser	7 MGS	1 Rifleman No 6 Co 1st Bn
				'Command with Baggage' MGS man
		2 on 1st Bn paylist		2 Rifleman No 7 Co 1st Bn [24th Jan]
72	Sgt Maj	William Fry	9 MGS	Sergeant No 4 Co 1st Bn [2nd Feb]
73	R'man	Joseph Fuller	6 MGS	Rifleman No 7 Co 1st Bn
				'Missing 16th Jan'

74	R'man	John Gallagher	2 MGS	Rifleman No 7 Co 2nd Bn 'General Hosp Portsmouth 4th Feb' (Gallougher)
75	R'man	John Gardner	9 MGS	Rifleman No 5 Co 1st Bn [2nd Feb]
76	R'man	Robert Gilchrist	9 MGS	Rifleman No 7 Co 1st Bn [1st Feb] 'Sick at Plymouth'
77	Corp	William Gillis	6 MGS	Rifleman No 7 Co 1st Bn [2nd Feb] (Gilles)
78	R'man	Josiah Goddard	8 MGS	Rifleman No 4 Co 1st Bn [2nd Feb] (Joshua Goodard)
79	R'man	James Gough	1 MGS	Rifleman No 1 Co 1st Bn 'Sick at Plymouth 26th Jan' (Goff)
80	Sgt	William Graham	6 MGS	Rifleman No 1 Co 1st Bn [15th Feb]
81	R'man	William Green	4 MGS	Rifleman No 3 Co 1st Bn [2nd Feb] (Greene)
82	Sgt	William Griffin	1 MGS	Rifleman No 9 Co 1st Bn 'Missing 5th Jan' (William Giffen)
83	R'man	John Hall	1 MGS	Rifleman No 3 Co 1st Bn [2nd Feb]
84	Corp	William Hall	8 MGS	Rifleman No 1 Co 2nd Bn
85	Sgt	William Hall	11 MGS	Sergeant No 8 Co 1st Bn [18th Feb]
86	Sgt	William Hall	1 MGS	Rifleman No 2 Co 1st Bn [2nd Feb]
87	Bugler	Robert Hannah	1 MGS	Bugler No 8 Co 2nd Bn
88	R'man	Thomas Harding	11 MGS	Rifleman No 3 Co 1st Bn [20 th Feb]
89	R'man	Robert Harling	9 MGS	Rifleman No 2 Co 1st Bn [2nd Feb]
90	R'man	Benjamin Harris	3 MGS	Rifleman No 7 Co 2nd Bn
91	R'man	Israel Harvey	8 MGS	Rifleman No 2 Co 1st Bn [11th Feb]
92	Sgt	William Hinde	11 MGS	Corporal No 1 Co 1st Bn [24th Feb]
93	Sgt	Joseph Hindle	14 MGS	Rifleman No 7 Co 2nd Bn
94	R'man	Thomas Holmes	10 MGS	Rifleman No 4 Co 1st Bn [2nd Feb]
95	R'man	David Hughes	6 MGS	1 Rifleman No 1 Co 2 Bn Montgomery, Weaver. MGS man
		2 on 2nd Bn paylist		2 Rifleman No 8 Co 2nd Bn Pembroke, Labourer.
96	R'man	Patrick Hussey	10 MGS	Rifleman No 6 Co 1st Bn [31st Jan]
97	R'man	Charles Jones	7 MGS	Rifleman No 6 Co 1st Bn [24th Jan]
98	Corp	Richard Jones	2 MGS	Sergeant No 3 Co 1st Bn [20th Feb]
99	R'man	Thomas Jones	3 MGS	Rifleman No 1 Co 1st Bn [18th Feb] 'Sick at Plymouth'
100	R'man	Michael Joyce	9 MGS	Rifleman No 1 Co 1st Bn [18th Feb]
101	R'man	George Kay	3 MGS	Rifleman No 7 Co 1st Bn [1st Feb] 'Sick at Plymouth'
102	R'man	Samuel Keen	7 MGS	Rifleman No 3 Co 1st Bn [31st Jan] 'Sick at Portsmouth'
103	R'man	William Kellaugher	11 MGS	Rifleman No 1 Co 2nd Bn
104	R'man	Thomas Kelly	9 MGS	Rifleman No 5 Co 2nd Bn
105	R'man	Denis Kennedy	1 MGS	Rifleman No 8 Co 1st Bn [28th Jan]
106	R'man	Thomas Kinslow	3 MGS	Rifleman No 1 Co 2nd Bn (Kinchlow)

107	R'man	John Lamont	13 MGS	Rifleman No 5 Co 1st Bn [2nd Feb]
108	R'man	David Law	11 MGS	Rifleman No 6 Co 1st Bn [2nd Feb]
109	Corp	George Law	12 MGS	Rifleman No 6 Co 1st Bn [2nd Feb]
110	Corp	William Law	1 MGS	Rifleman No 1 Co 1st Bn [28th Jan]
				'Sick at Plymouth'
111	R'man	Samuel Long	4 MGS	Rifleman No 9 Co 2nd Bn
				(Only a John Long on 1st Bn)
112	R'man	Samuel Lovatt	9 MGS	Rifleman No 9 Co 1st Bn [11th Feb]
113	Sgt	Michael Malone	5 MGS	Corporal No 3 Co 2 Bn
114	R'man	John Martin	8 MGS	Rifleman No 4 Co 1st Bn [27th Jan]
				'Sick at Plymouth'
115	R'man	David McDonald	3 MGS	Corporal No 8 Co 2nd Bn
116	Sgt	John McDonald	7 MGS	Sergeant No 7 Co 1st Bn [2nd Feb]
117	R'man	John McDougall	1 MGS	Corporal No 8 Co 2nd Bn (McDougald)
118	R'man	Hugh McLeod	6 MGS	Rifleman No 7 Co 1st Bn
				'Prisoner of war, 16th Jan'
119	R'man	Alexander McRae	8/9 MGS	Rifleman No 7 Co 1st Bn [2nd Feb]
120	R'man	John Miller	1 MGS	Rifleman No 4 Co 1st Bn POW
				On MGS rolls as John should be Joseph.
121	R'man	Daniel Milton	6 MGS	Rifleman No 8 Co 2nd Bn
122	Corp	John Monk	3 MGS	Rifleman No 1 Co 2nd Bn
123	Sgt	John Moran	11 MGS	1 Rifleman No 2 Co 2nd Bn
				Mayo, Labourer. MGS man
				2 Rifleman No 3 Co 2nd Bn
		3 on 2nd Bn paylist		Westmeath, Labourer.
				3 Rifleman No 5 Co 2nd Bn
				Roscommon, Labourer.
124	R'man	Joseph Morgan	1 MGS	Rifleman No 5 Co 1st Bn [26th Jan]
				'Sick at Plymouth'
125	R'man	Anthony Mullins	3 MGS	Rifleman No 2 Co 2nd Bn
				'Sick Villafranca, Spain'
126	R'man	Charles Murphy	6 MGS	Not on 1st or 2nd Bn paylist in 71st Foot
127	Corp	John Murphy	12 MGS	1 Rifleman No 3 Co 1st Bn [2nd Feb]
		3 on 1st and 1 on 2nd Bn paylist		2 Rifleman No 5 Co 1st Bn [2nd Feb]
				MGS man
				3 Rifleman No 5 Co 1st Bn [2nd Feb]
				4 Rifleman No 2 Co 2nd Bn
128	Sgt	John Murphy	7 MGS	1 Rifleman No 3 Co 1st Bn [2nd Feb]
		3 on 1st and 1 on 2nd Bn paylist		2 Rifleman No 5 Co 1st Bn [2nd Feb]
				3 Rifleman No 5 No 1st Bn [2nd Feb]
				MGS man
				4 Rifleman No 2 Co 2nd Bn
129	R'man	John Murray	1 MGS	1 Rifleman No 1 Co 2nd Bn
				Galway, Labourer.
		2 on 2nd Bn paylist		2 Rifleman No 7 Co 2nd Bn
				Dublin, Butcher.

130	R'man	Nicholas Myers	6 MGS	Rifleman No 2 Co 2nd Bn
131	Sgt	John Naughton	4 MGS	Rifleman No 4 Co 1st Bn [19th Feb] 'Sick at Plymouth'
132	R'man	James Neasmith	2 MGS	Rifleman No 7 Co 1st Bn [2nd Feb.9] (Nesmith)
133	QMS	William Nicholson	1 MGS	Bugler No 1 Co 1st Bn [2nd Feb]
134	R'man	William Niven	9 MGS	Rifleman No 1 Co 1st Bn [2nd Feb] (Nevan)
135	Sgt	Robert Nunn	7 MGS	Rifleman No 9 Co 1st Bn [2nd Feb]
136	R'man	James O'Neil	7 MGS	1 Rifleman No 2 Co 2nd Bn Wexford, Miller. MGS man.
		2 on 2nd Bn paylist		2 Rifleman No 1 Co 2nd Bn Wicklow, Labourer. 'Missing 2nd January, Spain'
137	R'man	Thomas Osborne	4 MGS	Rifleman No 7 Co 2nd Bn 'On furlough 17th Feb to 17th April'
138	R'man	John Palmer	12 MGS	Rifleman No 7 Co 1st Bn [2nd Feb]
139	R'man	William Parkinson	5 MGS	Rifleman No 9 Co 1st Bn [11th Feb]
140	R'man	Oliver Peacock	9 MGS	Rifleman No 1 Co 1st Bn [2nd Feb]
141	R'man	William Pegler	1 MGS	Bugler No 1 Co 2nd Bn
142	R'man	James Petty	12 MGS	Rifleman No 9 Co 1st Bn [2nd Feb] (Joseph Pettie)
143	R'man	William Prestage	5 MGS	Rifleman No 2 Co 2nd Bn
144	R'man	Benjamin Pring	11 MGS	Rifleman No 8 Co 1st Bn [28th Jan] 'Sick at Plymouth'
145	R'man	James Rawledge	7 MGS	Rifleman No 6 Co 1st Bn [17th Feb] (Rowledge)
146	R'man	James Reaburn	1 MGS	Rifleman No 9 Co 1st Bn [24th Feb] 'Sick at Plymouth'
147	Sgt	John Reakes	10 MGS	Corporal No 6 Co 1st Bn [2nd Feb]
148	R'man	William Rhodes	9 MGS	Rifleman No 2 Co 2nd Bn
149	R'man	William Rind	3 MGS	Not on 1st or 2nd Bn paylist Volunteer with 92nd Foot
150	R'man	James Roleston	4 MGS	Rifleman No 7 Co 1st Bn [1st Feb] 'Sick at Plymouth' (Roulstone)
151	Sgt	Charles Ross	7 MGS	Corporal No 7 Co 1st Bn [2nd Feb]
152	R'man	Richard Rouse	8 MGS	Rifleman No 6 Co 1st Bn [2nd Feb] 'Sick at Plymouth'
153	R'man	James Russell	4 MGS	Rifleman No 7 Co 1st Bn [2nd Feb]
154	R'man	William Russell	6 MGS	Rifleman No 10 Co 2nd Bn
155	Sgt	John Rutledge	8 MGS	Rifleman No 9 Co 2nd Bn
156	R'man	George Saunders	1 MGS	Rifleman No 9 Co 1st Bn [24th Jan] 'Sick at Plymouth'
157	R'man	John Scorgie	1 MGS	Rifleman No 1 Co 1st Bn [2nd Feb]
158	R'man	William Sharp	8 MGS	Rifleman No 9 Co 1st Bn [3rd Feb] 'Sick at Plymouth'
159	R'man	William Shaughnessy	3 MGS	Rifleman No 10 Co 2nd Bn

160	R'man	James Shields	2 MGS	Rifleman No 6 Co 1st Bn
				'Missing 16th January'
161	R'man	Joseph Sipson	1 MGS	Rifleman No 1 Co 1st Bn
				'Missing 3rd January'
162	R'man	Benjamin Slaughter	2 MGS	Rifleman No 5 Co 1st Bn [26th Jan]
				'Sick at Plymouth'
163	Corp	Michael Smart	10 MGS	Rifleman No 4 Co 1st Bn [19th Feb]
164	R'man	Thomas Smart	3 MGS	Rifleman No 4 Co 1st Bn [31st Jan]
165	R'man	William Smith	6 MGS	1. Rifleman No 2 Co 2nd Bn
		2 on 2nd Bn paylist		2 Rifleman No 8 Co 2nd Bn, MGS man
166	R'man	William Smithers	5 MGS	Rifleman No 8 Co 2nd Bn
				'On command on board ship'
167	R'man	John Smyth	12 MGS	1 Rifleman No 6 Co 1st Bn [26th Jan]
				(John Smith) MGS man
		2 on 1st Bn paylist		2 Rifleman No 7 Co 1st Bn
				'Prisoner of war 16th Jan' (John Smith)
168	R'man	William Sperry	9 MGS	Rifleman No 4 Co 1st Bn [19th Feb]
169	R'man	James Steele	6 MGS	Rifleman No 6 Co 1st Bn [2nd Feb]
170	R'man	James Stevens	11 MGS	Bugler No 4 Co 1st Bn [2nd Feb]
171	R'man	Jonathan Stubbs	10 MGS	Rifleman No 3 Co 2nd Bn
172	QMS	David Sutherland	1 MGS	Sergeant No 4 Co 1st Bn [24th Jan]
173	R'man	Edward Sutherland	8 MGS	Rifleman No 1 Co 2nd Bn
174	R'man	George Sutherland	9 MGS	Rifleman No 7 Co 1st Bn [2nd Feb]
175	R'man	John Symington	11 MGS	Rifleman No 7 Co 1st Bn [2nd Feb]
176	R'man	Edward Taggen	10 MGS	Rifleman No 5 Co 1st Bn [27th Feb]
				'Sick at Plymouth' (Teagan)
177	R'man	John Tatt	6 MGS	Corporal No 4 Co 1st Bn [2nd Feb]
178	R'man	William Taylor	1 MGS	1 Rifleman No 1 Co 1st Bn [20th Feb]
				2 Rifleman No 6 Co 1st Bn [17th Feb]
		2 on 1st and 2 on 2nd Bn paylist		3 Bugler No 10 Co 2nd Bn MGS man
				4 Rifleman No 5 Co 2nd Bn
179	Corp	Joseph Teacey	2 MGS	Rifleman No 4 Co 1st Bn [2nd Feb]
				(Tracey)
180	R'man	John Thomas	4 MGS	1 Rifleman No 3 Co 1st Bn [19th Feb]
				2 Rifleman No 5 Co 1st Bn
		3 on 1st Bn paylist		'Missing 16th January'
				3 Rifleman No 6 Co 1st Bn [2nd Feb]
				MGS man
181	R'man	Thomas Thomas	1 MGS	Rifleman No 3 Co 1st Bn [19th Feb]
182	Corp	James Tomlinson	8 MGS	Rifleman No 10 Co 2nd Bn
183	Corp	Edward Tonkinson	9 MGS	Corporal No 8 Co 1st Bn [2nd Feb]
184	R'man	Charles Underhill	1 MGS	Rifleman No 9 Co 2nd Bn
185	R'man	William Usher	8 MGS	Rifleman No 5 Co 1st Bn [19th Feb]
186	R'man	James Warberton	8 MGS	Rifleman No 5 Co 1st Bn [19th Feb]
187	R'man	John Ward	10 MGS	Rifleman No 4 Co 1st Bn [27th Jan]
188	R'man	Peter Ware	3 MGS	Rifleman No 2 Co 2nd Bn (Weir)

189	R'man	Thomas Webb	2 MGS	Rifleman No 9 Co 1st Bn [19th Feb]
190	R'man	William Wheatley	1 MGS	Rifleman No 4 Co 1st Bn [9th Feb] 'Sick at Plymouth'
191	R'man	William Wilkinson	2 MGS	Rifleman No 1 Co 1st Bn [28th Jan] 'Sick at Plymouth'
192	R'man	Joseph Witham	7 MGS	Rifleman No 2 Co 1st Bn [11th Feb]
193	R'man	Henry Wright	4 MGS	Rifleman No 8 Co 1st Bn [2nd Feb]
194	R'man	William Wright	10 MGS	Rifleman No 6 Co 1st Bn [2nd Feb]
195	R'man	David Wylie	6 MGS	Rifleman No 3 Co 2nd Bn (Weeley)

Additional names of MGS men not awarded the clasp for Corunna

1	Sub	Charles Eaton	7 MGS	Lieutenant in 1st Bn
2	R'man	William Allinson	2 MGS	Rifleman No 5 Co 1st Bn [19th Feb]
3	QMS	Isaac Bagshaw	2 MGS	Rifleman No 8 Co 1st Bn
4	R'man	John Burns	6 MGS	Rifleman No 9 Co 1st Bn
5	Sgt	Thomas Chambers	3 MGS	Rifleman No 4 Co 1st Bn
6	Sgt	Hugh Fraser	1 MGS	Sergeant No 6 Co 1st Bn [2nd Feb] (William Fraser)
7	R'man	John Grant	1 MGS	Rifleman No 8 Co 1st Bn
8	R'man	Thomas Laurison	9 MGS	Rifleman No 6 Co 1st Bn [19th Feb] (Lorrison)
9	Sgt	Alexander McLeod	9 MGS	Rifleman No 9 Co 1st Bn
10	R'man	Thomas Robinson	8 MGS	Rifleman No 1 Co 1st Bn

2nd Bn MGS men on paylist not awarded the clasp for Corunna

R'man	James Bennett No 9 Co	R'man	David Beattie No 5 Co
R'man	Stephen Bedford No 2 Co	R'man	Joseph Bell No 7 Co
Sgt	Patrick Brown No 2 Co	R'man	James Cavanagh No 3 Co
R'man	Michael Connor No 9 Co	R'man	James Crooks No 5 Co
R'man	Edward Donaghoe No 7 Co	R'man	Michael Fagan No 9 Co
R'man	Edward Farmer No 7 Co	Sgt	Hugh Fraser No 3 Co
Corp	William Grant No 7 Co	R'man	Christopher Grimes No 2 Co
Sgt	Robert Hayes No 3 Co	R'man	John Lowe No 7 Co
R'man	Charles McPherson No 3 Co	R'man	John Mahar No 3 Co
R'man	James Mason No 3 or 5 Co	R'man	James Mitchell No 2 Co
R'man	John O'Brian No 2 Co	R'man	Joseph Piers No 7 Co
R'man	Peter Price No 2 Co	R'man	Edward Rochford No 5 Co
R'man	Bartholomew Rogers No 7 Co	R'man	John Smith No 2 or 3 Co
R'man	George Smith No 5 Co	R'man	Daniel Stott No 2 Co
Bugler	Maurice Wildes No 7 Co		

2nd Battalion 95th Landing at Mondego Bay
1st August 1808

Death of Lieutenant Ralph Bunbury, 2nd Battalion 95th at Obidos
15th August 1808

1st Battalion Rifles Retreat to Corunna

1st Battalion 95th at the Battle of Corunna
16th January 1809

Military General Service Medal

Official Entitlement
and
Actual Entitlement

		ROL	VIM	COR	TAL	BUS	BAR	F'O	C'R	BAD	SAL	VIT	PYR	S/S	NVL	NIV	ORT	TOU
CAPTAINS:																		
ALEXANDER CAMERON	5 MGS	•	VIM	COR								VIT						
		•	VIM	COR														
WILLIAM COX	7 MGS	ROL	VIM	•								VIT	PYR		NVL	NIV	ORT	
		ROL	VIM	•														
JOHN KENT RECEIVED ROL & VIM, 50TH REGT	5 MGS	ROL	VIM	•					C'R	BAD	SAL							
		ROL	VIM	•														
JONATHAN LEACH	12 MGS	ROL	VIM	•		BUS		F'O	C'R	BAD	SAL	VIT	PYR		NVL	NIV		TOU
		ROL	VIM	•														
HON HERCULES PAKENHAM	2 MGS	ROL	VIM	•														
		ROL	VIM	•														
SMITH RAMADGE	2 MGS	•	VIM	COR														
		•	VIM	COR														
LIEUTENANTS:																		
WILLIAM BOOTH IN 95TH FOR COR ONLY	4 MGS	•		COR								VIT					ORT	TOU
		•		COR														
JOHN R BUDGEN	8 MGS	•		COR			BAR					VIT	PYR		NVL	NIV	ORT	TOU
		•		COR														
A. E. GREGORY	1 MGS	•		COR														
		•		COR														
WILLIAM HALLEN	6 MGS	•		COR								VIT	PYR		NVL		ORT	TOU
		•		COR														
DUDLEY HILL	4 MGS	ROL	VIM	•		BUS			C'R									
		ROL	VIM	•														
JOHN MOLLOY	8 MGS	ROL	VIM	•							SAL	VIT	PYR		NVL	NIV		TOU
		ROL	VIM	•														
HARRY SMITH	12 MGS	•	VIM	COR		BUS		F'O	C'R	BAD	SAL	VIT	PYR		NVL	NIV	ORT	TOU
		•		COR														
THOMAS SMITH	10 MGS	•	VIM	COR					C'R	BAD	SAL	VIT	PYR		NVL	NIV	ORT	TOU
		•		COR														

KEY: OFFICIAL   ACTUAL   • NOT ENTITLED

	MGS	ROL	VIM	COR	TAL	BUS	BAR	F'O	C'R	BAD	SAL	VIT	PYR	S/S	NVL	NIV	ORT	TOU
SUBALTERNS:																		
JOHN COX	10 MGS	ROL	VIM	•		BUS		F'O	C'R			VIT	PYR		NVL	NIV	ORT	
CHARLES EATON	7 MGS			•			BAR					VIT	PYR	s/s	NVL		ORT	TOU
WILLIAM HUMBLEY	12 MGS	ROL	VIM	COR		BUS	BAR				SAL	VIT	PYR		NVL	NIV	ORT	TOU
ASSISTANT SURGEON:																		
WILLIAM JONES	12 MGS	ROL	VIM	COR		BUS		F'O	C'R	BAD	SAL	VIT	PYR		NVL	NIV	ORT	TOU
SERGEANT MAJORS:																		
WILLIAM FRY	9 MGS			COR					C'R	BAD	SAL		PYR		NVL	NIV	ORT	TOU
JOHN THOMPSON	5 MGS	ROL	VIM	•		BUS						VIT						TOU
QUARTERMASTER SERGEANTS:																		
ISAAC BAGSHAW	2 MGS			•		BUS		F'O										
WILLIAM NICHOLSON	1 MGS			COR														
DAVID SUTHERLAND	1 MGS			COR														
BUGLE MAJOR:																		
JAMES MITCHELL	8 MGS	ROL	VIM	•								VIT	PYR		NVL	NIV	ORT	TOU

	MGS	ROL	VIM	COR	TAL	BUS	BAR	F'O	C'R	BAD	SAL	VIT	PYR	S/S	NVL	NIV	ORT	TOU
COLOUR SERGEANT:																		
JAMES DAVISON	7 MGS	•	VIM	•		BUS			C'R	BAD			PYR	s/s				TOU
SERGEANTS:																		
JAMES ANDERSON	9 MGS	•	VIM	COR				F'O	C'R	BAD	SAL	VIT	PYR					
STEPHEN BEDFORD	6 MGS	•	VIM	•				F'O	C'R	BAD	SAL			s/s				TOU
JOSEPH BOWLEY	10 MGS	ROL	VIM	COR		BUS			C'R	BAD	SAL	VIT	PYR					TOU
PATRICK BROWN	3 MGS	ROL	VIM	•	TAL	BUS												
ANDREW CARR	1 MGS	•	•	COR														
ANDREW CARR	11 MGS	•	VIM	COR				F'O	C'R	BAD	SAL	VIT			NVL	NIV	ORT	TOU
THOMAS CHAMBERS	3 MGS	•	•	•					C'R	BAD	SAL							
JOSEPH COWEN	9 MGS	•	VIM	COR		BUS			C'R	BAD	SAL	VIT					ORT	TOU
TOBIAS DIGBY	9 MGS	•	•	COR		BUS		F'O	C'R	BAD	SAL	VIT					ORT	TOU
ALEXANDER EASON	13 MGS	•	VIM	•		BUS		F'O	C'R	BAD	SAL	VIT	PYR		NVL	NIV	ORT	TOU
JAMES FARMER	9 MGS	•	VIM	COR		BUS			C'R	BAD	SAL	VIT	PYR					TOU
HUGH FRASER	1 MGS	•	VIM	COR														

Name	MGS	ROL	VIM	COR	TAL	BUS	BAR	F'O	C'R	BAD	SAL	VIT	PYR	S/S	NVL	NIV	ORT	TOU
WILLIAM GRAHAM	6 MGS	•	•	COR		BUS		F'O	C'R	BAD	SAL							
WILLIAM GRANT	1 MGS	•	VIM	•														
WILLIAM GRIFFIN	1 MGS	ROL	•	•														
WILLIAM HALL	11 MGS	•	•	COR		BUS		F'O	C'R	BAD	SAL	VIT	PYR	S/S			ORT	TOU
WILLIAM HALL	1 MGS	•	•	COR														
ROBERT HAYES	2 MGS	ROL	VIM	•														
WILLIAM HINDE	11 MGS	•	•	COR				F'O	C'R	BAD	SAL	VIT	PYR		NVL	NIV	ORT	TOU
JOSEPH HINDLE	14 MGS	ROL	VIM	COR		BUS	BAR		C'R	BAD	SAL	VIT		S/S	NVL	NIV	ORT	TOU
JOHN LOWE	8 MGS	ROL	VIM	•				F'O	C'R	BAD	SAL	VIT	PYR					
MICHAEL MALONE	5 MGS	ROL	VIM	COR								VIT	PYR					
JOHN MCDONALD	7 MGS	ROL	•	COR				F'O				VIT			NVL	NIV	ORT	TOU
ALEXANDER MCLEOD	9 MGS	•	•	COR		BUS		F'O	C'R	BAD			PYR	S/S	NVL	NIV	ORT	TOU
CHARLES MCPHERSON	6 MGS	ROL	•	COR		BUS		F'O	C'R	BAD	SAL	VIT						
JOHN MORAN	11 MGS	•	VIM	COR		BUS		F'O	C'R	BAD	SAL	VIT	PYR			NIV		TOU
JOHN MURPHY	7 MGS	ROL	•	COR		BUS		F'O	C'R	BAD	SAL	VIT						

Name		ROL	VIM	COR	TAL	BUS	BAR	F'O	C'R	BAD	SAL	VIT	PYR	S/S	NVL	NIV	ORT	TOU
JOHN NAUGHTON	4 MGS	•	•	COR					C'R	BAD	SAL							
JOHN NORTON	9 MGS	•	VIM	•	TAL			F'O	C'R	BAD	SAL	VIT	PYR					TOU
ROBERT NUNN	7 MGS	•	•	COR			BAR				SAL	VIT	PYR				ORT	TOU
JOHN REAKES	10 MGS	•	VIM	COR		BUS		F'O			SAL	VIT			NVL	NIV	ORT	TOU
EDWARD ROCHFORD	2 MGS	ROL	VIM	•														
CHARLES ROSS	7 MGS	ROL	VIM	COR		BUS			C'R	BAD	SAL							
JOHN RUTLEDGE	8 MGS	•	VIM	•			BAR					VIT	PYR		NVL	NIV	ORT	TOU
JOHN TATT	6 MGS	ROL	VIM	COR				F'O	C'R	BAD								
JOHN WHEELER	1 MGS	ROL	VIM	•														
CORPORALS:																		
ANDREW ASH	8 MGS	•	•	COR				F'O		BAD	SAL	VIT	PYR			NIV		TOU
DANIEL CROZIER	1 MGS	•	•	COR														
JOHN FISHER	1 MGS	•	•	COR														
WILLIAM GILLIS	6 MGS	•	VIM	COR								VIT	PYR				ORT	TOU
WILLIAM HALL	8 MGS	•	•	COR		BUS			C'R	BAD	SAL	VIT	PYR					TOU

		ROL	VIM	COR	TAL	BUS	BAR	F'O	C'R	BAD	SAL	VIT	PYR	S/S	NVL	NIV	ORT	TOU
RICHARD JONES	2 MGS	•	•	COR		BUS												
GEORGE LAW	12 MGS	•	•	COR		BUS		F'O	C'R	BAD	SAL	VIT	PYR	S/S	NVL	NIV	ORT	TOU
WILLIAM LAW	1 MGS		VIM	COR														
JOHN MONK	3 MGS	•	•	COR •			BAR					VIT						
JOHN MURPHY	12 MGS	•	•	COR		BUS		F'O	C'R	BAD	SAL	VIT	PYR		NVL	NIV	ORT	TOU
MICHAEL SMART	10 MGS	•	•	COR		BUS		F'O	C'R	BAD	SAL	VIT	PYR		NVL	NIV		
JAMES TOMLINSON	8 MGS	•	•	COR •								VIT	PYR	S/S	NVL	NIV	ORT	TOU
EDWARD TONKINSON	9 MGS	•	•	COR		BUS		F'O	C'R	BAD	SAL	VIT	PYR					TOU
JOSEPH TRACEY	2 MGS	•	•	COR		BUS												
BUGLERS:																		
WILLIAM CARDEN	11 MGS	•	•	COR		BUS		F'O	C'R	BAD	SAL	VIT	PYR	S/S			ORT	TOU
ROBERT HANNAH	1 MGS	•	•	COR														
JAMES STEVENS	11 MGS	•	•	COR		BUS		F'O	C'R		SAL	VIT	PYR		NVL	NIV	ORT	TOU
MAURICE WILDES	6 MGS	ROL	VIM	COR •								VIT	PYR				ORT	TOU

RIFLEMEN:

Name	ROL	VIM	COR	TAL	BUS	BAR	F'O	C'R	BAD	SAL	VIT	PYR	S/S	NVL	NIV	ORT	TOU
CHARLES ALLEN — 5 MGS	•	•	COR		BUS			C'R	BAD	SAL							
WILLIAM ALLINSON — 2 MGS	•	•	COR	TAL	BUS												
JOSEPH ARMS — 11 MGS	•	VIM	COR		BUS		F'O	C'R	BAD	SAL	VIT			NVL		ORT	TOU
JAMES ASHWORTH — 7 MGS	ROL	VIM	COR		BUS		F'O	C'R	BAD	SAL	VIT						
JOHN BALDWIN — 4 MGS	•	•	COR			BAR											
JACOB BARLOW — 5 MGS	•	VIM	COR				F'O	C'R	BAD		VIT	PYR					TOU
JAMES BARRETT — 2 MGS	•	VIM	COR	TAL													
DAVID BEATTIE — 9 MGS	ROL	VIM	COR				F'O	C'R	BAD	SAL	VIT	PYR					TOU
ARCHIBALD BELL — 1 MGS	ROL	VIM	COR														
JOHN BELL — 11 MGS	•	VIM	COR		BUS		F'O	C'R	BAD	SAL	VIT	PYR				ORT	TOU
JOSEPH BELL — 8 MGS	ROL	VIM	COR						BAD		VIT	PYR				ORT	TOU
HENRY BERRY — 11 MGS	•	•	COR		BUS		F'O	C'R	BAD	SAL	VIT	PYR		NVL	NIV		TOU
WILLIAM BERRY — 11 MGS	•	•	COR		BUS		F'O	C'R	BAD	SAL	VIT	PYR		NVL	NIV		TOU
TUTTLE BETTS — 3 MGS	•	VIM	COR														TOU

Name		ROL	VIM	COR	TAL	BUS	BAR	F'O	C'R	BAD	SAL	VIT	PYR	S/S	NVL	NIV	ORT	TOU
JOHN BIDWELL	8 MGS	•	•	COR		BUS			C'R	BAD	SAL	VIT	PYR					TOU
THOMAS BLOOMFIELD	3 MGS	•	•	COR					C'R	BAD								
EDWARD BOLTON	2 MGS	•	•	COR		BUS				BAD								
EDWARD BOWEN	7 MGS	•	•	COR				F'O	C'R	BAD	SAL	VIT						TOU
WILLIAM BOYD	4 MGS	•	•	COR				F'O		BAD	SAL							
RICHARD BROOM	4 MGS	ROL	•	COR					C'R	BAD	SAL							
JAMES BRYCE	9 MGS	•	VIM	COR				F'O	C'R	BAD	SAL	VIT	PYR		NVL			
JAMES BUCKLER	6 MGS	•	VIM	COR					C'R		SAL	VIT		S/S				
WILLIAM BUCKLEY	7 MGS	•	VIM	COR		BUS		F'O	C'R	BAD	SAL							
DAVID BURNET	6 MGS	•	•	COR				F'O	C'R	BAD		VIT	PYR					
JOHN BURNS	6 MGS	•	•	COR		BUS				BAD	SAL	VIT	PYR					TOU
JOHN BURR	8 MGS	•	•	COR		BUS		F'O	C'R	BAD	SAL		PYR					TOU
JOHN BURROWS	8 MGS	•	•	COR		BUS		F'O		BAD	SAL	VIT			NVL	NIV		
JAMES BYFORD	5 MGS	•	VIM	COR			BAR		C'R	BAD								
JAMES CAIRNS	12 MGS	•	VIM	COR				F'O	C'R	BAD	SAL	VIT	PYR		NVL	NIV	ORT	TOU

Name	MGS	ROL	VIM	COR	TAL	BUS	BAR	F'O	C'R	BAD	SAL	VIT	PYR	S/S	NVL	NIV	ORT	TOU
NEIL CAMERON	8 MGS	•	VIM	COR								VIT	PYR		NVL	NIV	ORT	TOU
THOMAS CANNING	6 MGS	ROL	VIM	•		BUS		F'O		BAD	SAL							
PATRICK CASEY	3 MGS	•	•	COR						BAD	SAL							
JAMES CAVANAGH	2 MGS	ROL	VIM	•														
ROBERT CLAXTON	7 MGS	•	•	COR		BUS				BAD	SAL	VIT					ORT	TOU
JAMES COLEMAN	12 MGS	•	VIM	COR		BUS		F'O	C'R	BAD	SAL	VIT	PYR		NVL		ORT	TOU
PATRICK CONNELL	2 MGS	•	VIM	COR														
OWEN CONNELLY	12 MGS	•	•	COR		BUS		F'O	C'R	BAD	SAL	VIT	PYR		NVL	NIV	ORT	TOU
THOMAS CONNELLY	2 MGS	•	•	COR			BAR											
JOHN CONNOR	1 MGS	•	•	COR														
MICHAEL CONNOR	1 MGS	ROL	•	•														
JOHN CONWAY	7 MGS	•	•	COR				F'O		BAD	SAL	VIT	PYR					TOU
JAMES COOKE	13 MGS	•	VIM	COR		BUS		F'O	C'R	BAD	SAL	VIT	PYR		NVL	NIV	ORT	TOU
EDWARD COPE	7 MGS	•	•	COR		BUS	BAR					VIT	PYR				ORT	TOU
JOHN COX	1 MGS	•	•	COR														

Name	MGS	ROL	VIM	COR	TAL	BUS	BAR	F'O	C'R	BAD	SAL	VIT	PYR	S/S	NVL	NIV	ORT	TOU
JAMES CROOKS	6 MGS	•	VIM	•			BAR		C'R			VIT	PYR					TOU
THOMAS DALY	3 MGS	•	•	COR		BUS				BAD								
ROBERT DEACON	5 MGS	•	•	•						BAD	SAL	VIT	PYR					TOU
GEORGE DEMPSTER	9 MGS	•	VIM	COR		BUS		F'O	C'R	BAD	SAL	VIT	PYR					
TERRANCE DILLON	1 MGS	•	•	COR														
EDWARD DONAGHOE	3 MGS	•	VIM	•													ORT	TOU
JOHN DRUCE	1 MGS	•	•	COR														
JAMES DUNCAN	1 MGS	•	•	COR														
GEORGE DUNLOP	3 MGS	•	VIM	COR		BUS												
THOMAS EASTWOOD	6 MGS	•	•	COR		BUS		F'O	C'R		SAL	VIT						
HENRY ELDRIDGE	6 MGS	•	•	•			BAR			BAD	SAL	VIT	PYR					TOU
MICHAEL FAGAN	3 MGS	•	VIM	•								VIT	PYR					
BARTHOLOMEW FAIRHURST	10 MGS	•	•	COR		BUS			C'R	BAD	SAL	VIT	PYR		NVL	NIV	ORT	
JOHN FARLIN	5 MGS	•	•	COR								VIT	PYR				ORT	TOU
EDWARD FARMER	5 MGS	•	VIM	•					C'R	BAD	SAL	VIT						

203

	MGS	ROL	VIM	COR	TAL	BUS	BAR	F'O	C'R	BAD	SAL	VIT	PYR	S/S	NVL	NIV	ORT	TOU
JAMES FITZGERALD	5 MGS	•		COR		BUS		F'O	C'R	BAD								
JAMES FRASER	7 MGS	•	VIM	COR							SAL	VIT	PYR				ORT	TOU
JOSEPH FULLER	6 MGS	•	VIM	COR		BUS		F'O		BAD								
JOHN GALLAGHER	2 MGS	•	VIM	COR					C'R									
JOHN GARDNER	9 MGS	•		•					C'R	BAD	SAL	VIT	PYR	S/S			ORT	TOU
ROBERT GILCHRIST	9 MGS	•	VIM	COR		BUS		F'O	C'R	BAD	SAL	VIT						TOU
JOSIAH GODDARD	8 MGS	•		COR		BUS			C'R	BAD	SAL	VIT	PYR					TOU
JAMES GOUGH	1 MGS	•		COR														
JOHN GRANT	1 MGS	•		COR						BAD								
WILLIAM GREEN	4 MGS	•		COR		BUS			C'R	BAD								
CHRISTOPHER GRIMES	8 MGS	•	VIM	•		BUS		F'O	C'R	BAD	SAL		PYR					TOU
JOHN HALL	1 MGS	ROL	VIM	COR														
THOMAS HARDING	11 MGS	•		COR		BUS		F'O	C'R	BAD	SAL	VIT	PYR		NVL	NIV	ORT	
ROBERT HARLING	9 MGS	ROL	VIM	COR							SAL	VIT			NVL	NIV	ORT	TOU
BENJAMIN HARRIS	3 MGS	ROL	VIM	•														

		ROL	VIM	COR	TAL	BUS	BAR	F'O	C'R	BAD	SAL	VIT	PYR	S/S	NVL	NIV	ORT	TOU
ISRAEL HARVEY	8 MGS	•	VIM	COR				F'O	C'R	BAD	SAL	VIT	PYR					
THOMAS HOLMES	10 MGS	•	•	COR		BUS		F'O	C'R	BAD	SAL	VIT	PYR				ORT	TOU
DAVID HUGHES	6 MGS	•	•	COR			BAR					VIT	PYR					TOU
PATRICK HUSSEY	10 MGS	•	VIM	•		BUS		F'O	C'R	BAD	SAL	VIT	PYR					TOU
CHARLES JONES	7 MGS	•	VIM	COR					C'R	BAD		VIT	PYR					TOU
THOMAS JONES	3 MGS	•	VIM	COR													ORT	TOU
MICHAEL JOYCE	9 MGS	•	•	COR		BUS		F'O	C'R	BAD	SAL	VIT	PYR					TOU
GEORGE KAY	3 MGS	•	VIM	COR		BUS												
SAMUEL KEEN	7 MGS	•	•	COR				F'O	C'R	BAD	SAL	VIT					ORT	TOU
WILLIAM KELLAUGHER	11 MGS	•	•	COR	TAL	BUS		F'O	C'R	BAD	SAL	VIT	PYR	S/S				TOU
THOMAS KELLY	10 MGS	ROL	VIM	COR				F'O	C'R	BAD	SAL	VIT						TOU
REC. EGYPT OR MAIDA, 58TH REGT		ROL	VIM	•														
DENIS KENNEDY	1 MGS	•	•	COR														
THOMAS KINSLOW	3 MGS	•	•	COR			BAR		C'R									
JOHN LAMONT	13 MGS	•	•	COR		BUS		F'O	C'R	BAD	SAL	VIT	PYR	S/S	NVL	NIV	ORT	TOU
THOMAS LAURISON	9 MGS	•	VIM	COR		BUS		F'O	C'R	BAD	SAL	VIT	PYR					TOU

Name	MGS	ROL	VIM	COR	TAL	BUS	BAR	F'O	C'R	BAD	SAL	VIT	PYR	S/S	NVL	NIV	ORT	TOU
DAVID LAW	11 MGS	•	VIM	COR					C'R	BAD	SAL	VIT	PYR		NVL	NIV	ORT	TOU
SAMUEL LONG	4 MGS	•	VIM	•					C'R	BAD	SAL							
SAMUEL LOVATT	9 MGS	•	•	COR		BUS			C'R	BAD	SAL	VIT	PYR				ORT	TOU
JOHN MAHER	5 MGS	ROL	VIM	•		BUS		F'O	C'R	BAD								
ARTHUR MALONE RECEIVED EGYPT, 44TH REGT	2 MGS	ROL	VIM	•														
JOHN MARTIN	8 MGS	ROL	VIM	COR		BUS		F'O	C'R	BAD	SAL	VIT	PYR					
JAMES MASON	3 MGS	ROL	VIM	•			BAR					VIT						
DAVID MCDONALD	3 MGS	ROL	•	COR													ORT	TOU
JOHN MCDOUGAL	1 MGS	•	•	COR														
WILLIAM MCKAY	5 MGS	ROL	VIM	•					C'R	BAD	SAL	VIT						TOU
JOHN MCKITCHIE	2 MGS	ROL	VIM	•														
HUGH MCLEOD	6 MGS	ROL	VIM	COR					C'R	BAD	SAL	VIT						TOU
ALEXANDER MCRAE	9 MGS	•	VIM	COR		BUS		F'O	C'R	BAD	SAL	VIT						TOU
JOHN MILLER SHOULD BE JOSEPH MILLER	1 MGS	•	VIM	COR														
DANIEL MILTON	6 MGS	•	VIM	COR							SAL	VIT					ORT	TOU

		ROL	VIM	COR	TAL	BUS	BAR	F'O	C'R	BAD	SAL	VIT	PYR	S/S	NVL	NIV	ORT	TOU
JOSEPH MORGAN	I MGS	•		COR														
ANTHONY MULLINS	3 MGS	•		COR														
		ROL	VIM	COR					C'R			VIT						
CHARLES MURPHY	6 MGS	•	VIM	COR								VIT	PYR				ORT	TOU
RECEIVED VIM & COR, 71ST REGT			VIM	COR														
JOHN MURRAY	I MGS	•		COR														
NICHOLAS MYERS	6 MGS	ROL	VIM	COR		BUS											ORT	TOU
		ROL	VIM															
JAMES NEASMITH	2 MGS		VIM	COR														
			VIM	COR														
WILLIAM NIVEN	9 MGS	•		COR		BUS		F'O		BAD	SAL	VIT	PYR					TOU
				COR														
JOHN O'BRIAN	3 MGS	ROL	VIM	COR			BAR											
		ROL	VIM															
JAMES O'NEIL	7 MGS	•		COR					C'R	BAD	SAL	VIT	PYR					TOU
		ROL	VIM	COR														
THOMAS OSBORN	4 MGS	ROL	VIM	COR								VIT						
		ROL	VIM	COR														
JOHN PALMER	12 MGS	•	VIM	COR		BUS		F'O	C'R	BAD	SAL	VIT			NVL	NIV	ORT	TOU
			VIM	COR														
WILLIAM PARKINSON	5 MGS	•		COR		BUS		F'O	C'R	BAD								
		•		COR														
OLIVER PEACOCK	9 MGS	•		COR		BUS		F'O	C'R	BAD		VIT	PYR			NIV		TOU
		•		COR														
WILLIAM PEGLER	I MGS	•		COR														
		•		COR														
JAMES PETTY	12 MGS	•		COR		BUS		F'O	C'R	BAD	SAL	VIT	PYR		NVL	NIV	ORT	TOU
		•		COR														

	ROL	VIM	COR	TAL	BUS	BAR	F'O	C'R	BAD	SAL	VIT	PYR	S/S	NVL	NIV	ORT	TOU
WILLIAM PHILLIPS — 1 MGS	•	VIM	•														
JOSEPH PIERS — 8 MGS	ROL	VIM	•			BAR		C'R		SAL	VIT					ORT	TOU
WILLIAM PRESTAGE — 5 MGS	ROL	VIM	COR			BAR					VIT						
PETER PRICE — 10 MGS	ROL	VIM	•					C'R	BAD	SAL	VIT			NVL	NIV	ORT	TOU
BENJAMIN PRING — 11 MGS	ROL	VIM	COR		BUS		F'O	C'R	BAD	SAL	VIT	PYR					TOU
JAMES RAWLEDGE — 7 MGS	•	VIM	COR		BUS		F'O	C'R	BAD		VIT						TOU
JAMES RÉABURN — 1 MGS	•	VIM	COR														
WILLIAM RHODES — 9 MGS	•	VIM	COR		BUS		F'O	C'R	BAD	SAL	VIT					ORT	TOU
WILLIAM RIND — 3 MGS (RECEIVED COR, 92ND REGT)	ROL	VIM	COR														
THOMAS ROBINSON — 8 MGS	•	VIM	•		BUS		F'O	C'R	BAD	SAL	VIT		S/S				TOU
BARTHOLOMEW ROGERS — 1 MGS	ROL	VIM	•														
JAMES ROLESTONE — 4 MGS	•	VIM	COR						BAD	SAL							TOU
RICHARD ROUSE — 8 MGS	•	VIM	COR		BUS			C'R	BAD	SAL	VIT						TOU
JAMES RUSSELL — 4 MGS	•	VIM	COR		BUS		F'O										
WILLIAM RUSSELL — 6 MGS	•	VIM	•							SAL	VIT	PYR				ORT	TOU

Name	MGS	ROL	VIM	COR	TAL	BUS	BAR	F'O	C'R	BAD	SAL	VIT	PYR	S/S	NVL	NIV	ORT	TOU
GEORGE SAUNDERS	1 MGS	•	•	COR														
JOHN SCORGIE	1 MGS	•	•	COR														
WILLIAM SHARP	8 MGS	•	•	COR		BUS			C'R		SAL	VIT				NIV	ORT	TOU
WILLIAM SHAUGHNESSY	3 MGS	•	VIM	COR													ORT	
JAMES SHIELDS	2 MGS	•	VIM	COR														
JOSEPH SIPSON	1 MGS	•	•	COR														
BENJAMIN SLAUGHTER	2 MGS	•	•	COR						BAD								
THOMAS SMART	3 MGS	•	•	COR		BUS												TOU
GEORGE SMITH	3 MGS	ROL	VIM	•			BAR											
JOHN SMITH	2 MGS	ROL	VIM	•														
THOMAS SMITH	11 MGS	ROL	VIM	•		BUS			C'R	BAD	SAL	VIT		S/S	NVL		ORT	TOU
WILLIAM SMITH	6 MGS	•	•	COR			BAR		C'R		SAL	VIT						TOU
WILLIAM SMITHERS	5 MGS	•	•	COR								VIT	PYR				ORT	TOU
JOHN SMYTH	12 MGS	•	VIM	COR		BUS		F'O	C'R	BAD	SAL	VIT			NVL	NIV	ORT	TOU
WILLIAM SPERRY	9 MGS	•	VIM	COR		BUS		F'O				VIT			NVL	NIV	ORT	TOU

	ROL	VIM	COR	TAL	BUS	BAR	F'O	C'R	BAD	SAL	VIT	PYR	S/S	NVL	NIV	ORT	TOU
JAMES STEELE — 6 MGS	•	VIM	COR		BUS						VIT	PYR					TOU
DANIEL STOTT — 2 MGS	ROL	VIM	•														
JONATHAN STUBBS — 10 MGS	ROL	VIM	COR		BUS	BAR		C'R	BAD	SAL	VIT	PYR					
EDWARD SUTHERLAND — 8 MGS	•	•	COR		BUS			C'R	BAD	SAL	VIT	PYR					TOU
GEORGE SUTHERLAND — 9 MGS	•	VIM	COR	TAL	BUS		F'O	C'R	BAD	SAL	VIT						
JOHN SYMINGTON — 11 MGS	•	VIM	COR / TAL		BUS		F'O	C'R	BAD	SAL	VIT	PYR		NVL	NIV	ORT	
MGS LISTS VARY: EITHER COR / TAL	•	VIM	COR														
EDWARD TAGGEN — 10 MGS	•	•	•		BUS		F'O	C'R	BAD	SAL	VIT	PYR				ORT	TOU
WILLIAM TAYLOR — 1 MGS	•	•	COR														
JOHN THOMAS — 4 MGS	•	VIM	COR					C'R	BAD								
THOMAS THOMAS — 1 MGS	•	•	COR														
CHARLES UNDERHILL — 1 MGS	•	•	•														
WILLIAM USHER — 8 MGS	•	•	COR		BUS			C'R	BAD	SAL	VIT	PYR					TOU
JAMES WARBURTON — 8 MGS	•	•	COR				F'O	C'R	BAD		VIT			NVL	NIV		TOU
JOHN WARD — 10 MGS	•	•	COR		BUS		F'O	C'R	BAD	SAL	VIT	PYR				ORT	TOU
PETER WARE — 3 MGS	ROL	VIM	COR														

Name		ROL	VIM	COR	TAL	BUS	BAR	F'O	C'R	BAD	SAL	VIT	PYR	S/S	NVL	NIV	ORT	TOU
THOMAS WEBB	2 MGS		•	COR								VIT						
WILLIAM WHEATLEY	1 MGS		•	COR														
WILLIAM WILKINSON	2 MGS		•	COR								VIT						
JOSEPH WITHAM	7 MGS		•	COR					C'R	BAD	SAL	VIT	PYR					TOU
HENRY WRIGHT	4 MGS		•	COR			BAR		C'R	BAD								
WILLIAM WRIGHT	10 MGS		•	COR		BUS		F'O	C'R	BAD	SAL	VIT	PYR				ORT	TOU
DAVID WYLIE	6 MGS		VIM	COR								VIT	PYR	S/S				
		ROL	VIM	COR	•													
		ROL	VIM	•														

	ROL	VIM	COR
	41	107	195
LESS:	1*	2**	2***
	40	105	193

TOTAL CLASPS TO THE 95TH: 338

	ROL	VIM	COR
	63	109	153
LESS:	1*	2**	2***
	62	107	151

TRUE TOTAL OF CLASPS: 320

(* LESS KENT AT ROLIÇA ** LESS KENT AND MURPHY AT VIMEIRO *** LESS MURPHY AND RIND AT CORUNNA.)

Battle Orders

Battle of Roliça 17th August 1808

British Commander-in-Chief, General Sir Arthur Wellesley

1st brigade	General Rowland Hill	1/5th, 1/9th, 1/38th
2nd brigade	General Ronald Ferguson	1/36th, 1/40th, 1/71st and 6 guns
3rd brigade	Brigadier General Miles Nightingall	1/29th, 1/82nd and 6 guns
4th brigade	Brigadier General Barnard Bowes	1/6th, 1/32nd and 6 guns
5th brigade	Brigadier General Catlin Craufurd	1/50th, 1/91st
6th brigade	Brigadier General Henry Fane	1/45th, 5/60th, 2/95th and cavalry
Cavalry	Charles Taylor	20th Light Dragoons
Artillery	William Robe	18 guns (10 x 6 lbs, 5 x 9 lbs and 3 x 5.5 Howitzers)
Portuguese	Colonel Nicholas Trant	6th Caçadores, 12th, 21st and 24th Line, Portuguese dragoons

1/45th and 1/50th changed places before Vimeiro, Napier puts 1/45th, 1/50th and 1/91st all in Catlin Craufurd's brigade.

Total strength between 15,136 to 16,765 men and 18 guns.

French Officer Commanding, General de Division Henri Delaborde

General de Brigade	Thomières	3/2nd Leger	(Thomières, from Peniche)
		3/4th Leger	(Thomières, from Peniche)
		4th Swiss	(Thomières, from Peniche)
	(Brennier)	1/70th Ligne	(Brennier, from Lisbon)
		2/70th Ligne	(Brennier, from Lisbon)
Cavalry		26th Chasseurs à Cheval (from Lisbon)	
Artillery		8 guns	

Total strength between 4,350 to 4,400 men and 8 guns.

Battle of Vimeiro 21st August 1808

British Commander-in-Chief, General Sir Arthur Wellesley

1st brigade	Major General Rowland Hill	1/5th, 1/9th, 1/38th and 4 guns
2nd brigade	Major General Ronald Ferguson	1/36th, 1/40th, 1/71st
3rd brigade	Brigadier General Miles Nightingall	1/29th, 1/82nd
4th brigade	Brigadier General Barnard Bowes	1/6th, 1/32nd
5th brigade	Brigadier General Catlin Craufurd	1/45th, 1/91st
6th brigade	Brigadier General Henry Fane	1/50th, 5/60th, 2/95th and 6 guns
7th brigade	Brigadier General Robert Anstruther	2/9th, 2/43rd, 2/52nd, 2/97th and 6 guns
8th brigade	Brigadier General Worth Acland	2nd Queen's, 1/20th, 1/95th and 2 guns
Cavalry	Charles Taylor	20th Light Dragoons
Artillery	William Robe	18 guns, 3 batteries
Portuguese	Colonel Nicholas Trant	6th Caçadores, 12th, 21st and 24th Line, Portuguese dragoons

Total strength between 18,778 to 20,846 men and 18 guns.

French Commander-in-Chief, General de Division, Jean Andoche Junot

	General de Division Delaborde	
	General de Brigade Brennier	3/2nd, 3/4th Leger, 1/70th, 2/70th Ligne
	General de Brigade Thomières	1/86th, 2/86th Ligne, 4th Swiss
	General de Division Loison	
	General de Brigade Solignac	3/12th, 3/15th Leger, 3/58th Ligne
	General de Brigade Charlot	3/32nd, 3/82nd Ligne
Reserve	General Kellermann	1st Regt, 2nd Regt Grenadiers
Reserve	General de Brigade St. Clair	3rd Regt, 4th Regt Grenadiers
Cavalry	General de Division Margaron	26th Chasseurs à Cheval 3rd, 4th, 5th Dragoons, 1 Squadron volunteer cavalry
Artillery		4 batteries, 3 Foot, 1 Horse, 26 guns

Total strength between 12,694 to 13,910 men and 26 guns.

Battle of Corunna 16th January 1809

British Commander-in-Chief Sir John Moore

1st Division	Sir David Baird	
Warde's brigade		1st and 3rd Bns 1st Foot Guards
Bentinck's brigade		1/4th, 1/42nd, 1/50th
Manningham's brigade		3/1st, 1/26th, 2/81st
		Bean artillery

2nd Division	Sir John Hope	
Leith's brigade		51st, 2/59th, 2/76th
Hill's brigade		2nd Foot, 1/5th, 2/14th, 1/32nd
Craufurd's brigade		1/36th, 1/71st, 1/92nd
		Drummond artillery

3rd Division	Lieutenant General McKenzie Fraser	
Beresford's brigade		1/6th, 1/9th, 2/23rd, 2/43rd
Fane's brigade		1/38th, 1/79th, 1/82nd
		Wilmot artillery

Reserve Division	Major General Edward Paget	
Anstruther's brigade		20th Foot, 1/52nd, 1/95th
Disney's brigade		1/28th, 1/91st
1st Flank brigade	Colonel Robert Craufurd	1/43rd, 2/52nd, 2/95th
2nd Flank brigade	Brig Gen Charles Alten	1st and 2nd Light Bns King's German Legion
Cavalry	Lord Henry Paget	7th, 10th, 15th Hussars, 18th Light Dragoons, 3rd Light Dragoons King's German Legion, Dowman and Evelin horse artillery

Total strength 29,357 men.

Battle of Corunna 16th January 1809

French Commander-in-Chief, Marshall Nicolas Jean de Dieu Soult

1st Division	Merle	

Brigades of Reynaud, Sarrut, Thomières	2nd Léger 3 Bns
	4th Léger 4 Bns
	15th Ligne 3 Bns
	36th Ligne 3 Bns
Cavalry　　　La Houssaye	
Brigades of Marisy, Caulaincourt	17th, 18th, 19th, 27th Dragoons

2nd Division　　　Mermet	

Brigades of Gaulois, Jardon, Lefebvre	31st Léger 4 Bns
	47th Ligne 4 Bns
	122nd Ligne 4 Bns
	2nd Swiss Regt 2 Bns
	3rd Swiss Regt 1Bn
Cavalry　　　Franceschi	
Brigades of Debelle, Girardin	1st Hussars, 8th Dragoons, 22nd
	Chasseurs, Hanoverian Chasseurs

3rd Division　　　Delaborde	

Brigades of Foy, Arnaud	17th Léger 3 Bns
	70th Ligne 4 Bns
	86th Ligne 3 Bns
	4th Swiss Regt 1 Bn
Cavalry　　　Lorge	
Brigades of Vialannes, Fournier	13th, 15th 22nd 25th Dragoons
Artillery	36 canon

Total strength 24,200 men. (Exact figure not known.)

Notes on the Officers of the 1st Battalion 95th

Reference: WO 12 9522 25th June -24th September 1808
WO 12 9522 25th December-20th February 1809

Company No	Captain	Lieutenant	2nd Lieutenant
Worth Acland's force			
No 4 Co	Smith Ramadge	J. Duncan	W. Humbley
No 6 Co at Corunna		J. G. M'Cullock	
No 5 Co	Alexander Cameron	J. Logan	W. Clarke
No 7 Co at Corunna		D. McLeod	

Land in Portugal 19th/20th August - present at Vimeiro and Corunna.

Company No	Captain	Lieutenant	2nd Lieutenant
Sir John Moore's force			
No 1 Co	Amos Norcott (Maj)	J. Ward	J.C. Hope
No 1 Co at Corunna	Hon J. Stewart		
No 2 Co	John Ross	J. B. Hart	
No 2 Co at Corunna		Hon D. Arbuthnot	
		W. Pemberton	
No 3 Co	Peter O'Hare	H. G. Smith	C. Eaton
No 3 Co at Corunna		W. Eeles	
		J. Travers	

Land in Portugal 29th August - present only at Corunna.

Company No	Captain	Lieutenant	2nd Lieutenant
Sir David Baird's force			
No 4 Co	Charles Beckwith	J. Uniacke	J Budgen
		P. Reilly	
No 5 Co	Hon H. Pakenham*	J. McDermid	
	(*From 2nd Bn 95th)	J. Layton	
No 8 Co	George Miller	W. Hallen	
		S. Patrickson	
No 9 Co	George Elder	H. Lee	T. Smith
		A. Coane	

Land in Spain 26th October present at Corunna. Lt Charles Noble killed at Corunna 16th January 1809. Captain Latham Bennett died of wounds 11th January 1809.

Company numbers at Vimeiro and Corunna 1st Battalion 95th

	Vimeiro	Corunna	
Moore	{ No 1 Co Norcott	No 1 Co Norcott	
	No 2 Co Ross	No 2 Co Ross	
	No 3 Co O'Hare	No 3 Co O'Hare	
		No 4 Co Beckwith	} Baird
Acland	{ No 4 Co Ramadge	No 5 Co Pakenham	
	No 5 Co Cameron	No 6 Co Ramadge	
		No 7 Co Cameron	
		No 8 Co Miller	} Baird
		No 9 Co Elder	

Notes on the Officers of the 2nd Battalion 95th

Reference: WO 12 9579 25th June-24th September 1808
WO 12 9580 24th December-February 1809

Company No	Captain	Lieutenant	2nd Lieutenant
Sir Arthur Wellesley's force			
No 1 Co	Jeremiah Crampton	R. Bunbury	T. Cochrane
No 3 Co at Corunna		W. Cox	J. Cox
No 2 Co	Jasper Creagh	T. Diggle	H. Manners
No 2 Co at Corunna		D. Hill	J. Molloy
No 3 Co	Jonathan Leach	W. Johnston	
No 7 Co at Corunna		B. Keappock	
No 4 Co	Hon H. Pakenham	T. McNamara	
No 5 Co at Corunna		M. Pratt	
		W. Scott	
Sir David Baird's force			
No 10 Co at Corunna	Daniel Cadoux	W. D. Bedell	C. Ogilvie
		W. Booth	R. Stevenson
No 8 Co at Corunna	Thomas Drake	W. Clark	A. Stewart
		F. Edmondstone	
No 1 Co at Corunna	Loftus Gray	V. Grantham	
		J. Mercer	
No 9 Co at Corunna	John Jenkins	J. Perceval	
		N. Travers	

The lieutenants and 2nd lieutenants are listed alphabetically as it is not known which officers belonged to which company.

Company numbers at Roliça/Vimeiro and Vigo/Corunna 2nd Battalion 95th

	Roliça/Vimeiro	Vigo/Corunna
Wellesley	No 1 Co Crampton	No 1 Co Gray
	No 2 Co Creagh	No 2 Co Creagh
	No 3 Co Leach	No 3 Co Crampton
	No 4 Co Pakenham	No 5 Co Pratt
		No 7 Co Leach
Baird	Gray	No 8 Co Drake
	Cadoux	No 9 Co Jenkins
	Jenkins	No 10 Co Cadoux
	Drake	

The Companies of the 95th Rifles for
Roliça, Vimeiro and Corunna

Sir Arthur Wellesley's force

Major Robert Travers with four companies 2nd Battalion 95th Rifles; Captains, Jeremiah Crampton, Jasper Creagh, Jonathan Leach and the Honourable Hercules R. Pakenham left Dover on the 8th June 1808 and sailed for Cork in Ireland. Then onto Portugal, arriving at Figueira da Foz in Mondego Bay on the 1st August 1808, where they were placed in General Henry Fane's brigade.

Obidos 15th August 1808. Lieutenant Ralph Bunbury, Riflemen William Dodd, James Martin and Mathew Maxwell killed. Hercules Pakenham and 6 Riflemen wounded amongst them Thomas Wall.

Roliça 17th August 1808. 17 Riflemen killed. Captain Jasper Creagh, Lieutenants Dudley Hill, Thomas Cochrane and 30 Riflemen wounded.

Vimeiro 21st August 1808. 3 sergeants, 34 Riflemen killed. Lieutenants Henry Manners, Dudley Hill, William Johnston, William Cox, 3 sergeants and 40 Riflemen wounded.

Brigadier General Worth Acland's force

Colonel Thomas Sidney Beckwith with two companies 1st Battalion 95th Rifles; Captains Alexander Cameron and Smith Ramadge embark from Harwich early July 1808 and arrive at Porto Novo at the mouth of the river Maceira on the 19th August 1808. Disembarking on the 20th August. In General Acland's brigade.

Vimeiro 21st August 1808. Casualties for Vimeiro not known.

Sir John Moore's force

Major Dugald Gilmour with three companies of the 1st Battalion 95th Rifles; Major Amos Norcott, Captains John Ross and Peter O'Hare march to Harwich on the 8th April 1808 and set sail for Sweden on the 9th April but but never land. Set sail for Portugal and arrived at Maceira near Peniche disembarking between the 25th and the 28th August 1808.

After Vimeiro both the two companies 1st Battalion and the four companies 2nd Battalion are placed in General Fane's brigade.

These companies are joined by the three companies 1st Battalion at Torres Vedras at the end of August 1808.

Then in early September the five companies 1st Battalion move across the Tagus to Villa Viciosa and the four companies 2nd Battalion move to near Lisbon.

Sir David Baird's force

Major Norman M'Leod with four companies 1st Battalion;
Captains Charles Beckwith, George Elder, George Miller, Latham Bennett
Colonel Hamlet Wade with four companies 2nd Battalion;
Captains Daniel Cadoux, Thomas Drake, Loftus Gray and John Jenkins
land at Corunna on the 26th October 1808.

The strength of the Rifles on the 20th December 1808 at Trianon Convent: Four companies under Major M'Leod and five companies under Colonel Beckwith making a total of nine companies 1st Battalion; four companies under Major Travers and four companies under Colonel Wade, making a total of eight companies 2nd Battalion.

The 1st Battalion were attached to the Reserve under Sir Edward Paget and the 2nd Battalion were under Brigadier General Robert Craufurd. The 2nd Battalion covered the retreat to Vigo where they embarked on the 21st January 1809 and returned to Portsmouth on the 1st February 1809.
1st Battalion acted as rearguard under Sir John Moore.

Cacabelos 3rd January 1809. It was mainly Amos Norcott and Peter O'Hare's companies with some 15th Hussars which held back the advancing French army. Rifleman Thomas Plunket shot dead General Colbert.

2 sergeants and 17 Riflemen killed, Captain Bennett who later died of wounds on the 11th January and Lieutenant Eeles were wounded. 4 sergeants and 44 Riflemen were taken prisoner of war.

Corunna 16th January 1809. Lieutenant Charles Noble, 1 sergeant and 10 Riflemen killed. 8 Riflemen taken prisoner. The 1st Battalion set from Corunna on the 17th January 1809 and arrived home at Spithead on the 24th January to the 28th February 1809.

Bibliography

A Boy in the Peninsular War. Robert Blakeney, edited by Julian Sturgis.
Murray, London 1899.
A Dorset Rifleman. Eileeen Hathaway, Dorset 1996.
A Journal of a Cavalry Officer, the Corunna Campaign 1808-1809. Captain Gordon.
A History of the Peninsular War Vol. 1. Charles Oman MA, Oxford 1902.
Britannia Sickens. Michael Glover, Leo Cooper.
British Battles on Land and Sea. Vol 1 & 2. Field-Marshal Sir Evelyn Wood VC,
Cassell & Co 1915.
Corunna. Christopher Hibbert, Gloucestershire 1996.
Digest of service 1st Battalion Rifle Brigade from its formation in 1800.
Battalion Press 1885.
Fragments of Voyages and Travel. Captain Basil Hall R. N., 1831.
History of the Rifle Brigade. Sir William Cope, London 1877.
History of the War in the Peninsula Vol 1. Sir William F. P. Napier KCB,
Frederick Warne & Co Ltd, London.
History & Campaigns of The Rifle Brigade 1800-1813. Willoughby Verner, London.
History of the 52nd Regiment 1755-1816. M. S. Moorsom.
History of the XX Regiment.
Letters from the Peninsula. Sir William Warre, London 1909.
Life in Wellington's Army. Anthony Brett James, London 1972.
Mark Isambard Brunel. Paul Clements, Longmans 1970.
MGS Medal Roll 1793-1814. Lieut Colonel F. S. S. Brind.
MGS Medal Roll.1793-1814. Lieut Colonel Kingsley Foster.
MGS Roll. edited by A. L. T. Mullen, 1990.
MGS Medal Roll 1793-1814. 'A. J. N.'
Napoleon and Europe. L. C. F. Turner, Frederick Warne & Co Ltd 1973.
Recollections of Rifleman Harris. Benjamin Harris, edited by Henry Curling, 1848.
Rifle Green at Waterloo. George Caldwell & Robert Cooper,
Bugle Horn Publications 1990.
Rough Sketches of the Life of an Old Soldier. Lieut Colonel Jonathan Leach CB,
London 1831.
The Spanish Ulcer. David Gates, London 1986.
Twenty-Five Years in the Rifle Brigade. William Surtees, Muller 1973.
Wellington in the Peninsula 1808-1814. Jac Weller, London 1962.
Wellington Studies Vol 1. C. M. Woolgar, Hartley Institute,
University of Southampton 1996.
Where Duty Calls Me. William Green, edited by John & Dorothea Teague, 1975.

Index

1ST FOOT: 75, 91, 156

1ST FOOT GUARDS: 75, 91, 123, 139, 156, 159

1ST LIGHT INFANTRY KGL: 70, 77, 91

2ND LIGHT INFANTRY KGL: 70, 77, 91

2ND QUEEN'S: 43, *66*, 77, 91, 156

3RD BUFFS: 78

3RD LIGHT DRAGOONS KGL: 77, 91, 105, 107, 108, 153, 167

4TH: 77, 91, 156, 159

5TH: 16, 24, 34, 35, 37, *39*, 40, 43, *66*, 77, 91, 156

6TH: 16, 24, *39*, 43, 59, *66*, 78, 91

7TH HUSSARS: 75, 88, 91, 153, 167

8TH DRAGOONS: 92

9TH: 16, 24, 34, 35, 37, *39*, 40, 43, 49, 54, *66*, 77-79, 91

10TH HUSSARS: 75, 84, 88, 91, 92, 100, 105, 108, 128, 153

11TH: 75, 91, 156, 161

15TH HUSSARS: 75, 88, 90-92, 105, 112, 122, 123, 125, *126*-128, 130, 153

18TH HUSSARS: 78, 153

18TH LIGHT DRAGOONS: 89, 91, 100, 107, 108

20TH: 16, 43, *66*, 77, 91, *126*, 128, 132, 147, 156, 159, 164

20TH LIGHT DRAGOONS: 16, 25, 26, 30, 43, 45, 49, 56, 57, 78

23RD: 75, 91, 164

25TH: 156

26TH: 75, 91

27TH: 78

28TH: 77, 91, *126*, 128-131, 136, 146-150, 156, 159, 164

29TH: 16, 24, 33, 34, 37, *39*, 40, 43, 59, *66*, 78

32ND: 16, 24, *39*, 43, 59, *66*, 77, 78, 91, 156

35TH: 156

36TH: 16, 24, *39*, 43, 59, *66*, 77, 91

38TH: 16, 24, *39*, 43, *66*, 77, 91

40TH: 16, 24, *39*, 41, 43, 44, 47, 59, *66*, 78

42ND: 77, 91, 156, 159, 160, 161

43RD: 16, 42, 43, 49, 54, 55, 59, 61, *66*, 75, 77, 86, 91, 101, 103, 106, 144

45TH: 16, 19, 24, *39*, 43, *66*, 74, 78

50TH: 16, 24, *39*, 42, 43, 45, 49-55, 59, 61, *66*, 78, 91, 156, 159

51ST: 91, 132, 156

52ND: 16, 42, 43, 49, 54, *66*, 69, 70, 77, 91, 105, *126*, 128, 129, 131-133, 147, 156, 157, 159, 164

53RD: 75

59TH: 75, 91, 156

5/60TH: 16, 19, 23, 24, 26, 28-31, 34-*39*, 40, 42, 43, 45, 49-51, 53, 54, 61, 64, *66*, 70, 77, 80, 86, 95

71ST: 16, 24, *39*, 43, 59, *66*, 77, 91, 156

76TH: 75, 91, 156

79TH: 74, 77, 79, 91

81ST: 75, 91, 156

82ND: 16, 24, 37, *39*, 40, 43, 59, *66*, 78, 91

91ST: 16, 24, *39*, 43, *66*, 77, 91, 99, 128, 129, 145, 147, 156, 159, 164

92ND: 77, 91, 156

1/95TH RIFLES: 16, 17, 42, 43, 55, 64, *66*, 69-*71*, 75, 77, 79, 80, 82, 91, 94, *97*, 114, 122, 125-127, 133, 148, 156, *162*-164, 167

2/95TH RIFLES: 16, 19, 20, 22-24, 26-29, 31, 34-*39*, 40, 42, 43, 45, 49, 50, 52-54, 56, 62, 64-*66*, 69, *71*-78, 82, 83, 85, 91, 93-95, *97*, 99, 100, 103, 108, 110, *162*, 167

97TH QUEEN'S GERMANS: 16, 43, 49, 54, *66*, 78

ROYAL HORSE ARTILLERY: 128, 131

ABRANTES: 29, 77, *97*

ACLAND, WORTH: 16, 17, 25, 41-44, 47, 48, 55, 60, *66*, 69, *71*

ALAEJOS: 89, 90

ALAMTEJO: 70

ALCANTARA: 77, 80

ALCOBAÇA: 25, 26, *71*

ALCOENTRE: 29

ALMARAZ: 78

ALMEIDA: 75, 76, 78, 79, *97*

ALTEN, CHARLES: 77, 90, 91, 111, 114, 141, 214

ANSTRUTHER, ROBERT: 16, 17, 25, 41-44, 47, 49-51, 53-55, 60, *66*, *71*, 76, 77, 91

ARAGON: 90

AREVALO: 78

ARMS, JOSEPH: 120

ASTORGA: 81-85, 88, 96, *97*, 98, 104, 108-110, 112, 113, 142, *162*

AZAMBUGEIRA: 36, *39*

BADAJOZ: 25, 78, 90, 173

BAIRD, SIR DAVID: 75, 77, 78, 81, 83-86, 88, 90, 91, 93-97, 99, 100, 121, 135, 139, 142, 156, 158-160

BALL, RICHARD: 151

BATALHA: 25, 26, *71*

BAXTER, THOMAS: 143, 163

BECKWITH, CHARLES: 75

BECKWITH, SIR THOMAS SIDNEY: 17, 42, 94, 128-130, 143, 154, 159

BELEM: 70

BELVEDER, CONDE DE: 84

BEMBIBRE: 114, 121, 125, *126*

BENAVENTE: 88, 90, 95, *97*, 104-111, 136, 141, *162*

BENNETT, LATHAM: 75, 133, 134, 137, 151

BENTINCK, LORD WILLIAM: 77, 80, 85, 91, 153, 156, 159, *165*

BERESFORD, WILLIAM CARR: 77-80, 91, 166, 167

BERTHIER, LOUIS: 90

BETANZOS: 82, 84, *97*, 143-148, *162*
BILBAO: 84
BLAKE, JOACHIM: 81, 84
BLAKENEY, ROBERT: 136, 137, 146, 150, 151
BONNET, GENERAL: 114
BOWES, BARNARD: 24, *39*, 43, 44, 48, 58, 59, *66*
BRENNIER, GENERAL: 47-49, 54, 58, 59, *66*
BRILLOS: 27
BROTHERWOOD, WILLIAM: 53, 56
BROWN, JOHN: 141
BRUCKELY, WILLIAM: 141
BRUNEL, SIR MARC ISAMBARD: 168
BULMER, THOMAS: 99
BUNBURY, RALPH: 27-29
BURCELLES: 70
BURGOS: 84, 90
BURK, JOHN: 143
BURKE, THOMAS: 120
BURRARD, SIR HARRY: 44, 60, 61, 67
CABILOS: *126*
CACABELOS: 82, 86, *97*, 124-*126*-128, 135, 137, 151, *162*
CADOUX, DANIEL: 76
CALDAS: 26, *71*
CAMERON, ALEXANDER: 17, 42, 55, 69, 148-151
CARRALTO, MARQUÉS DE: 84
CASTAÑOS, GENERAL: 85, 87, 90
CASTILLO DE SAN ANTONIO: *165*, 166
CASTILLO DE SAN DIEGO: *165*, 167
CASTLEREAGH, LORD ROBERT: 75
CASTRO GONZALO: 96, 100, 101, 104, 105, *162*
CASTRO NUEVO: 94
CASTRO PIPA: 100, *162*
CELORICO: 77, 78
CERCAL: 36, 40
CHARLES VI, KING: 14
CHARLOT, GENERAL: 49, 51, 53, 54, *66*
CINTRA: 67, 69-*71*, 74
CIUDAD RODRIGO: 80, 86, *97*
CLARK, JOHN: 120
CLARK, THOMAS: 113
COCHRANE, THOMAS: 32, 38
COCKAYNE, JOSEPH: 56, 62, 65
COIMBRA: 17, *71*, 77, 78, 80, *97*
COLBERT, AUGUSTE: 128, 131, 133
COLUMBEIRA: *39*
COMBARROS: 114
COMPOSTELA: 139
CONSTANTINO: 138, *162*
CORDER, JOHN: 143
CORUNNA: 17, 18, 75, 77-79, 81-89, 95, *97*, 110, 111, 113, 121, 125, 136, 137, 141-143, 145-149, 151, 152, 155-157, 160-*162*, 164, *165*, 166, 168, 173-175
COULTER, JOHN: 120
COX, WILLIAM: 72, 73, 109
CRADOCK, SIR JOHN: 78
CRAMPTON, JEREMIAH: 16, 32
CRAUFURD, CATLIN: 23, 24, 30, *39*, 43, 44, 48, 59, *66*, 91, 156, *165*

CRAUFURD, ROBERT: 90, 91, 93, 95, 96, 98, 99, 101-103, 105, 107, 108, 111, 114-119, 121, 127, 139-141, *162*, 167
CREAGH, JASPER: 16, 38
CUBILOS: 122
CURTRO: 137
DALRYMPLE, SIR HEW: 67, 70, 75
DEBELLE, GENERAL: 114, 215
DELABORDE, HENRI: 25, 27, 29-31, 33-37, 40, 47, 53, 54, 153, *165*
DISNEY, : 91
DODD, WILLIAM: 28
DOUGHTER, HUGH: 64, 65
DOVER: 16, *71*
DOYLE, PATRICK: 28
DRAKE, FRANCIS: 76
DUGGIN, WILLIAM: 28, 38, 65
DURANGO: 84
EELES, CHARLES: 133, 134, 163
EIRIS: 156
EL BODON: 80
EL BURGO: 147, 148, 151, 152, 156, *165*
ELDER, GEORGE: 75
ELVAS: 29, 77, 78, 80
ELVINA: 153, 155, 156, 158-160, *165*
EPINAR: 78
ESPINOSA: 84
EVORA: 17
FALMOUTH: 75, 76
FANE, HENRY: 19, 22-26, 31, 35, *39*, 41-45, 48-52, 55, 56, 60, *66*, 69, 70, 77, 78, 91
FERGUSON, ROBERT: 119
FERGUSON, RONALD: 22-24, 30, 31, 35, *39*, 41, 43, 44, 48, 58-61, *66*, 161
FIGUEIRA DA FOZ: 17, *71*
FLANAGAN, PATRICK: 120
FLETCHER, GEORGE: 151
FONCEVADON: 113, 114, *162*
FORENCAVA: 125
FOY, GENERAL: 161
FRANCESCHI, GENERAL: 89, 146, *165*
FRASER, ALEXANDER: 32, 38
FRASER, MCKENZIE: 90, 91, 96, 101, 105, 106, 121, 139, 157, 158, *165*
FREIRE, BERNADINO: 20
FRERE, JOHN: 81
GILLASPIE, JOHN: 52, 65
GILMOUR, DUGALD: 69
GIFFEN, WILLIAM: 138
GODOY, MANUEL: 14, 15
GRAJAL DEL CAMPO: 94
GRAY, JOHN: 120
GRAY, LOFTUS: 76
GREEN, WILLIAM: 137, 154, 157, 167
GUARDA: 77
HALL, BASIL: 154, 155
HALLAGHAN, WILLIAM: 141
HARRIS, BENJAMIN: 21, 22, 28, 32, 33, 52, 53, 56, 61-64, 72, 73, 93, 95, 117, 121, 140, 141

HART, JOHN, MICHAEL & PETER: 53
HARWICH: 16, *71*, 75, *97*
HENDERSON, HENRY: 121, 141
HEREDIA, JOSEPH: 87
HERRERIAS: 135-138, *162*
HIGGINS, TERRANCE: 115
HILL, DUDLEY ST LEGER: 38, 65, 121
HILL, ROWLAND: 24, 30, 31, 40, 43, 44, 48, 59, 60, 77, 91, 156, *165*, 166
HOPE, SIR JOHN: 77, 80, 81, 85, 86, 88, 90, 91, 95, 96, 99, 101, 105, 106, 121, 139, 155, 156, 158, 160, 161, 164
HOWARD, DANIEL: 118, 119
HUGHES, AMBROSE: 120
HUGHES, JAMES: 120
HUNT, EDWARD: 120
IMPERIAL GUARD: 107, 108, 114
JACKSON, RICHARD: 101, 102
JAGGER, BENJAMIN: 118
JENKINS, JOHN: 76
JESSOP, HENRY: 42
JOHN, PRINCE REGENT OF PORTUGAL: 14
JOHNSTON, WILLIAM: 218
JUNOT, JEAN ANDOCHE: 14, 25, 29, 36, 40, 44-48, 54-56, 58, 59, 61, 67, 69, 78, 80, 90, 114
KEARNEY, DANIEL: 120
KELLERMANN, FRANÇOIS: 47, *55*, *66*-68, 74
KELLY, MAURICE: 28
KERRIGAN, PATRICK: 120
LA BAÑEZA: 83, 85, 88, *97*, 109, 110, *162*
LA HOUSSAYE, GENERAL: 132, 159, *165*
LA RUA: *162*
LAKE, GEORGE: 33, 34, *39*, 42
LAMBETH, JAMES: 120
LAPISSE, GENERAL: 114
LAVOS: 21-24, *71*
LEACH, JONATHAN: 16, 25, 32, 49, 62, 64, 72, 73
LEES, JOHN: 151
LEFEBVRE-DESNOUETTES, CHARLES: 78, 85, 90, 107, 108
LEIRIA: 24-26, 68, *71*, 78, 80
LEITH, JAMES: 91, 156, *165*
LEÓN: 84, 90, 99, 109, 110, 113
LINCOLN, JOHN: 120
LISBON: 14, 17, 25, 40, 45, 46, 59, 60, 62, 67, 68, 70, *71*-73, 77, 78, 80, 86, 90, *97*, 154
LISTON, ROBERT: 79
LOISON, GENERAL: 17, 25, 29, 30, 35, 36, 40, 47, 48, 69
LOURINHA: 40, 41, 47, 48, 58, 59
LUGO: 82, 84, *97*, 135, 136, 139, 141-144, *162*, 163
M'GUIRE, WILLIAM: 116
M'LEOD, NORMAN: 75, *97*
MACEIRA: 41, *66*, *71*
MACEIRA BAY: 41, 44, 69
MADRID: 14, 15, 75, 81, 85-88, 90, 113, 114
MAFRA: 40, 69
MANNERS, HENRY: 218
MANNINGHAM, COOTE: 91, 156, 158, 160, *165*
MANSILLA: 96

MARANSIN, GENERAL: *66*
MARGARON, GENERAL: *66*
MARIANO RIDGE: 47, 58, 59
MARTIN, JAMES: 28, 218
MAXWELL, MATHEW: 28
MAYORGA: 90, 92, 100, *162*
MCCARTHY, CHARLES: 115
MCLAUCHLIN, PATRICK: 120, 121
MERLE, GENERAL: 132, 152, *165*
MERMET, GENERAL: *165*
MGS MEDAL: 174
MICHAEL, HENRY: 143
MILES, WILLIAM: 113
MILLER, GEORGE: 75
MOLLOY, JOHN: 53
MONCEY, MARSHAL: 78
MONDEGO BAY: 17, 18, 19, 25, 41, 69
MONTACHIQUE: 36, 40
MOORE, SIR JOHN: 16, 60, 67, 69-*71*, 75-78, 81, 84-90, 92, 94-97-99, 105, 106, 109-115, 117, 121, 123-125, 127, 129, 132, 135, 136, 138, 139, 141, 143, 144, 146, 147, 152-154, 156-*162*, 166-168
MORGAN, JEREMIAH: 141
MORTIER, ÉDOUARD: 78, 90
MULLEN, STEWART: 61
MURAT, JOACHIM: 15
MURPHY, JOHN: 50
NAPOLEON: 14, 15, 23, 68, 70, 80, 81, 84, 86, 88, 90, 95, 99, 100, 108, 113, 114
NEY, MICHEL: 78, 84, 95, 114, 142
NIGHTINGALL, MILES: 24, 30, *39*, 43, 44, 48, 58, 59, *66*
NOBLE, CHARLES: 161, 163
NOGALES: 135, 136, 138, 139, *162*
NORCOTT, AMOS: 69, 128, 129, 143, 149, 161
O'HARE, PETER: 69, 128, 129, 145, 157
O'NEIL, JAMES: 120
OBIDOS: 25-30, 33, 37, *39*, 40, *71*
OPORTO: 17, *71*
ORENSE: 111, 113, 121, 139, 142, *162*
OZA: 156, *165*
PAGET, HON EDWARD: 70, 80, 90, 91, 94, 125-129, 132, 135, 139, 143, 144, 146-149, 151, 156-159, 164, *165*
PAGET, LORD HENRY: 88-92, 100, 101, 107, 108
PAKENHAM, HON HERCULES ROBERT: 16, 26-29, 50, 95
PALAFOX, JOSEPH: 85
PALAVEA: *165*
PALAVIA ABAXO: 158, 161
PANTON, WILLIAM: 32, 33, 38
PENICHE: 25, 41, 47, *71*, 212, 218
PILKINGTON, THOMAS: 120
PINHEL: 78
PLAZA MAJOR: 124
PLUNKET, THOMAS: 133
POMBAL: 78
PONFERRADA: 114, *126*, *162*
POOLE, THOMAS: 139
PORT, THOMAS: 120

PORTO NOVO: *71*
PUEBLA: 94
QUELUZ: 73
QUENTIN, GEORGE: 84
QUINTA DA BUGAGLIERA: 36
RAMADGE, SMITH: 17, 42, 69
REINOSA: 85
RIBADAVIA: 140, *162*
RICHARDS, JAMES: 120
RIDGWAY, THOMAS: 64
RIGNIE, PATRICK: 100
RIVER AVIA: 140
    CARRION: 85, 88, 94, 95
    CUA: *126*, 127
    DOURO: 17, 89, 114
    EBRO: 85
    ESLA: 96, 99, 100, 101, 103, 104, 107, 108
    MACEIRA: 41, 45, 48, *66*
    MAYOR: 80
    MERO: 148, 152
    MIÑO: 82, 115, 121, 139, 140
    MONDEGO: 17, *71*
    SIL: 127
    TAGUS: 68, 70, *71*, 76-78, 80
    ZIZANDRE: 68
ROBE, WILLIAM: 43, 52, 54
ROBERTS, HENRY: 120
ROLIÇA: 25, 27-31, 35-37, *39*-42, 45, 47, 53, *71*, 72, 76, 86, 174, 175
ROMANA, MARQUÉS DE LA: 81, 84, 95, 96, 109, 110, 138
ROSS, JOHN: 69
ROSTEN, THOMAS: 115
RUEDA: 89
RUNA: 36
SACAVEM: 78
SAHAGÚN: 92, 95-97-99, 106, *162*
SALAMANCA: 77-81, 84-86, 88-90, *97*, 106
SALDANA: 90, 95
SAMMON, JOHN: 33, 38
SAN CHRISTOBAL: 156-159, *165*
SAN DOMINGO FLORES: *162*
SAN JUAN, GENERAL: 87, 88
SAN MIGUEL: 100, *162*
SANTA LUCIA: 156, *165*
SANTA ROQUE: *165*
SANTABAS: 94
SANTAREM: 29, 67
SARAGOSSA: 90, 95
SEGOVES: 90
SHRAPNEL, HENRY: 52
SIDDOWN, JOSEPH: 120
SIMMONS, GEORGE: 45, 46
SLAUGHTER, BENJAMIN: 171, 173
SOBRAL: 70
SOLIGNAC, GENERAL: 48, 49, 58-61, *66*
SOMOSIERRA: 86, 87
SOULT, NICOLAS JEAN DE DIEU: 78, 85, 90, 92, 95, 99, 109, 114, 131, 142, 153, 154, 158, 159

SPENCER, SIR BRENT: 16, 17, 19, 20, 24, 27, 28
ST. CLAIR, GENERAL: 54, *66*
ST. CYR, LAURENT: 78
STEPHENS, CORNELIUS: 100
STEWART, JAMES: 76
SULLIVAN, JOHN: 120
SURTEES, WILLIAM: 93, 102, 104, 107, 108, 110, 140, 141
TALAVERA: 73, 78, 90
TAYLOR, CHARLES: 43, *56*, 57
THOMIÈRES, GENERAL: 49-54, *66*
TINSDALE, ROBERT: 100
TOLEDO: 58
TOMAR: 68
TORDESILLAS: 88, 89
TORO: 89, 94
TORRES VEDRAS: 40, 45, 60, 61, *66*, 68, 70, *71*
TRANCOZA: 80
TRANT, NICHOLAS: 20, 30, 31, 35, *39*, 41-44, 48, *66*
TRAVERS, ROBERT: 16, 26-29, 50, 57, *97*
TRIANON: 92, *97*, *162*
TUDELA: 85
VAL DES ORUES: 142
VALDERAS: 106, 107
VALDESTILLOS: 90
VALENCIA DE DON JUAN: 95, 96, 99, 100
VALLADOLID: 77, 84, 88-90, 114
VALONGO RIDGE: 41, 46-48
VENTOSA: 48, 58-60, *66*
VICTOR, CLAUDE: 78
VIGO: 82, *97*, 111, 113, 115, 141, 152, *162*, 167
VILLA MAYOR: 90
VILLA VICIOSA: *71*
VILLAFRANCA: 78, 82, 86, 88, *97*, 110, 111, 123, 125, *126*-129, 131, 135, 136, 142, *162*
VILLALON: 90
VILLAPANDO: 94
VILLARIS: 88
VIMEIRO: *39*-50, 52, 54-56, 58-60, 64, *66*, 67, 69, *71*, 72, 76, 86, 174, 175
VITTORIA: 84
VIULLONIA: 90
WADE, HAMLET: 76, *97*, 102, 119
WALL, PATRICK: 120
WALL, THOMAS: 28
WALTON, JOHN: 101, 102, 163
WARDE, HENRY: 91, *165*
WATERS, JOHN: 90
WEATHERALL, JOSEPH: 120
WELLESLEY, SIR ARTHUR: 15-20, 23-26, 28-31, 33, 34, 36, 37, 40-42, 44-49, 51, 53-56, 59-61, 67, 68, 70, *71*, 75
WILSEY, THOMAS: 151
WILSON, GEORGE: 120
WYNN, ROBERT: 141
YUIL, ALEXANDER: 120
ZALADA: 83, 85, 110-112
ZAMORA: 88-90